How Ottawa Decides

Planning and Industrial
Policy-Making 1968–1980

The Canadian Institute for Economic Policy has been established to engage in public discussion of fiscal, industrial and other related public policies designed to strengthen Canada in a rapidly changing international environment.

The Institute fulfills this mandate by sponsoring and undertaking studies pertaining to the economy of Canada and disseminating such studies. Its intention is to contribute in an innovative way to the development of public policy in Canada.

Other titles available in the Canadian Institute for Economic Policy Series are:

The Monetarist Counter-Revolution: A Critique of Canadian Monetary Policy 1975–1979
Arthur W. Donner and Douglas D. Peters

Canada's Crippled Dollar: An Analysis of International Trade and Our Troubled Balance of Payments
H. Lukin Robinson

Unemployment and Inflation: The Canadian Experience
Clarence L. Barber and John C. P. McCallum

Canadian Institute for Economic Policy
Suite 409 350 Sparks St., Ottawa K1R 7S8

How Ottawa Decides

Planning and Industrial Policy-Making 1968–1980

Richard D. French

James Lorimer & Company, Publishers
in association with the
Canadian Institute for Economic Policy
Toronto 1980

The opinions expressed in this study are those of the author alone and are not intended to represent those of any organization with which he may be associated.

ISBN 0-88862-369-0 cloth
ISBN 0-88862-368-2 paper

6 5 4 3 2 1   80 81 82 83 84 85 86

Canadian Cataloguing in Publication Data
French, Richard D., 1947-
How Ottawa decides

ISBN 0-88862-369-0 bd.   ISBN 0-88862-368-2 pa.

1. Canada - Economic policy - 1971-   *
2. Canada - Politics and government - 1968-   *
3. Industry and state - Canada. I. Canadian Institute for Economic Policy. II. Title.

HC115.F73   330.971'0644   C80-094264-7

Additional copies of this book
may be purchased from:

James Lorimer & Company, Publishers
Egerton Ryerson Memorial Building
35 Britain Street,
Toronto M5A 1R7, Ontario

Printed and bound in Canada

Contents

Foreword

It is now recognized that the major problems facing the Canadian economy are structural in nature and that their resolution will take time. Correcting a serious international payments deficit, as well as imbalances in our industrial structure, in our regional economies, in our labour force and so on, will require a sustained effort over the longer term. How the federal government organizes itself to face these issues in the coming years will, to a large extent, determine the kind of country we will have in the year 2000. The policy-making mechanisms that are set in place must reflect the political commitment to attack such fundamental problems.

The machinery of government is of crucial importance to the development of economic policy. The Canadian Institute for Economic Policy is publishing this study in pursuit of a wider understanding of the interaction of participants in various federal institutions in the development of national priorities, such as industrial strategy. The attempts over the last twelve years to improve the planning process in the Government of Canada in general, and to formulate an industrial strategy in particular, are well described by Richard French. Hopefully the lessons learned from this period will help us to devise more realistic ways of handling the difficulties of policy-making for an increasingly uncertain economic future.

The Institute hopes that this study will be actively discussed by our decision-makers and the public. The analysis and the conclusions are those of the author and do not necessarily reflect the views of the Institute.

R. D. Voyer
Executive Director

vii

Acknowledgements

Many people have aided in the research for this study. I appreciate the willing co-operation of a number of public servants and politicians whose generosity in time, information and opinion has been essential. It is not in the nature of such a study that they can be publicly recognized, nor is it likely that any one of them will be fully satisfied with the treatment of the events in which he or she played a leading role. Within these rather substantial constraints, I hope that they will accept the study in the spirit in which it is offered—as an analysis intended to beg correction and amplification from those best placed to provide them.

Fortunately, some obligations are easier to discharge. It is evident that I owe an intellectual debt to two leading students of Canadian public policy: Douglas Hartle and Bruce Doern. Hartle is both a protagonist in the story and a perceptive analyst of the theory and practice of public management in Canada. In both respects, his role is central. Bruce Doern's extensive contribution to the literature of federal public policy constitutes, like Hartle's, an elemental part of the intellectual under-pinnings of the field. For example, Richard Phidd and Bruce Doern's *The Politics and Management of Canadian Economic Policy* (Macmillan, 1978) represents a valuable framework for the specific analysis undertaken here.

I thank my research assistant, Robin Schweitzer, for yeoman's service in newspaper files and libraries, in particular those of the Science Council of Canada, the Library of Parliament, and the Department of Industry, Trade and Commerce, the co-operation of whose staffs is gratefully acknowledged. Certain portions of the treatment of the cabinet committee system have been reproduced from my article "The Privy Council Office: Support for Cabinet Decision-Making" in Richard Schultz *et al* (eds.), *The Canadian Political Process* (3rd ed., 1979), with the kind permission of the publishers, Holt, Rinehart and Winston of Canada, Limited.

The Canadian Institute for Economic Policy and its Executive Director, Roger Voyer, have provided everything an author could ask in the way of patient support, encouragement and editorial assistance.

viii

Introduction

This is a study of public planning. It is an examination of the capacity of the Government of Canada to attack complex public problems, problems which imply the involvement of diverse institutions, the commitment of substantial resources and the creation of a number of policies and programs.[1] In the latter part of the study, the government's attempts during the Seventies to plan for a particular facet of economic policy, namely, industrial policy, are considered.

The study, however, is *about*, rather than *in*, planning or economic policy. It is not, for example, my intention to draw conclusions about what Canada's industrial policy ought to be, though it is important to examine in general terms what others have had to say on the subject. Rather, this is a study of how government organizes itself to undertake policy-making, and how the participants in that process—notably, the bureaucrats—behave. As such, it is a contribution to a growing literature which emphasizes the importance of permanent officials in the policy process and which attempts in various ways to illuminate their role within the context of constitutional, economic and political theory, and of bureaucratic culture. The focus of governing Canada is now less in Parliament than in the executive branch: the Prime Minister and ministers, assembled periodically in cabinet, as they are counselled, supported and no doubt at times frustrated, by officials. The study attempts to explore interactions within the bureaucracy, and between officials and ministers, with a view to relating these phenomena to some of the broader contours of recent Canadian political economy.

Whatever is original herein arises from the extensive use of confidential interviews with individuals who participated directly in the events described. The study is, therefore, a kind of "internal history" of the concept of planning and the constructions placed upon it within the Government of Canada during the Seventies. It discusses attempts to rationalize decision-making techniques in government, the ideological and intellectual variations among such attempts, and the clash of interests they engendered. Its focus is essentially upon the institutions of government. Its thesis is that a close examination of the behaviour

ix

of officials and ministers within these institutions will illuminate the "public history" of the period, 1968–1980. The paralysis of the newly elected majority government from July 1974 to the imposition of wage and price controls in the fall of 1975, and the drastic budget cuts of August 1978, are among the events so examined.

The use of confidential interviews does not permit the reader the opportunity to judge the primary evidence for himself.[2] It is impossible to undertake descriptive analysis of policy-making behaviour in Canada without encountering this problem in one form or another. Ultimately, the reader can only assess the utility and verisimilitude of the analysis itself. If he believes the issues dealt with are significant, he must ask whether the analysis is consistent with the public events it purports to underly. Is it internally consistent? Are there others available? If so, how do they compare with this analysis? Finally, is the analysis useful? Does it clarify issues, alter our view of events, affect our thoughts or actions regarding the future?

The intention of this study is to add depth to the picture of the heroic attempts made to improve planning in the Government of Canada, especially during 1968–1975, and to follow the chequered history of one classic planning problem, industrial strategy, over the last decade. To the best of my knowledge, neither of these issues has yet received systematic treatment, though of course a great deal of material of a fragmentary nature has been written about both.

Chapter 1 discusses the definition of planning to be used in the study, and briefly describes the central decision-making process within which different planning systems developed. Chapter 2 outlines the major argument, that there were three distinct forms of planning operating within the federal government during the Seventies. The next four chapters attempt to demonstrate how this framework helps us to understand resource allocation and fiscal policy (Chapter 3), the Priorities Exercise of 1974–75 (Chapter 4), and the history of industrial strategy (Chapters 5 and 6). Chapter 7 analyses the Clark administration's reforms in the central decision-making process and Chapter 8 draws some general conclusions.

Planning and the Central Decision-Making Process 1

"Planning" is perhaps the most multifacetted, the most protean concept to have eluded students of government over the last twenty years. The subject suffered a near fatal dose of academic attention in the Sixties. Even as the theoreticians were worrying away at it, governments the world over were "trying the experiment", that is, attempting to implement planning, invariably with indifferent success.

An examination of one nation's experience requires a pragmatic definition of planning. This definition of planning avoids the "scholasticism" of the academic literature on the subject, in favour of immediate utility for historical analysis.

> *Planning* is the attempt to place government policies and programs within a suprasectoral or national context to permit political decision-making about their relationships and relative priority.

Such a view of planning involves a level of aggregation higher than that of policies or programs. Planning attempts to relate and compare policies and programs originally developed within various particular sectors, as an *ensemble*. Planning implies political choice of overriding criteria within which the competing claims of different sectors to the limited resources of government will be rationalized. It implies the identification by ministers of dominant concerns to which policies and programs conceived within the parochial context of a given sector must be bent.

This definition of planning accords reasonably well with the more prescriptive version adopted by the (Lambert) *Royal Commission on Financial Management and Accountability:*

> The sound management of government . . . requires that certain basic operations be carried out. These are planning, budgeting, directing and co-ordinating, controlling, and evaluating. The essential first step involves the development of a forward plan which, within the framework of

1

decisions about the amount of revenue to be available and total expenditures to be made, would determine how resources should be allocated to implement policies and programs that reflect the Government's priorities.[1]

The definition used here captures what was loosely understood as planning in the Government of Canada over the last decade, makes it possible to explore the essentials of that experience and permits some broad conclusions. It maximizes the empirical content of the notion of planning for a particular time and place. Its purpose is to help fill out an overall sketch, or *gestalt*, about planning in the national context. The attempt at historical precision will, no doubt, be at the expense of failing to contribute to such academic topics as "disjointed incrementalism" versus "comprehensive" policy-making, the joys of "mixed scanning", or the subtle distinctions inherent respectively in indicative, normative and central planning.[2] The important debates for present purposes take place not in academic journals but in the cabinet chamber and bureaucratic boardrooms.

One final point about this definition of planning. It focusses on intragovernmental efforts to plan, on the attempt to mobilize federal institutions and resources to achieve particular public objectives. On occasion, the achievement of these objectives may require substantial co-operation from other organizations, such as provincial governments or private enterprise. Indeed, there is a major tradition of public discussion and research literature which construes this last kind of public-private co-operation as "planning". From the perspective adopted here, planning may, but need not, involve the extragovernmental or public-private dimensions. Thus, the public-private dimension is not the central concern of the study as a whole. It is the exercise and implementation of choice within the federal cabinet and bureaucracy which is primarily at issue. Such decision-making would be an essential pre-requisite even where—as in industrial strategy—a broader notion of planning, bridging the public and private sectors, might well apply.

The Cabinet Committee System

The forum or framework within which planning took place was a central decision-making process whose essential features had been established during the latter half of the Sixties, in the Pearson and first Trudeau administrations. A good deal has been written about the elements of the central decision-making process. These elements will be summarized here: the cabinet committee system, the Treasury Board and the expenditure budget process. Each may be explored in greater depth through the references footnoted in the summaries which follow.

Cabinet is the instrument by which ministers concert their views to arrive at government policies which they all, by the political conventions which we inherited from Great Britain, must accept and publicly support. It is also the instrument by which the perspectives of different ministerial portfolios are brought to bear on major policy problems, which rarely respect the essentially arbitrary structuring of public issues into government departments by confining themselves within the boundaries of any one department. Cabinet is where the interplay of the political, portfolio and personal interests of ministers takes place. It is the crucial decision-making forum for the political executive.

Under Prime Minister Trudeau,[3] the full cabinet of thirty-plus ministers bore collective responsibility for all government policy presented as such before the public and Parliament. The decision-making process was structured in such a way as to provide each minister with the right to express his or her point of view on any of the several hundred issues of public policy submitted annually by individual ministers for decision by their colleagues. That is, each minister had a potential opportunity, at a meeting of full cabinet during which the entire volume of proposed policy which had reached a critical stage was on the table, to persuade colleagues of the virtues of his or her point of view on any item of policy.

Much of the intensive study and discussion of policy issues raised in Memoranda to Cabinet, however, took place in the various cabinet committees. One of Prime Minister Trudeau's most distinctive personal contributions to Canadian government was to formalize a system of standing committees of cabinet, building upon a base of sporadic experience of *ad hoc* committees over previous decades, and specifically on the rudiments of a regular practice which had emerged toward the end of the Pearson administration.

A number of reasons have been invoked for the establishment of the cabinet committee system. The Prime Minister was anxious to use the limited time which ministers have to devote to joint decision-making as efficiently as possible, to reduce the lack of co-ordination resulting from what he saw as the excessive autonomy of individual ministers in the Pearson cabinet, and to reinforce the decision-making prerogatives of ministers as opposed to the influence of permanent officials.

Ministers lead incredibly harassed lives; ministerial time has been called "the rarest of government commodities" and "the scarcest resource in Ottawa".[4] The duties of preparation for and participation in cabinet compete, often unsuccessfully, with a myriad of other calls on

3

ministerial time: the constituency, the House of Commons, the department, the party, travel, speech-making and so forth. It is evident that issues can be discussed in greater depth, and with greater participation by any given minister, if they are intensively studied by a committee of four to eight, than if each must be explicitly considered in the full cabinet of some thirty or so ministers.

The Prime Minister described his desire to prevent unduly independent ministers from operating at cross-purposes with one another as follows:

> Ministers tended to be their own bosses in their own sections and therefore their deputy ministers, to the same extent, tended to be their own bosses too. They didn't have to submit their policies to the countervailing forces or to the cross-stimulation, or cross-fertilization, for all I know, of other ministers and other departments. That's the way I've been trying to make the government function, by telling a minister look, before you do something with such and such a program, you must realize the impact it will have on another department.[5]

Thus, a formal committee system required each minister to consult his colleagues regarding new policy or program initiatives. This aspect of the Trudeau reforms has been christened "the advent of collegiality".[6]

The attempt to reassert the political responsibility of ministers relative to the bureaucracy had at least four aspects to it, as the Prime Minister explained in 1975:

> First, we wanted more decisions to be taken at the ministerial level. Second, we wanted to ensure that ministers had soundly researched alternatives from which to choose. Third, we wanted to aid ministers to make a conscious choice of priorities in the full knowledge of the real pressures which were being placed on their colleagues. Fourth, we wanted to extend dialogue between ministers and officials, and not just officials from their own department.[7]

Accordingly, the Privy Council Office, acting on behalf of the Prime Minister as the secretariat to the cabinet and its committees, encouraged ministers to consult their colleagues, demanded the presentation in Cabinet Memoranda of genuine alternatives for political choice, attempted (as we shall see) to support ministerial selection of priorities, and managed a committee process in which senior departmental officials played active roles.

There were nine major cabinet committees in the Trudeau cabinet committee system (see Figure 1).[8] The first five committees represented an attempt to divide the major substantive policy spheres of the federal government into identifiable and (to the extent possible) coherent sectors.

4

Figure 1 – MAJOR CABINET COMMITTEES AND THEIR SECRETARIATS DURING THE TRUDEAU ADMINISTRATIONS[8]

Committee	Secretariat
Culture and Native Affairs External Policy and Defence Economic Policy Social Policy Government Operations	Operations Division, Privy Council Office
Legislation and House Planning Priorities and Planning	Plans Division, Privy Council Office
Federal-Provincial Relations	Federal-Provincial Relations Office
Treasury Board	Treasury Board Secretariat

The Priorities and Planning Committee was a critical organizational element in the Trudeau administrations' planning ambitions, and its role changed as those ambitions evolved. Its general function, however, was to set the overall tone and direction of government policy, by choosing priorities, initiating major policy reviews, assigning certain responsibilities to other cabinet committees and considering the most pressing and politically important issues. Priorities and Planning was a committee unlike the others. It special status was underlined by the fact that it was the only committee with closed participation: whereas any minister could attend any other committee meeting, whether or not he had been formally designated a member by the Prime Minister, attendance by non-members at Priorities and Planning was by invitation only. The Prime Minister personally chaired the Priorities and Planning Committee.

The relationship between cabinet committees and the full cabinet was structured as follows. Ministers consulted their cabinet colleagues regarding public problems through the vehicle of the Memorandum to Cabinet, which presents the issues and alternatives, and concludes with a recommended course of action: for example, the adoption of a particular policy or the establishment of a particular program. These Memoranda to Cabinet were drawn up in the minister's department after extensive study, and signed by the minister.

After discussion in the appropriate committee (or more rarely, committees), the Memorandum would be forwarded along with the committee's recommendation, in the form of a Committee Report, for consideration by full cabinet. In principle, any Committee Report could be reopened by any minister in full cabinet. In practice, cabinet spent most of its time on major issues listed on its Main Agenda. Most items of cabinet business (and thus most Memoranda and Committee Reports) were listed on the Annex to the Agenda, and most Annex items got approval "on the nod"—that is, without further explicit discussion in full cabinet. However arrived at, cabinet's decisions constituted government policy and were embodied in documents known as Records of Decision. Records of Decision directed the actions of ministers and officials.

The staff of the Privy Council Office organizes, co-ordinates and communicates the results of cabinet committee and cabinet meetings. The Office is organized in parallel with the cabinet committee system. Each cabinet committee is served by a secretariat headed by an Assistant Secretary to the Cabinet and consisting of from three to about eight other officials. PCO staff must seek to maintain an overview of government policies and programs and, in particular, a continuing sense of the "cutting edge" of issues and problems which are likely to require collective decision by ministers within the foreseeable future. The elaborate and complex system of decision-making which they manage on behalf of the Prime Minister gives them considerable responsibility and influence. PCO staff advise departmental officials about the preparation of Memoranda to Cabinet, establish agendas for cabinet committee and cabinet meetings, brief the Prime Minister and committee chairmen on Memoranda to Cabinet once formally submitted, and draft Committee Reports and Records of Decision.

All of these functions are sensitive. Consider the latter two. In briefing the Prime Minister or a committee chairman on a Memorandum, the PCO official is counterposing his overview of developments in the policy sector and his experience with cabinet and its committees against the substantive expertise of departmental officials. This is an exercise which calls for some care, because the systematic frustration of departmental ambitions, if it is seen to arise from PCO officials (as opposed to the decisions of ministers), may create tension or kill initiative in departmental ranks. Thus the PCO official must try not to second-guess the department on technical matters. He will try to tap sources of information and advice in the various departments concerned without allowing himself to become the instrument of the ambitions of any one. He will try to tap the expertise of the appropriate officers in the Program Branch of the Treasury Board Secretariat, who will often have a more detailed grasp of the policies, programs and personalities in any given department than he does. And he will try to use the experience of his superiors, especially (when the issue is important enough) the Secretary and the Deputy Secretaries to the Cabinet, who will often provide judgments or directions based upon sources of information unavailable to him.

The end result of this exercise should be that the PCO official develops a grasp of the fundamentals of the issue, of the differences of view among departments and ministers upon it, and of the quality of the Memorandum. He will use this assessment to brief the committee chairman, in order to assist him in conducting the meeting and to minimize waste of time, especially insofar as it may arise from preoccupation with peripheral issues or from prolonged confrontations between ministers.

After a committee or cabinet meeting, a second highly sensitive task is undertaken: the drafting of Committee Reports or Records of Decision, respectively. This responsibility, to formulate the first systematic expression of government policy at its source, is complicated by the personal style of most Canadian ministers and the norms governing their collective behaviour. Ministerial discussions will often meander from issue to issue, abandoning policy questions while any consensus may remain largely implicit, without any formal specification of the resolution of the issues at stake. The extent to which this occurs will, of course, depend upon the chairman and the nature of the matters under discussion. Even where clear and precise differences among ministers arise, chairmen will often prefer to guide their colleagues onto other issues without any definitive summing up; the norms required by cabinet solidarity prohibit embarrassing any minister by dwelling any more than absolutely necessary on the fact that he or she has "lost" the debate. While discussion in cabinet is somewhat more structured and formal than in committee, the finalization of Records of Decision has often required enormous efforts of drafting and consultation by PCO officials.

The Prime Minister, through the Secretary to the Cabinet, is the final arbiter of the content of Records of Decision, while committee chairmen will oversee the efforts of secretariat officials drafting Committee Reports. Ministers and officials recognize the difficulty of these functions. Aggressive ministers and deputy ministers see the stage of drafting Committee Reports and Records of Decision as an important point in the process at which pressure may be brought to bear, perhaps to achieve objectives which failed to attract ministerial attention or support. The fairness with which the Prime Minister, the Secretary to the Cabinet and PCO officials fulfill these responsibilities is continually monitored by other ministers and senior officials. If there were systematic doubt as to the legitimacy of Records of Decision, the collective responsibility essential to the system could be jeopardized.

Thus it is not only the Prime Minister and PCO officials whose participation in the system offers opportunities for influence. Indeed, the cabinet committee system is a classic demonstration of the organizational truism that structures, rules and procedures do not dampen political activity, but simply render it more complex and more subtle. Departmental ministers and officials are far from powerless to affect the treatment of particular issues by cabinet,[9] and there are some entertaining accounts in the literature as to how this can occur.[10] Likewise, central agencies other than the PCO have a great deal at stake in the operations of the cabinet committee system, and a more detailed examination of central agency interaction within that forum is essential to the analysis in this study.

Any reform as thorough-going and far-reaching as Prime Minister Trudeau's of cabinet operations alters the balance of political and bureaucratic power to the displeasure of some, and inevitably occasions criticism of one sort or another. It is not necessary to consider all of this criticism here and indeed there is little consensus on the issues in any case. It is worth mentioning, however, certain bureaucratic and ministerial perceptions of the Trudeau cabinet committee reforms. While the reforms are generally understood to have instituted much needed structure and control after the helter-skelter confusion of the Pearson years, some questioned whether the defects inherent in these virtues did not bring the whole exercise into question. In particular, the sophisticated analytical demands and cumbersome procedures were seen as serious barriers to decisive action, resulting in the constant delay of "analysis paralysis".[11] In the same way, the advent of collegiality, the insistence on collective decision-making within the committee system, is believed to have frustrated some capable ministers,[12] and the allegedly dominant role of certain senior PCO officials to have disheartened, even driven to early retirement, talented departmental officials.[13]

The Treasury Board as a Committee of Cabinet

The final major element in the Trudeau committee system was the Treasury Board, a cabinet committee with the general functions of management policy and expenditure control. The Treasury Board has a number of unique features.[14]

Although its members, like those of other cabinet committees, are named by the Prime Minister, the Treasury Board is the only committee to have a statutory basis. Its existence and functions are provided for in the *Financial Administration Act* and its members must be named by Order in Council. Thus, unlike other Trudeau committees, the ministers who composed the Treasury Board were publicly known. By statute, the chairman is the President of the Treasury Board, the Minister of Finance is a member, and there are four other members.[15]

Until the establishment of the Board of Economic Development Ministers in 1978–79, the Treasury Board was the only cabinet committee served by a secretariat which did not answer to the Prime Minister.[16] The Treasury Board Secretariat is an extremely important central agency, larger than the PCO, and with a great diversity of functions.

Finally, while other cabinet committees under the Trudeau administration had to have their recommendations endorsed by full cabinet before these recommendations had the force of decisions which could be implemented, the Treasury Board had what was in practice final decision-making power over a large number, though not all, of the management issues coming within its purview.

The *Financial Administration Act* provides that the Treasury Board *may*, on behalf of cabinet, act on matters relating to:

    (i) "general administrative policy";

   (ii) "the organization of the public service . . . and the determination and control of establishments therein";

  (iii) "financial management";

  (iv) "the review of annual and longer term expenditure plans and programs of the various departments of Government, and the determination of priorities with respect thereto";

   (v) "personnel management in the public service, including the determination of terms and conditions of employment of persons employed therein";[17]

  (vi) the administration of various public service pension plans;[18]

 (vii) prescribing the form and frequency of financial accounting procedures in the public service.[19]

The *Act* provides that cabinet ("the Governor in Council") can assign further responsibilities to the Treasury Board and likewise can "amend or revoke" any action of the Treasury Board whatsoever.[20] Thus, to the degree that the Treasury Board exercises independent decision-making power, it does so in a legal and constitutional sense at the suffrance of full cabinet.

The *Financial Administration Act* goes on to confer on the Treasury Board extensive powers in relation to the responsibilities set out above, as well as the power to make regulations covering the operations of government departments and agencies with respect to these areas.

9

Under its *Act*, the Treasury Board is required to become involved in a very large number of "housekeeping" questions for the government as a whole.[21] Its management policy responsibilities include its role as the employer of public servants and hence the negotiator for purposes of collective bargaining (conferred by the *Public Service Staff Relations Act*) and a myriad of other functions flowing from the *Financial Administration Act*, such as, for example, "control over the disposition of Crown property", "control over manpower utilization by departments", or "authorization of departments to enter into contracts and establishment of terms of such contracts".[22] Generally, the Treasury Board establishes policies to guide departmental management, and departments must consult the Treasury Board where they see a need to exceed the authority they have been allocated thereunder.[23]

The vehicle by which departments consult the Treasury Board is known as a submission. Where a cabinet committee may have from two to fifteen or so multipage Memoranda to Cabinet on its agenda for a given meeting, the Treasury Board will have over a hundred one- or two-page submissions on its agenda for each of its weekly meetings. Although the Board may also have new regulations, Committee Reports, or the occasional Memorandum to Cabinet to consider, the great bulk of its work consists of submissions. Each submission will be assessed within the appropriate branch of the Treasury Board Secretariat and a recommendation from the Secretariat to accept, reject, or modify the departmental proposal embodied in the submission will be made to ministers on the Treasury Board. If, say, a department wished to transfer funds intended for salaries to the procurement of equipment, the transfer would be analyzed within the Program Branch of TBS[24] (whose staff manage the expenditure budget process and thus are specialists in the budgets and programs of particular departments and agencies). On the other hand, if the contracting for the procurement itself involved anything out of the ordinary, the submission would be analyzed within the Administrative Policy Branch[25] of TBS. These two branches handle most of the thousands of submissions annually, with a smaller number of personnel-related matters requiring recommendations from the Personnel Policy Branch.[26]

A submission may occasion one of three responses from the Treasury Board. It may be approved, approved on conditions, or it may be rejected. In either of the last two cases, a formal "decision letter" is sent to the department which sponsored the submission, outlining the Treasury Board response. The Secretariat's goal is to have the process of submission, analysis, Board meeting and decision take no more than three weeks.

In cases where a minister refuses to accept the Treasury Board's

10

rejection of a submission, he may appeal to full cabinet, in which case a Treasury Board document embodying the decision, called a "referral form", goes forward to cabinet.

In management policy, the Treasury Board and its Secretariat have an extraordinarily demanding role. It is they who must set regulations and policies which reach far into the domain of departmental management, it is they who must police these regulations and policies, it is they who must say "No!" to the usually well-meant ambitions of departments and agencies. For departmental personnel, the Treasury Board and its staff are the most omnipresent bogeymen in the never-ending intrabureaucratic manoeuvring between co-ordinator and co-ordinatee. The Lambert Commission referred to "the distrust which prevails in so many cases today between departments and the Treasury Board."[27] The Commission did not exaggerate the tensions which developed over the last fifteen years of managerial reforms sponsored by the Treasury Board. Consider this from a senior departmental manager:

> With its extended managerial mandate, the Treasury Board Secretariat loaded itself with high-powered, and high-priced, analytical talent... There is an iron law of talent: talent demands a means of expression. When it is associated with a central control agency, it is as natural as breathing for talent to seek expression through the exercise of power. There is only so much power lying around; the supply is limited. What is acquired by one must therefore be subtracted from another. To the considerable extent to which the analytical talent of the Treasury Board staff has intervened in internal departmental decision-making, it has been sapping the line manager of authority and it has been imposing its judgment on departmental operations without any continuing responsibility for the consequences.[28]

Here again, we see a central agency encountering departmental resistence, just as the implantation of the cabinet committee system inspired similar rumblings of discontent from departmental ministers and officials.

What, it may be asked, has all this detailed managerial policy to do with planning as this study defines it? Very little, no doubt. That is the point. Although Treasury Board responsibility in the area of management policy provided the instrument through which a number of managerial systems were introduced into the bureaucracy, the Board as a committee of cabinet was largely preoccupied by the tedious operational necessities of an enormous and complex bureaucracy. Thus, the popular image of the Treasury Board as expenditure manager, implying surely "the attempt to place government policies and programs within a suprasectoral or national context to permit political decision-making about their relationships and relative priority" is misleading to say the least. If planning was going on, it was not the Treasury Board as a committee of ministers that was doing it.

There are some important corollaries to this point. First, the Treasury Board was a cabinet committee of entirely marginal interest and prestige among Liberal ministers.[29] There were two reasons for this: ministers saw little of political appeal or direct interest in the unending flood of submissions and, when there was, ministers hated to deny their colleagues the means to achieve their aspirations. Rejecting a colleague's initiative in the name of an abstraction like "administrative consistency" or "fiscal responsibility" came extremely hard to Canadian ministers; log-rolling and backscratching were the instinctive reactions. Thus, Treasury Boards under Trudeau consisted, aside from the President and the Minister of Finance, of relatively junior ministers, and of Ministers of Supply and Services or Public Works, whose portfolios had a great deal at stake in Treasury Board policies and their enforcement. Successive Ministers of Finance ignored their Treasury Board membership, virtually never attending meetings. Second, all this led in turn to the isolation of the President of the Treasury Board, as the only minister whose portfolio involved both an intrinsic incentive to control expenditure and the explicit mandate to do so. This gave the President and the staff of the Program Branch of the Secretariat the important but lonely role of managing the expenditure control process with negligible support from the Board as such. It made the President and his staff highly dependent for success in this enterprise on the support of the only ministers whose portfolios did not involve an incentive to spend, the Prime Minister and the Minister of Finance, and of the central agencies which reported to them. The working out of this relationship is a central part of the planning story.

The Expenditure Budget Process

The government's revenue and expenditure budgets indubitably represent a plan, and the processes of developing them a forum for planning, within which the relationships between the three ministers and their central agencies are critical. As Phidd and Doern have pointed out,

> ...the government's expenditure budget reflects the internal conflicts within the governmental system while the economic budget reflects the broader conflicts within the economy and society and the strategies which the government considers to be an appropriate response. Even without the formal publication of a plan the government's budget represents a form of planning by identifying and highlighting issues of choice and change.[30]

12

The expenditure budget process as it evolved during the Trudeau administration has been treated in some detail elsewhere.[31] This summary is limited to features essential to a grasp of its place within the central decision-making process. The expenditure budget process is an elaborate set-piece competition among departments, recurring in annual cycles, and refereed by the central agencies. The prizes are shares of the resources, whose expenditure for particular purposes the government of the day will propose for Parliament's approval in the form of spending legislation called Estimates. The process begins some fourteen months before the Main Estimates are tabled in Parliament and about sixteen months before the beginning of the fiscal year in question. Figure 2 provides a general schematic outline of the expenditure budget process under Prime Minister Trudeau.

The essence of the expenditure budget process was the intense intraexecutive politics necessary for the reconciliation of the following three elements:

    (i) The Fiscal Framework (not specifically referred to in Figure 2);

    (ii) Departmental Budgets;

    (iii) The Expenditure Guidelines, set by cabinet.

Once these elements had been melded into the Estimates, the process of Parliamentary approval was relatively *pro forma.*

The Fiscal Framework is the Department of Finance's contribution to the expenditure budget process.[32] More than a year before the beginning of the fiscal year in question, the Department of Finance assesses the fiscal capacity of the economy within the context of the outlook for the year, considering such indicators as rate of growth of the economy, employment levels, inflation, the stability of the currency and so forth. On the basis of this analysis, and within the context of Keynesian and (since the mid-Seventies) monetarist assumptions regarding the achievement of countercyclical or stabilization goals for the economy, the Department and the Minister will propose to cabinet "whether the economy should be stimulated or controlled, and the extent to which this should be by tax or by expenditure changes".[33]

During the Seventies, then, the Minister of Finance recommended to cabinet an overall fiscal policy known as the Fiscal Framework which was discussed in detail in the first instance by the Cabinet Committee on Priorities and Planning. The resulting Record of Decision, after consideration by full cabinet, would set specific levels for the budgetary deficit and for the total cash requirements of the government. In arriving at these figures, the expected level of revenues for the year would be forecast and target levels of expenditure established.

13

FIGURE 2-THE EXPENDITURE BUDGET PROCESS UNDER PRIME MINISTER TRUDEAU

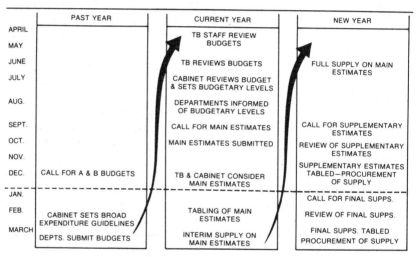

	PAST YEAR	CURRENT YEAR	NEW YEAR
APRIL		TB STAFF REVIEW BUDGETS	
MAY			
JUNE		TB REVIEWS BUDGETS	FULL SUPPLY ON MAIN ESTIMATES
JULY		CABINET REVIEWS BUDGET & SETS BUDGETARY LEVELS	
AUG.		DEPARTMENTS INFORMED OF BUDGETARY LEVELS	
SEPT.		CALL FOR MAIN ESTIMATES	CALL FOR SUPPLEMENTARY ESTIMATES
OCT.		MAIN ESTIMATES SUBMITTED	REVIEW OF SUPPLEMENTARY ESTIMATES
NOV.			
DEC.	CALL FOR A & B BUDGETS	TB & CABINET CONSIDER MAIN ESTIMATES	SUPPLEMENTARY ESTIMATES TABLED—PROCUREMENT OF SUPPLY
JAN.			CALL FOR FINAL SUPPS.
FEB.	CABINET SETS BROAD EXPENDITURE GUIDELINES	TABLING OF MAIN ESTIMATES	REVIEW OF FINAL SUPPS.
MARCH	DEPTS. SUBMIT BUDGETS	INTERIM SUPPLY ON MAIN ESTIMATES	FINAL SUPPS. TABLED PROCUREMENT OF SUPPLY

Source: Program Branch, Treasury Board Secretariat, 1978.

The Fiscal Framework guided the President of the Treasury Board and the Secretariat in subsequent work on the expenditure budget for that year. Their task was to negotiate the allocation of the revenues and borrowings, on which cabinet had agreed, among the competing expenditure proposals of the departments and agencies of government, within priorities set by cabinet. Departmental spending ambitions were contained in Departmental Budgets, and the cabinet's priorities were embodied in Expenditure Guidelines.

Departmental Budgets were called by Treasury Board nearly a year and a half before the beginning of the fiscal year, before the Fiscal Framework for that year had been settled. After what was often a lengthy and complex process of internal negotiation and deputy ministerial arbitration among aggressive departmental managers, departments submitted to TBS their spending proposals in the form of what are called Program Forecasts, a little over a year before the fiscal year began. These Departmental Budgets, or Program Forecasts, were divided into "A" and "B" budgets. The "A" budget covered forecasts of expenditure to maintain current levels of service in programs which had already been approved and were part of the current expenditure budget. The "A" budget represented how much faster one had to run in order not to lose ground. The "B" budget covered forecasts of expenditure for new programs and/or expansion or improvements of existing programs. "B" budget proposals, in the aggregate, represented the total amount of "new money" the government would have to find in order to undertake all of the new initiatives departments would have liked to see undertaken. As new initiatives, most "B" budget items would not only have to survive the vetting of the expenditure budget process by competing successfully for limited *resources* against other "B" budget items, but also gain *policy* approval through a Memorandum to Cabinet in the cabinet committee system. "B" budget items required both resourcing and policy approval before they could be implemented. What is important from the expenditure theory point of view is that the "B" package provided Treasury Board with a sense of the degree of inconsistency between departmental aspirations and the resource limitations set by the Fiscal Framework.

With increasing frequency toward the end of the Seventies, departments were asked to develop "X" budgets of lowest priority programs which were to be dropped in order to achieve targets for spending limits in the Fiscal Framework.

About the time the staff of the Program Branch of TBS began to study Departmental Budgets intensively, cabinet issued the Fiscal Framework. TBS and PCO officials then submitted for the consideration of the Committee on Priorities and Planning, and of cabinet, suggestions for marginal changes within the total package of departmental budgetary proposals: priorities for the allocation of new money and/or for cutting to achieve spending limits. The results of these deliberations were known as the Expenditure Guidelines.

The Expenditure Guidelines provided a framework within which the Treasury Board, its President and the Treasury Board Secretariat, negotiated with each minister and department to reduce the total spending package to meet the requirements of the Fiscal Framework. These negotiations represented the guts of the budgetary process. They were highly political and often bitter and protracted, with disappointed ministers on occasion seeking to go over the heads of the Board and its President by appealing to the full cabinet.[34]

As early as 1971, "the difference between the sum of funds requested by departments and agencies for the ensuing year, and the sum eventually authorized" was estimated to be "on the order of $500,000,000".[35] And in some years, the manpower allocations ultimately approved for the "A" and "B" budgets combined were less than those which departments had originally sought in "A" budget forecasts alone.

These negotiations were typically completed by late spring or summer (i.e. several months before the start of the fiscal year). The final disputes were resolved by cabinet, which then approved the total package in early fall. Main Estimates were prepared, approved by Treasury Board in December, and tabled in Parliament in February, two months before the beginning of the fiscal year.

After Main Estimates, there were, during the fiscal year, two sets of Supplementary Estimates submitted to Parliament. These Supplementary Estimates were typically composed of miscellaneous expenditure proposals which had been approved by cabinet committees after and outside the annual expenditure budget cycle. These are packages of individual and unrelated items which changing political or economic circumstances, ministerial or departmental flashes of inspiration, or other factors pushed through the cabinet committee system for approval, one by one. They were typically not subject to the full rigour of vetting intrinsic to the annual cycle and this had important implications, which are examined in Chapter 3.

In theory, then, the expenditure budget process provided a place for each actor in the executive branch decision-making process: departments and their ministers, Finance and its minister, the Treasury Board, its Secretariat and its President, the PCO, the Committee on Priorities and Planning, full cabinet and the Prime Minister. Its product, the expenditure budget, represented a crucial expression of the government's priorities, the point at which its diverse policies and

16

programs "must somehow be brought together into an integrated and hopefully harmonious whole".[36] Given what is at stake, given the logic of public sector incentives and given the complexity of the process itself, it is obvious that the expenditure budget process offered manifold opportunities for tactics and gamesmanship, intended to maximize individual or institutional interests at the expense of the collective ones the process was designed to serve. This was even more true to the extent that there was not any consensus as to the precise nature of these collective interests, nor, as we shall see, any single actor or institution which succeeded in claiming a franchise on their interpretation and defence. As Hartle put it, the heart of the matter "is that there is a perpetual conflict among interests which must be resolved, and that [an essentially arbitrary] procedure must be devised which legitimizes the outcome to the point where those who perceive themselves to be losers are willing to acquiesce in their losses or are willing to fight for what they desire through legitimate [i.e. generally recognized] channels".[37]   •

Three Planning Systems 2

It is now difficult to find planners in Ottawa. People describe themselves as policy advisors, co-ordinators, evaluators, managers, but rarely as planners. The notion currently evokes an unappealing image within the bureaucracy: a highly formal, rigid, rational, systematic and ultimately sterile attempt to frame the current and future actions of government through a series of elaborate planning exercises. This negative image of planning—sometimes called "technocracy" and its practitioners, "technocrats"—is the product of a Canadian experience which is distinctive in flavour though not unique in kind. That experience is the subject of this chapter.

(When to this intragovernmental concept of planning is added the public-private dimension mentioned in Chapter 1, negative overtones of a *dirigiste* and interventionist role for government in the economy of the country are added along with it. *This* concept of planning is stigmatized in certain segments of public opinion as "socialism" and its proponents, "socialists". Such issues arise again in the discussion of industrial strategy in Chapters 5 and 6).

Planning was not always so out of fashion. To the contrary. In the late Sixties and early Seventies, it was an idea in good currency: elaborate procedures and structures were established in the name of planning, and ambitious careers were launched within them. Why all the enthusiasm for planning, and substantial reforms to implement it, during this period?

In Canada, a convergence of factors common to many Western governments with features specific to this country produced a substantial impetus for planning, particularly after the advent of Prime Minister Trudeau in 1968. The postwar period, and especially the late Fifties and Sixties, saw democratic governments move far beyond the traditional concerns of defence, diplomacy and a modicum of economic infrastructure. They increased dramatically their involvement and expenditure in areas such as culture, social services, research, education and regulation of the marketplace. Emanations of the state came to affect the lives of more and more citizens in a direct and tangible way, to attract more and more of their attention, and to demand more and more of their income in the form of taxes. As organizations outside government grew and as physical problems of cities, transportation and environment accumulated, public tolerance of the disadvantages of these developments diminished, and government was expected to respond. The arrival of the pervasive state in the postwar period was the greatest single factor behind recognition of the need for improved planning of the activities of Western governments.

Along with the expansion in the role and complexity of government, and to some extent abetted by it, came an explosion of activity in the social sciences. The analysis of public problems became a series of esoteric specialties, requiring lengthy formal training. The social science disciplines traditionally relevant to government, such as economics and political science, grew apace, and they were joined in the Sixties by an overlapping group of "horizontal" disciplines—cybernetics and modelling, systems analysis, technological forecasting and futurology—which attempted to knit together the concerns of the traditional disciplines. These new analytical approaches emphasized the interdependence of hitherto distinct fields of activity. There was enormous optimism about the knowledge emerging from these forms of analysis and about its potential effectiveness in the solution of public problems. There was a belief on the part of social scientists that their disciplines were approaching the kind of certainty that characterizes the natural sciences, and hence that their results could be implemented within public programs with the same kind of confidence that attends the use of a "hard" technology. This positivist view of the social sciences, very typical of the Sixties,[1] is one of the many misleading ways in which that hardy perennial, "knowledge is power", returns to haunt us.[2] The rhetoric of planning in the late Sixties and early Seventies is shot through with superficial metaphors between governing and planning, on the one hand, and information sensing and processing technologies, on the other. These metaphors were meant to convey a sense of the vast possibilities of rational analysis of policy, predicated on the social sciences. More or less fashionable forms of corporate planning drew on this movement. They were first translated into the public sector by Robert McNamara at the U.S. Department of Defense, and spread from there into most Western governments.

The classic Canadian statement of this enthusiasm was embodied in Prime Minister Trudeau's speech to the Liberal Policy Conference of 1969, in Harrison Hot Springs, British Columbia.[3] In a speech filled with references to "genetic engineering", "satellite broadcasting", "supersonic aircraft" and organ transplants, the Prime Minister offered a vision of political parties as "society's radar".[4] He went on:

> We, however, are aware that the many techniques of cybernetics, by transforming the control function and the manipulation of information, will transform our whole society. *With this knowledge, we are wide awake, alert, capable of action; no longer are we blind, inert pawns of fate.*[5]

What is significant, though nowhere explicitly confronted in the speech, is that the Prime Minister confounded the undoubtedly dramatic social impacts of "hard" technology in areas like medicine and communications, with the use of "soft" technologies like cybernetics by individuals and governments to control the future:

> With the refinement of our techniques for forecasting and planning, we are coming to realize that the image we hold of our future is itself an important element of that future.[6]

While the social sciences indeed offered aid to governments undertaking unprecedented responsibilities, the optimism of the Sixties has been tempered by the experience of the Seventies. Even as philosophers are discovering the inadequacy of the positivist view of the social sciences—that is, admitting that the social sciences are far indeed from the certainties of the natural sciences—policy analysts and government decision-makers are ruefully recognizing the technocratic hubris of the Sixties.

In 1968, all this was in the future, a future which looked very bright indeed to Canadians, who were bathing in the afterglow of Expo 67, feeling a new confidence and a new sense of possibility in the country. They were fascinated with a figure who manifested some entirely original features on the Canadian political scene: brilliance, style, irreverence, imagination and a genuine biculturalism. They gave Pierre Trudeau a landslide victory in the election of 1968. He returned to Ottawa with a quite extraordinary personal mandate and he used it in part to complete a major restructuring of central decision-making in the Government of Canada. Some of this restructuring had its roots in the previous administration; other aspects are inconceivable without the Prime Minister's personal ascendancy and the commitment by him and certain of his key advisors to a certain notion of planning. It was through Prime Minister Trudeau that the pressures on all governments to plan took their particular form within the Canadian context.

One factor was Trudeau's relatively recent arrival in Ottawa. Having been a Member of Parliament for only a few years and a minister for even fewer, the new Prime Minister moved to put his own stamp on the decision-making process in order to tailor it to his own particular

20

style and approach.[7] Lacking the extensive network of personal acquaintance and the breadth of experience of a Lester Pearson, Trudeau was to create a system which was more formal, more explicitly forward-looking and more overtly rational than its predecessors.

Trudeau and his advisors were determined not to continue the government-by-crisis pattern which characterized the Diefenbaker and Pearson administrations. Trudeau had been horrified by the succession of scandals, threatened resignations, cabinet leaks and other upsets which made the Pearson minority administrations a continuing exercise in improvisation by the Prime Minister. He wanted to avoid such untidy government at all costs.[8]

Somewhat in parallel to these developments, the traditional and cohesive elite of Canadian public servants, the experienced generalists known as the mandarins, were gradually being taken by age and infirmity from the Ottawa scene. Their style of co-ordination and decision-making, based on longstanding personal acquaintance and broad experience, seemed less appropriate for a larger government grappling with issues of great technical complexity.[9] A new generation of technocrats, whose claim to involvement in the solution of public problems lay in their formal training and substantive expertise rather than in seniority and experience, saw in the planning movement an ideal instrument to speed the supplanting of the mandarinate and their own succession to power. In addition to the importance of expertise, implicit in the technocrats' claims was the argument that the cohesion of the mandarinate was undesirable to the extent that it presented cabinet ministers with a single concerted bureaucratic viewpoint on an issue, thus preventing cabinet and ministers from exercising their democratic responsibility to choose between alternatives. The restructuring of the decision-making system in order "to ensure that it is ministers who make decisions" would also ensure that the analytical skills of the new generation could be exercised from positions of substantial influence within the system.

The new Prime Minister and certain of his closest aides were probably intellectually and culturally well prepared for the rationalism of the planning movement. The Prime Minister and those of his associates who had been educated in the classical colleges of Québec shared an instinct for the kind of Cartesian clarity and symmetry represented by the comprehensive frameworks of objectives and instruments which the social scientist-apostles of planning of the Sixties were offering. Trudeau had written in 1964:

> ... the state—if it is not to be outdistanced by its rivals—will need political instruments which are sharper, stronger, and more finely controlled than anything based on mere emotionalism: such tools will be

21

made up of advanced technology and scientific investigation, as applied to the fields of law, economics, social psychology, international affairs and other areas of human relations; in short, if not a pure product of reason, the political tools of the future will be designed and appraised by more rational standards than anything we are currently using in Canada today.[10]

A second group in the Trudeau entourage were the engineers, notably Jim Davey, Program Secretary in the Prime Minister's Office, whose attempts to apply to the problems of governing systems concepts from industrial engineering and project management, led in precisely the same direction. During the first Trudeau administration (1968–72), terms borrowed from engineering and high technology contributed a patina of pseudo-sophistication to the argot of the enthusiasts in the Prime Minister's and Privy Council Offices, and elaborate charts intended to capture and interrelate the government's many planning exercises provided an often bizarre iconography for the corridors of power.

While the Prime Minister himself was always fascinated by those with a capacity for abstraction, it is unclear how seriously he took the kind of idiot fringe of futurology, elaborate chart construction and "thinking the unthinkable" which was tolerated on the margins of the Prime Minister's and Privy Council Offices between 1968 and 1972. He probably knew little about it. As a symbol for the rest of the bureaucracy, however, it was significant.

The commitment to planning, policy formulation and co-ordination which was to be less personal and less informal remained fundamental to the Prime Minister's vision of his administration. Institutions, forms and procedures were to be designed for a multiplicity of actors to take the place of the experience and *savoir-faire* of a few. The scope of individual ministerial initiative and the influence of the mandarinate was to be reduced in favour of a more corporate and collegial style of decision-making by cabinet. The whole movement of structural and procedural reform, though in some cases it simply advanced developments already in train under Pearson, took on a distinctive cachet from the political momentum of the Prime Minister and the rationale which he and his advisors invoked for the changes.

It is the officials and ministers of the central agencies of government, those which exist to co-ordinate and control the activities of the so-called line departments (which deliver programs to the public), who must be responsible for planning in the sense of our definition:

> The portfolios of these ministers cut across special interest lines for they reflect the several dimensions of the *collective* concerns of Cabinet.

22

Their task is to ensure that, insofar as is possible, the *full* policy line of the party is both balanced and feasible given the immutable constraints. To acquiesce in the face of each of the narrow demands of the ministers who pursue, as they are expected to pursue, the special interest of special interest [line] portfolios would be to generate an unbalanced and/or infeasible policy package. In a sense, these collective interest portfolios, to a greater or lesser extent, can be thought of as emanations of the Prime Minister who is responsible for the overall reconciliation of particular interests.[11]

Thus it is in the central agencies, such as the Privy Council Office (PCO), the Department of Justice, the Treasury Board Secretariat (TBS) and the Department of Finance that we expect to see sectoral policies and programs rationalized within the context of national government. And it is no surprise that it is the central agencies, notably the PCO (of which the Prime Minister is minister) and the TBS (of which the President of the Treasury Board is minister) that design and advocate new structures and procedures within which such rationalization is to take place.[12]

It is an important part of central agency mythology that the role of co-ordinator and controller is carried out in strict neutrality, its only purposes being such unexceptionably general ones as ensuring that it is ministers and not officials who take important decisions, guarding the public purse, ensuring that government actions conform to law, ensuring prudence and probity in administration, ensuring fairness in public employment and the like. However, as Phidd and Doern note, "intrabureaucratic organization and management are the focal points of micro-politics, requiring a more explicit analysis of the role of government and the state, and of the intellectual developments in management, budgeting and the behaviour of organizations."[13] Key in turn to these issues are exactly the manifestations in central agencies of individual and institutional interests, whose existence central agency mythology denies. And what Phidd and Doern say about the economic sector applies to all sectors of government:

> ... economic-policy goals, although frequently discussed by economists as technical problems, have important philosophical implications which guide "agency philosophies". If a given philosophical position takes precedence then the bureaucratic structure will reflect this in a reorganization of some kind.[14]

The "agency philosophies" of certain central agencies, and the reorganizations and bureaucratic micropolitics which are occasioned by the development and competition of such philosophies, are essential to the analysis which follows.

23

The examination of attempts to plan is greatly complicated by the fact that individual and agency philosophies compromise the assessments of those within the system whose access to information would otherwise render them best qualified:

> ... the judgment of success is made within the same normative ethos which produced the new techniques and procedures, and significantly those making the judgment are already burdened with roles which commit them to the ... strategy.[15]

On the other hand, analysis by scholars using only public documentary sources proves unduly dependent upon the application of a body of theory of doubtful relevance to a body of information, inadequate in detail, and inevitably reflective more of the aspirations of reform than of tangible accomplishments.

This study's approach to planning cannot be definitive. It attempts, however, to place the contributions of other sometime participant observers of planning within a somewhat more comprehensive framework,[16] and to make more precise and systematic distinctions within the variety of post-1968 initiatives than some scholarly observers have wished to make.[17] It argues that there were not one but three different versions of planning as defined, that they emerged from three different central agencies, that they were predicated on different intellectual/disciplinary bases, that they originated from different historical roots, that they were advocated by different leading personalities within the bureaucracy, that they utilized different instruments within different timeframes and that they were focussed upon different elements within the central decision-making process. In short, that there were three different agency philosophies about planning during the major part of the last decade. While they were not mutually incompatible in a logical sense, their different origins, institutional sponsorship and individual advocacy often made them in practice incongruent if not irreconcilable. Each version of planning became a constraint on the others, with the result that the planning aspirations of the Sixties promised more than could be delivered. Furthermore, no single version of planning could be regarded as a success even on its own terms. They contended within a central decision-making process which, for all its theoretical consistency, ultimately failed to blend them. It could be demonstrated on paper that there was a place for everything.[18] Alas, everything was not in its place.

Planning theorists are fond of observing that "having no strategy is itself a strategy". Acquaintance with the central decision-making process as it developed under Prime Minister Trudeau—the cabinet committee system, the Treasury Board, the expenditure budget process—

24

might equally elicit the observation that such an apparatus inevitably "planned". That is, whatever the degree to which it may have been formally recognized, the government's package of policies and programs, and the relative levels of resources allocated to them, represented the product of "planning", in the sense that they logically implied

> ... the attempt to place government policies and programs within a suprasectoral or national context to permit political decision-making about their relationships and relative priority.

Precisely how did this planning take place? The Trudeau administration embraced three major versions of planning, or "planning systems". It is only by appreciating the nature of all three systems that discussion of future prospects for the enterprise of planning in Ottawa may move beyond speculation in the academy and self-serving reinterpretation by the bureaucracy: "to see the future in the present, seek the present in the past".

The "agency philosophies" of the three key central agencies—the Department of Finance, the Treasury Board and the Privy Council Office—were fundamentally incongruent with respect to their joint responsibility to lead the planning function in the Government of Canada. As a result, there were three planning systems operative within the central decision-making process, here identified as the Finance Planning System, the Treasury Planning System and the Cabinet Planning System. These names are simply labels for concepts used to order the better part of ten years of politico-bureaucratic history. These concepts have inevitable flaws and shortcomings, but they have advantages as a framework for analysis.

The three planning systems differed on a number of key dimensions: institutional sponsorship, intellectual/disciplinary base, historical origins, personal advocacy, timeframe, planning instruments employed and focus within the decision-making process. They also differed in the extent to which they were explicitly conceived as "planning" and in the degree to which they were initially or subsequently burdened with the images of planning which have become part of the administrative and political culture of Ottawa. Only one of these labels, the Cabinet Planning System, has an intrinsic historical validity; that is, it was used to describe a series of planning initiatives in the same way as it is used here. The other two labels are essentially arbitrary and to some extent misleading unless care is taken to identify them with the analysis attached to each. The particular influence of any one on any given event varied depending upon the nature of the issues at stake and the particular conjuncture of bureaucratic and national politics.

25

Furthermore, while each of them represents the agency philosophy about planning that was dominant within the agency or sub-unit of the agency in question, all of them were the subject of lively controversy and a degree of internal opposition from within the agency which sponsored them.

A common feature of the three planning systems was their insistence upon analytical capacity predicated upon formal education, rather than upon, say, judgment based on bureaucratic experience. As a result, the emergence of these planning systems during the Sixties, and particularly the impetus which the Cabinet and Treasury Planning Systems received during 1968–72 from the advent of Prime Minister Trudeau, triggered an equally dramatic reaction within most line departments and agencies. As the central agencies added personnel skilled in economics and policy analysis, personnel who in turn transformed the central decision-making process by increasing the demand for formal and comprehensive analysis within it, departments and agencies were forced to follow suit. Without their own experts, departmental deputy ministers were unable to navigate through the central decision-making process and to negotiate with the central agency gatekeepers who had achieved pivotal positions within the process. Thus, in the early Seventies, each department created its own policy-analysis unit, planning branch and/or program evaluation group, a process that was greatly aided by the fact that the Treasury Board Secretariat was leading the drive for planning and analysis and therefore more than well-disposed toward departmental requests for resources to be directed to such purposes.

The emergence of planning and analysis in the central agencies and its spread through the departments was equivalent, at what is generally known in the public service as the "working level", to the deputy ministerial change of generations from mandarins to technocrats. Neither occurred overnight. Between 1965 and 1975, however, the whole notion of policy and objectives as conceptual frameworks, above and beyond particular programs, and knitting such programs together, spawned a profound change in the atmosphere, norms, prestige structure and career patterns in the federal public service.[19] Where program management and broad experience were once the sole qualifications of any significance, a new, parallel and in many ways attractive career path in the policy, planning and analysis functions opened up. It offered those who pursued it significantly greater remuneration and mobility.

If individuals who could qualify for such positions—and it was a sellers' market from 1969 to 1975—made impressive and in some cases spectacular careers, departmental experience with the new planning groups has been mixed at best. While analysts themselves typically rationalize their ineffectiveness with such standard public service clichés as the suspect machinations of "politics", the obtuseness of "bureaucrats", or the failure to get "access to the top", their difficulties were much more profound.[20] The assumptions of the planning systems were completely unable to come to grips with the realities of governing at the national level. The process of central decision-making under Prime Minister Trudeau demanded a surfeit of analysis from both central agencies and line departments. On balance, this surfeit of analysis served less to reduce the elements of intuition and power brokerage in political decision-making than to distract the attentions of ministers and to alter the language within which political behaviour was couched.

The Finance Planning System

The Finance Planning System had more to do with economics than finance, nor did it, ostensibly, pretend to plan in the sense we have defined. Were one to accept the interpretations of the Department of Finance's role and of the expenditure budget process provided by insiders,[21] or utilize a normative or prescriptive definition of what planning in a national context ought to be, it might appear that there was no separate Finance Planning System. However, the way in which the Department of Finance chose to exercise its mandate over the last decade, and the implications of that choice for the way in which planning occurred within the central decision-making process, make it essential to recognize the existence of a distinct and powerful, even if largely unacknowledged, Finance Planning System.

The Finance Planning System was based, of course, in the Department of Finance. Its intellectual roots lie in classical macroeconomics: the Keynesian faith and its monetarist reinterpretation. Its historical origins lie in the widespread adoption of Keynesian policies by postwar Western governments. Thus, it antedated the enthusiasm for "planning" which came in the Sixties, an enthusiasm which was encouraged by, but not logically derivative from, the very success of Keynesian policy. Furthermore, the Finance Planning System, though it demanded extensive and sophisticated analytical capacity, did not partake of the cycle of enthusiasm and disillusion which began with the arrival of an explicit public commitment to planning in 1968. Its role in the ultimate fate of those explicit planning efforts has never been addressed as such.

The foundations of the Finance Planning System were laid during the Sixties by Robert Bryce, deputy minister of the Department from 1963–1970, and the mandarin's mandarin. The system was embodied in the behaviour of successive Ministers of Finance, but the key personality for our appreciation of the Finance Planning System in the Seventies is Simon Reisman, the aggressive and experienced deputy minister of the Department from 1970–1974. Reisman was the uncompromising protagonist of a certain view of the economy and of the role of government within it, and hence, of a certain view of the Department of Finance. Reisman's ideas did not dominate by the force of his personality alone. Far from it. Although there were significant internal differences, Reisman's views represented a majority viewpoint within the Department, having more to do with the ideology of mainstream Western economics than with any kind of "coerced consensus". Reisman's lengthy and successful bureaucratic career, however, gave him the *savoir-faire* and personal contacts to be a formidable force in central decision-making.

The Finance Planning System comprehended the major instruments of economic policy, in particular the principal levers used to manage demand in the economy in the interests of stabilization of the business cycle. Through the Fiscal Framework, with its limits on aggregate federal expenditure and its particular taxation and expenditure components, through the management of public debt and through regulation of the supply of money and credit, the Department of Finance (and the Bank of Canada) sought to achieve the classic goals of Keynesian economics: maximum employment, contained inflation, growth and international monetary balance. An element central to Finance's perception of its role during the first half of the Seventies was its confidence in the ability to attain these goals through "fine tuning" of the economy on a relatively short term basis. This was the essence of a "steady as she goes" macroeconomic policy, which assumed that structural problems would in time take care of themselves. In contrast, the Cabinet Planning System continually tried to push Finance into a medium term perspective which would necessarily have to confront the structural issues.

Perhaps the single dimension most significant to an understanding of the Finance Planning System as a separate entity is its focus within the decision-making process. For what made the traditional responsibilities of the Finance portfolio into an implicit attempt to plan was the determination of successive ministers and senior officials during the Trudeau era to cling resolutely to the prerogatives historically unique to the Minister of Finance, rather than to attempt an active leadership role in a burgeoning economic sector, a role which would have had to be played within a cabinet committee system which Finance officials perceived as dominated by the Prime Minister and the Privy Council Office.

28

In order to appreciate how this came about, one must come to grips with the dual role of the portfolio, and with its historical development. As Phidd and Doern have described it:

> The Minister of Finance in his capacity as head of the department performs at least two distinct but closely inter-related roles. First, he performs a role as an initiator of policy in that he has primary responsibility for the preparation and presentation of the budget. He is the minister primarily responsible for fiscal policy issues and decision-making. Second, the Minister of Finance reacts to policy initiatives from other departments since he has an important responsibility for financial management. In this second role the Minister of Finance performs a broad economic management role, i.e., he assesses the impact of more particularistic aspects of departmental policies on the overall economy of the country. He makes major decisions relating to the politics and economics of taxing and spending.[22]

The essence of my analysis is that Finance chose to protect its primacy as an "initiator of [stabilization] policy" so jealously as to jeopardize its effectiveness in the "broad economic management role". While it may not have been entirely successful, this was nevertheless the implicit strategy for much of the Trudeau era.

In the Fifties and early Sixties there were, of course, few internal alternatives to Finance; insofar as the government had economic policies, they were largely the creations of the Department. In the years which followed, however, a number of developments seemed to threaten the hegemony of the Department of Finance in the economic sector. First, new goals, both redistributive (on the basis of income and region) and structural (foreign investment, competition policy), were added to the traditional Keynesian ones.[23] Second, new economic techniques, including the development of microeconomics, diversified the very notion of economic policy by directing attention toward new problems, developing new instruments to deal with them and introducing new ideological alternatives to those underlying the "fine tuning" approach of classical macroeconomics. For example, the management of supply factors such as research and development or highly qualified manpower came to be seen as a legitimate part of the government's role in managing the economy. Third, these new goals, techniques and instruments came in large part to be embodied in new economic portfolios rather than in the Department of Finance: " ... the gradual evolution of new economic portfolios ... demonstrated the first major movement away from the relatively more exclusive concern with the macrolevel Keynesian manipulation of aggregate expenditure and taxation".[24] Finally, the emergence of other central agencies with ambitious roles in the fiscal and economic areas, notably the splitting of the

Treasury Board Secretariat from the Department of Finance and the expansion of the Privy Council Office to serve an elaborate cabinet committee system, further altered the policy environment of the Department.

At first, the new socioeconomic departments, such as Consumer and Corporate Affairs or Regional Economic Expansion, or those revitalized, like Manpower and Immigration or Industry, Trade and Commerce, tended to be staffed by alumni of the Department of Finance. Co-ordination in the economic sector was maintained in the prototypical Ottawa style of direct but informal personal contact. Soon, however, the economic policy sector, like the government as a whole, outgrew this style of co-ordination. The new departments provided attractive career opportunities for economists, who were recruited directly, without a sojourn at Finance. The Department, however, chose not to play an active leadership role through senior interdepartmental committees or the cabinet committee system. It chose to protect what it saw as distinctly its own—the traditional goals and instruments of stabilization policy—by fighting the collegiality of the Trudeau cabinet committee system with respect to these prerogatives, and by adopting a predictable, if not rigid, posture toward the social or economic initiatives advanced by other departments through the interdepartmental and cabinet committee systems. Successive Ministers of Finance never regarded their chairmanship of the Economic Policy Committee of the Trudeau cabinet as an opportunity to exercise leadership, probably because that Committee was embedded within a committee system which they and their officials could not control. On the other hand, they resisted PCO pressure to open up the development of the revenue budget—traditionally the unique responsibility of the Minister of Finance—to collective participation by ministers of the Priorities and Planning Committee. Furthermore, Finance bitterly resented even the appearance of the development of economic expertise in the Privy Council Office or the Prime Minister's Office.[25] In brief, in the interests of preserving what it saw as the essence of economic policy from the hands of the profane outside the Department, Finance either abdicated entirely from, or compromised its legitimacy in, the role of leadership across the broad range of such policy. This indeed preserved a degree of independence,[26] but at some considerable cost to the policy-making process.

This Finance position, faced with the other economic portfolios and a central decision-making process demanding increased participation, was of course rationalized by a distinctive ideology. To describe it is to caricature it, but it is typical of all Finance/Treasury portfolios in the Anglo-Saxon countries, for it derives from the dominant schools of macroeconomic theory. Although it has recently been suggested that central agencies in the Government of Canada promote government intervention,[27] this is at a minimum an oversimplification. As Hartle has pointed out, additional government intervention simply complicates life for central agency officials.[28] Intrinsic to Finance's concern with the purity and integrity of what it saw as "economic" (i.e. the Department's stabilization) instruments, was a reflex anti-interventionism, a confidence in the allocation of resources by the market,[29] and a sense that these essentials must be protected at all costs:

> Departments are constantly coming up here with ill-conceived ideas which would either screw up the economy and/or employ an economic instrument, like taxation, for a social or cultural goal. I find it satisfying and exciting to see these policy proposals shot down by our boys [in Finance] purely on the grounds of economics.[30]

Furthermore, the Finance approach was not solely anti-interventionist. Its concern for the integrity of the Fiscal Framework, for example, led it to play an equally conservative role with respect to departmental proposals for major infrastructure investments or fiscal transfer programs. Beleaguered by competitors in its own backyard, second-guessed by the other central agencies and faced with major expenditure proposals from departments whose ministers and management did not share the Department's basic assumptions, Finance failed to find any criterion of general economic policy more sophisticated than a reflex anti-spending posture. The more the Department fought off pressures to open up its own policy initiation responsibilities, and the more inflexible and predictable its reaction to the initiatives of others presented through the cabinet committee system, the more suspect its credibility and good will within that system. It was not until the late Seventies that the Department's quasi-siege mentality began to lift, under the pressure of controls, the budget cuts of August 1978 and the creation of the Board of Economic Development Ministers. By that time, both sides would argue that the damage had been done: one, that essential social programs and investments had not been developed owing to the intransigence of Finance; the other, that precisely the economic misfortunes against which the Department had fought an unsuccessful but appropriate rearguard action had come to pass.

It was, then, Finance's aloof posture relative to the cabinet committee system and its rigidity in reacting to the socioeconomic initiatives of other departments which suggests that the Department was not part of a single government-wide planning mechanism, but rather represented its own. This Finance Planning System focussed upon the Minister of Finance, his deputy and the independent prerogatives of the Department, and emphasized the "fine tuning" of the economy within a relatively short term framework. In Finance's successful opposition, say, to the guaranteed annual income proposals which emerged from Health and Welfare following the Social Security Review in 1975, or to the proposals for major public investments in the infrastructure for Western grain handling of roughly the same period, the narrow criteria informing the Finance Planning System become clear. There obviously was, within that system, a distinct and independent "attempt to place government policies and programs within a suprasectoral or national context to permit political decision-making about their relationships and relative priority". And that attempt revealed again and again how priorities ought to be structured, by demonstrating again and again a particular agency philosophy: "the historic and continuing preference of Finance portfolios for basic monetary and Keynesian concepts and instruments of economic management and their preference for using the business enterprise as the focus of insuring appropriate changes in economic behaviour".[31] In a world of uncertainty, Finance clung to what it knew. This may not have been ill-judged. Indeed, the Lambert Royal Commission *Report* may be read as an exercise in nostalgia for the days in the Fifties and early Sixties when Finance rode tall in the saddle, budgetary deficits were minimal and taxpayers were glad of it.[32] The fact remains that the Finance approach constituted a separate version of planning, resistant to the collegiality of the Trudeau cabinet committee system with respect to the Department's prerogatives in budgetary development. It was no more than a begrudging participant in that system when, in the defence of liberal economics and fiscal sanity, it became necessary to react to the interventionist and/or spending proposals emerging from line departments. Its own horizons were resolutely limited to those of the stabilization instruments it employed. Certain officials in the Cabinet Planning System saw in this a crippling lack of vision, which precluded the emergence of any coherent picture of the medium or long term.

The Treasury Planning System

The Treasury Planning System was based in the Planning Branch of the Treasury Board Secretariat, particularly during 1969 to 1973, when that Branch was founded and enjoyed a fleeting pre-eminence under Deputy Secretary to the Treasury Board, Douglas Hartle. Its intellectual/disciplinary roots lay, like those of the Finance Planning System, in economics, but here the emphasis was not on classical macroeconomics. Rather, the Treasury Planning System was rationalized, through

Hartle's writing, within planning theory, and embodied, through the analyses carried out within the Branch, in advanced applied microeconomics. The historical origins of the Treasury Planning System are to be found in the "modernization" of government financial and other management techniques occasioned by the report in 1962 of the (Glassco) *Royal Commission on Government Organization.* The Treasury Planning System is one expression of that part of the Glassco logic which led to the introduction of the Planning, Programming, Budgeting System, Management by Objectives, the Operational Performance Measurement System and other new managerial techniques, into the public service between 1965 and 1975. This was the logic of the search for the public sector approximation of private enterprise's "bottom line" and for the operational control and clarified political choices consequent thereon. The story of the Treasury Planning System is a mere chapter in an ongoing saga which most recently starred the Auditor General, the Controller General and the (Lambert) *Royal Commission on Financial Management and Accountability.* It is in many ways, however, one of the most illuminating chapters of all.

The Treasury Planning System rested upon the premise that the reconciliation of the Fiscal Framework and the government's priorities as embodied in Expenditure Guidelines on the one hand, with departmental expenditure proposals on the other, must be undertaken in the light of evaluations of the "effectiveness of the programs in achieving government's objectives" and the "efficiency with which programs are being administered".[33] It was the role of the Planning Branch of TBS to develop these evaluations and to stimulate and assist departments themselves to undertake them. It seemed obvious that evaluations would greatly assist the Program Branch in the detailed management of the expenditure budget system, as well as aid ministers in making major resource allocation decisions. Over the medium term—say, on the order of five years—the systematic culling of ineffective programs would provide significant fiscal "elbow room" for the government.

The main instruments of the Treasury Planning System were, first, the Planning, Programming, Budgeting System and the other new management techniques adopted in the wake of Glassco and, second, the analytical apparatus of applied microeconomics, including econometric model building. The post-Glassco reforms in management systems forced the development by line (operating) departments of program objectives, input data and output data in a framework which was to permit the application of the sophisticated, rigorous and increasingly quantitative methods being developed by the Planning Branch. The nominal decision-making focus of the Treasury Planning System was thus on the Treasury Board and on the role of its President and Program Branch in the expenditure budget process and in the cabinet committee system.

During the heyday of the Treasury Planning System, the Secretary to the Treasury Board was Al Johnson, an enthusiastic believer in its premises and approach. On his arrival at the Treasury Board in 1970, Johnson saw the expenditure budget process and the Treasury Planning System as the twin foundations for a more systematic approach to government decision-making. The System's comprehension of the relevant techniques would imply a role for the Treasury Board Secretariat which would encompass not merely management, but a major part of basic policy-making as well.

The key personality in the Treasury Planning System, however, was Douglas Hartle, or rather, the two Douglas Hartles: one, the sometime Deputy Secretary (Planning) to the Treasury Board and proponent of rational planning, and the other, the Professor of Political Economy at the University of Toronto and critic of technocratic management in the public sector. His Treasury Board advocacy of improved evaluation and strategic planning, and his later revaluations of the Treasury Board experience, chart the dawn and demise of the Treasury Planning System.

Unlike the Finance Planning System, the Treasury Planning System was clearly and unequivocally identified as part of the planning enterprise not only by virtue of the institutional label, "Planning Branch", but also for theoretical reasons intrinsic to the enterprise of evaluation. As Hartle put it at the time,

> Evaluative and strategic planning are, it can be seen, inextricably related. Evaluation proceeds from the policy instruments to their effects on goals. Strategic planning proceeds from the desired attainment of goals to the selection of the mix of policy instruments best able to achieve them using the information produced through evaluation.[34]

As a Johnny-come-lately Branch in a Secretariat which had only recently emerged as a portfolio separate from the Department of Finance, the Planning Branch had to try harder. It lacked the traditional prerogatives and prestige of Finance, but it sought to compensate by riding the wave of planning enthusiasm which accompanied the arrival of the Trudeau government, and by excelling analytically.

Hartle was always ready to articulate the benefits of a more systematic and quantitative approach to planning and evaluation. His ideas achieved wide exposure in the bureaucracy in the early Seventies. Thus the Treasury Planning System partook of the image of governmental planning which was widespread at that time, although that image stemmed from both the Treasury and Cabinet Planning Systems and from the technocratic aura then surrounding the Prime Minister. Some scholarly accounts have tended to confound both systems under the rubric of "decisional technology",[35] but they were at best complementary in principle and exclusive in practice. Indeed, the Treasury Planning System demanded in theory a far more systematic framework of government goals and objectives than the Cabinet Planning System was able to provide and this was one among a number of factors leading to its ultimate frustration. The Planning Branch of TBS attempted at one point to deliver precisely such a systematic and rigorous framework for cabinet approval, but the attempt was beaten back by PCO officials, jealous of their own and the Prime Minister's franchise on the Cabinet Planning System as the ultimate mechanism for the determination of government goals and objectives. This left the Treasury Planning System with a no more than piecemeal, haphazard and ultimately unsatisfactory role in expenditure decision-making. For good reasons of its own, the Program Branch of the Treasury Board Secretariat was no more generally receptive to the Planning Branch's program evaluations than the Privy Council Office was to its attempt to establish a broader framework of goals and objectives. As Secretary to the Treasury Board, Al Johnson proved unwilling to force his Planning Branch's evaluations on his Program Branch. To the extent that it implies a Secretariat commitment to a certain version of planning, the "Treasury Planning System" is thus a misnomer. In retrospect, it appears as an intellectual *tour de force* without an audience to appreciate it. Given a cabinet committee system operated by the PCO, a Treasury Board immersed in the administrivia of submissions, a Secretariat dominated by the Program Branch, and a Program Branch preoccupied by the micropolitics of day-to-day management of the expenditure budget process, Douglas Hartle and his brain trust constantly found themselves all dressed up with no place to go.

Nevertheless, the Treasury Planning System represented Canada's most determined and intellectually sophisticated attempt to break out of the vicious circle of conceptual and political difficulties which have plagued program evaluation. What precisely was the Planning Branch trying to do?

The base on which Hartle and his colleagues thought they were building, to wit, the post-Glassco managerial reforms and especially the Planning, Programming, Budgeting System, was far less firm than they can be forgiven for believing at the time. In 1971, the first heretical views emerged in print from the Canadian bureaucracy: "It is now some six years since the wave of "modern" swept in in the wake of the *Glassco Report*. It has been a costly wave and its net benefits are doubtful".[36] Hartle himself, after he left the public service in the mid-Seventies, became an eloquent and searching critic.[37] As the Lambert Commission was to say of the Planning, Programming, Budgeting System, Operational Performance Measurement System, and Management by Objectives, "None of them proved an effective means of gaining control of the planning and expenditure processes".[38]

All this was in the future, however, when Hartle arrived in Ottawa to establish the Planning Branch of the Treasury Board Secretariat. His background as an academic economist and as secretary to the (Carter) *Royal Commission on Taxation,* and his forceful personality quickly attracted an extraordinary array of analytical talent. The Planning Branch of TBS, along with the Privy Council Office, became the implicit ideal underlying the enormous expansion in planning and policy groups in departments in the early Seventies. Unlike many of these groups, however, the intellectual quality of the Planning Branch was not *ersatz.* It may well be that the Planning Branch's most lasting and important contribution lay in its role as a funnel into the bureaucracy of outstanding public servants: Ian Stewart went on to become deputy minister of Energy, Mines and Resources; Russell Robinson, assistant deputy minister of Welfare; and Mark Daniels, assistant deputy minister in Regional Economic Expansion. All cut their teeth as directors under Hartle, and they in turn trained a number of other bright young men who graduated from the Planning Branch to important positions elsewhere in the bureaucracy.

Hartle's basic objective was to achieve a major improvement in the evaluation of efficiency and effectiveness of government programs by analysing the budgetary data produced by the Planning, Programming, Budgeting System with the most advanced microeconomic techniques. The Planning, Programming, Budgeting System, instituted originally in 1965–66, involved a basic alteration in the form of federal government budgeting:

> From the predominantly incremental budgeting in terms of expenditure categories (salaries, travel, postage, rent, repairs), which prevailed prior to 1965, there has been a significant shift in emphasis to planning and budgeting in the context of defined (or re-defined) departmental objectives and sub-objectives, and of programs and activities designed to meet these objectives structured in a manner to facilitate planning and subsequent evaluation of achievement.[39]

This budgetary restructuring was based on the following concepts, according to a Treasury Board Manual of 1969:

   (a)   the setting of specific objectives;
   (b)   the systematic analysis to clarify objectives and to assess alternative ways of meeting them;

(c)   the framing of budgetary proposals in terms of programs directed toward the achievement of the objectives;

(d)   the projection of the costs of these programs a number of years in the future;

(e)   the formulation of plans of achievement year by year for each program; and

(f)   an information system for each program to supply data for the monitoring of achievement of program goals and to supply data for the reassessment of the program objectives and the appropriateness of the program itself.[40]

In brief, participants in the budgeting process—departmental managers, central agency analysts, deputy ministers, ministers, parliamentarians—were henceforth to be in a position to consider the amounts and trends in resources allocated to particular functions, subfunctions and programs of government (e.g. Justice, Correctional Services, Police Protection...) as well as to particular objects of expenditure (e.g. accommodation, salaries, travel,...) for a particular department. The PPB System attempted to emphasize resource allocation in an overall governmental and departmental context, rather than decisions about incremental increases in categories of expenditure—"standard objects" —which were not conceived within the context of the purposes of government.

On the basis of this reform and others in train which shared its premises and purposes, Hartle and his group moved in two main directions. Hartle himself wrote a number of papers in the early Seventies whose purpose was to explicate, extend and clarify the logic of program evaluation—an exercise which inevitably, both in theory and in practice, broached in a fundamental way the entire process of strategic planning in government. Secondly, his staff, who compensated for their modest numbers by being both bright and aggressive, searched out some of the most significant and problematic of government programs on which to conduct exemplary evaluations. They hoped to produce evaluations which would be crucial to decision-making about the programs in question, to develop the technology of evaluation, and to transfer to departments the will and the technology to evaluate. We shall consider the underlying theory and then the practice of evaluation by the Treasury Planning System.

Hartle's attempt to articulate a coherent and logically complete version of evaluation in the public sector culminated in 1972 with two papers, "The Objective of Government Objectives" and "A Proposed System of Program and Policy Evaluation". The first of these, published much later in revised form, was preoccupied with the relative roles of ministers and officials in the establishment of objectives, and with bureaucratic advice about objectives, policy and program evaluation.[41] The second article, however, was published during Hartle's tenure of office, in *Canadian Public Administration* in 1973. It is a particularly illuminating contemporary expression of the ambitions of the Treasury Planning System.

The abstract of the article reads as follows:

> The objective of this paper is to outline a conceptual framework which integrates and renders operational the governmental decision-making functions of policy and program evaluation, strategic planning, and priority problem identification. Meeting this objective involves three tasks: (1) identifying ministerial goals, and classifying those with similar characteristics into "goal areas"; (2) specifying statistical indicators suitable for measuring the extent to which particular goals are being realized, and estimating values for these goal achievement indicators assuming no change in policy; (3) identifying policy instruments that affect goals, and estimating changes in goal achievement indicators associated with changes in these instruments.[42]

While in the 1973 paper, Hartle recognized many of the conceptual and practical difficulties attendent upon evaluation and planning, there was none of the pessimism that marked his post-Treasury Board writings. These began in 1976 and can be read as a sustained assault on the practicality of many of the things for which the Treasury Planning System and Hartle himself stood between 1969 and 1973. As Hartle saw it in 1973,

> Although it would be a mistake to try to minimize these problems or to over-emphasize the value of what has been achieved, experience to date strongly suggests that: (a) much more analysis of existing policies and programs needs to be and can be done; (b) the techniques and resources required to pursue more adequately the evaluation of policies and programs either are available or can be made available; (c) a relatively few changes in the system would yield great returns.
>
> These changes include: (i) the development and general adoption of an inclusive, common set of operationally defined evaluative criteria; (ii) the collection on a continuing basis by departments and agencies of the data required to assess their programs and policies in the light of these criteria; (iii) more time could be found in the tight schedules of ministers for the presentation of the results of the evaluation of current and prospective programs so that they could be more fully taken into account in their decisions. This would reinforce the work of officials in this direction.[43]

Despite the problems, then, there was a great deal that could and should be done. Existing and proposed programs cried out for rigorous evaluation; there was a vast field of opportunity open to a government that would be prepared to make "a relatively few changes in the system [that] would yield great returns".

Another central feature of the 1973 paper was that its thorough-going treatment of the logic of policy and program evaluation led inevitably to planning and priority choice. Hartle saw evaluation and planning as "inextricably related" and this drew the Treasury Planning System into inevitable confrontation with the Cabinet Planning System. The abstract of the paper included the term "priority problem identification", a dead give-away that Hartle was in the PCO's back-yard.[44] Indeed, the paper represented a far more systematic account of the implications of the rhetoric of planning emanating from the PCO than that fragmentary rhetoric itself was ever able to convey. Considering Hartle's articulation of the elements of strategic planning, one can almost sense in the crabbed prose the origins of the PCO's intuitive reluctance to follow the logic to its conclusion, that is, one can sense the ultimate unsuitability of the approach to its intensely political context:

> Evaluation is, in turn, one of five elements of what we will call strategic planning. These elements are: (1) forecasts of the changes in the indicators of goal achievement that would occur in the absence of changes in the policy instruments; (2) the assignment by ministers of priorities to the present or emerging problems identified on the basis of this information; (3) identification of the kinds of policy instrument changes that might be used to meet these high-priority problems; (4) assessment of their relative effectiveness, taking into account any positive or negative effects on other goals (prospective evaluation); (5) selection by ministers of the changes in the policy instruments that would most effectively resolve the highest priority problems of the Government.[45]

Hartle, too intellectually honest to obscure the implications of his argument and the difficulties besetting it, but as yet too faithful to rational ideals to surrender it, went on to provide a meticulous sketch of his proposed conceptual framework. He touched on "The Goals of Government", "Goal Achievement Indicators", "The Inventory of Policy Instruments" and "The Classification of Policies and Expenditure Programs by Goal Area". He concluded that

> In reality it is impossible to evaluate the joint effects of all conceivable bundles of policy instruments on the realization of all of the government's goals. It is equally impossible to devise *the* strategic plan that optimizes the degree to which all goals are realized simultaneously in the light of the preferences of ministers when conflicts among goals are involved. *The problem is to move from the definition of the task that is conceptually perfect but hopelessly impractical to one where material progress can be made without losing the fundamental insights provided by the framework.*[46]

39

If this indeed was "the problem"—and Hartle stressed the need to move forward in implementing a framework for evaluation and strategic planning, rather than endlessly debating the merits of various schemes in the abstract—what was the Treasury Planning System doing in the way of evaluation, as opposed to theorizing about it? Hartle and his group used their "hunting license" to select the most substantial as well as analytically vulnerable of programs. They carried out major reviews of the effectiveness of social programs such as manpower training, direct job creation and youth employment; of economic development programs such as the regional development subsidies of the Department of Regional Economic Expansion, the industrial research and development incentives operated principally by the Department of Industry, Trade and Commerce, the involvement of Devco in coal mining, and the operations of Atomic Energy of Canada Limited; and of agricultural programs such as dairy price support. Considerable sophisticated analysis was done around other major issues, such as potential industrial benefits from major aircraft procurement and cost modelling of proposed guaranteed income schemes.

These evaluations had varying degrees of impact on the decision-making process. Hartle's enthusiasm and intellect created a superb *esprit de corps* within the Planning Branch. There was very considerable progress in the technology of evaluation. Hartle's forcefulness guaranteed that the results of the Branch's work would gain a hearing within the Treasury Board and cabinet committee system. But the Deputy Secretary's strength of character was not an unmixed blessing. His brilliance and determination, and that of his staff, threatened and intimidated vested bureaucratic interests at almost every turn. This applied not only to departmental managers whose programs were or might be evaluated, but also central agency officials in Finance, PCO and TBS.

Despite the high quality of the analysis, Hartle seemed unable to operate with, rather than against, the norms and expectations of the participants in the central decision-making process. As one observer put it, "It doesn't matter whether you throw champagne or gingerale into the wind. It still comes back in your face. Hartle never learned to work with his back to the wind."

Moreover, Hartle and Johnson made an important tactical error in the early Seventies, by trying to fill the economic policy vacuum created by the reticence of Finance. In cabinet committee discussions of major program proposals from departments, they moved beyond the managerial and expenditure aspects of the proposals, to argue before ministers the broader economic implications. By thus representing a possible counterweight to Finance, they alienated the most important potential ally the Treasury Planning System might have secured.

Finally, ministers often refused to "bite the bullet", as the Planning Branch saw it. It turned out that the analytical vulnerability of a program had far less to do with its political vulnerability than the logic of evaluation had assumed, for that logic factored out bureaucratic and political conflict, ignoring the system of incentives bearing on ministers and officials. The Treasury Planning System was a commercial failure but an artistic success, and not only in the sense that it improved the technology of evaluation. At least as important was its discovery of the powerful symbiosis of the conceptual and political difficulties attendant upon evaluation, and its role in seeding its brightest staff, newly chastened by this discovery, into key positions in major program departments.

To the extent that the Planning Branch might have succeeded in inserting its evaluations into a receptive decision-making process, it would have become so powerful as to have to be dismantled. If, in the end, the demise of the Treasury Planning System did not occur in quite this way—it ultimately went out with a whimper rather than a bang—it would nevertheless be quite wrong to see it as a failure. Although a failure on its own terms, these terms were of a kind of technocratic hubris which demanded failure. There was a dignity, born of intellectual honesty, in Hartle's eventual eulogies for the System.

Hartle wrote in a later revision to his 1972 paper on objectives, finally published in 1976, "...even if made operational on a vast scale, ministers would never accept the proposed evaluation scheme as more than one of many sources of intelligence".[47] Hartle and the Planning Branch had learned the hard way by 1973 what the Cabinet Planning System did not discover until two or three years later: planners bring another, but not the only, perspective to the determination of public policies.

The Cabinet Planning System
The Cabinet Planning System was the creation of the Privy Council Office. It was developed initially as part and parcel of the cabinet committee system and in particular around the Committee on Priorities and Planning, which, along with cabinet as such, was its decision-making focus. Its historical roots may be traced to the emergence of an embryonic cabinet committee system in the waning years of the Pearson administration, as well as to the first explicit attempts to identify priorities in the summer of 1966 and the spring of 1967.[48] On this modest base was built the central decision-making process, and an elaborate and evolving Cabinet Planning System within it.

This system was at once the most influential—because the best integrated into cabinet operations and connected to the Prime Minister —and least intellectually rigorous of the three planning systems which coexisted between 1968 and about 1975. It was based on an eclectic (critics said incoherent) mixture of corporate planning theory, cybernetics and systems, with a smattering of technological forecasting and futurology. There is no official version of the intellectual inspiration for the Cabinet Planning System, nor has there yet been an account of that system sufficient to sort out its debts to the vast planning literature of the later Sixties. Laurent Dobuzinskis referred to "decisional techniques...more or less directly inferred from cybernetics"[49] and Doern remarked:

> ...the presence of Prime Minister Trudeau and his advisors seems to indicate a change in the philosophy and in the conceptualization of policy-making. Much of it seems to be congruent, on a philosophical plane, with those political scientists who have argued that we ought to view the political system in cybernetic terms as a goal-seeking and error-correcting information system that "will learn how to learn".[50]

Both Dobuzinskis and George Szablowski have emphasized the optimality motif of planning rhetoric, that is, its commitment to a comprehensive searching-out of alternative solutions and selection of the one best overall, in preference to adoption of an incremental or "satisficing" solution.[51] Szablowski cited planning theorists, Yehezkel Dror and Amitai Etzioni, the former of whom consulted for the Privy Council Office during the first Trudeau administration. Two leading participants in the Cabinet Planning System, Michael Kirby and Hal Kroeker, described the implementation of the new approach this way:

> In its more comprehensive form, this concern for planning was characterized by the "systems" approach. This approach was almost a total rejection of the personalized manner of policy-making in the 1950s and early 1960s. In the systems approach, structure and process become the main determinants of policy, that is, the management of government became institutionalized and formal. Emphasis was placed on designing the right structure which would enable the identification of potential problems along with the development of the best policies...only less sophisticated and capable government than Canadians should expect in Ottawa would be unable to control emerging problems or would be so totally irresponsible as to neglect or ignore them.[52]

None of these authors chose to distinguish between a Treasury Planning System and a Cabinet Planning System, let alone identify a Finance Planning System.

The intellectual/disciplinary origins of the Cabinet Planning System were elusive compared to those of the Finance or Treasury Planning Systems, because the Cabinet Planning System was conceived in closer proximity to the untidy realities of collective decision-making by ministers. Unlike the Treasury Planning System, which constantly sought to place a rational *analysis* before ministers, the Cabinet Planning System constantly sought first and foremost to create on the foundation of the cabinet committee system a rational *process* and *framework* through which ministers could make decisions. While the Planning Branches of TBS and PCO shared most of the classic assumptions of rational planning, together represented its apotheosis to the bureaucracy, Parliament and the media, and shared the popular image of "planning", the two planning systems in a sense represented opposite sides of the same coin. Where the Treasury Planning System as articulated by Hartle emphasized rigorous evaluation of existing policies and programs, and reallocation of resources accordingly, the Cabinet Planning System emphasized a more proactive approach, involving the forecasting of future problems and opportunities, and the design of policies to protect the public interest by anticipating such developments. While neither system would in theory reject these distinguishing features of the other, their differing institutional sponsorship made the contrasting emphases natural. In practice, the selective evaluations carried out within the Planning Branch of TBS represented an inductive medium term approach to strategic planning initiated by officials. The Cabinet Planning System, on the other hand, represented a deductive approach to planning, ostensibly initiated by ministers in their responses to the credo of that System: "what kind of Canada do we want in the year 2000?" Indeed, PCO officials in the early Seventies were suspicious of the Treasury Planning System's aggressive evaluation activity centred on the Planning Branch of TBS. They saw it as tending to minimize departmental self-evaluation and erode the responsibility of ministers for the programs in their own portfolio. The PCO agency philosophy highlighted the role of the individual and collective responsibilities of ministers, for whose exercise of these responsibilities and expression of preferences the PCO was in theory no more than a neutral vehicle. On the other hand, Treasury, Finance and departmental officials felt, especially between 1968–72, that the claim of the PCO Plans Division to no more than transmit to the bureaucracy the aggregated preferences and priorities of ministers was disingenuous if not self-serving; the products of the Cabinet Planning System were packaged in a way transparently reflective of the agency philosophy of the packagers, a relatively small group within the prime ministerial bureaucracy. It should be noted, however, that before 1972 there was substantial social interaction between leading ministers and key figures in the PCO and PMO. To that extent, claims of a meeting of the minds between politicians and the "Cabinet Planners" may not have been without foundation.

These tensions are reflected in an article by Michael Pitfield, the key personality behind the Cabinet Planning System. When he was Secretary to the Cabinet in 1975, Pitfield wrote "Techniques and Instruments for Policy Formulation". This paper's retrospective treatment of the reforms of 1965–75 is a remarkable contrast to the post-Treasury Board writings of Douglas Hartle, and even to the lengthy treatment of planning by two former members of the prime ministerial bureaucracy (and close associates of Pitfield), Michael Kirby and Hal Kroeker.[53] For Pitfield, with the restraint appropriate to his sensitive post, and despite his central role in the reforms at issue, managed to touch upon planning only in passing, almost timidly:

> In talking about objectives, I do not want to get into a debate about the desirability of planning, the utility of abstract goals, and whether or not intellectual sophistication has any place in something as strictly practical and realistic as politics and government. Suffice to say that I am talking about objectives simply in the sense of a government knowing what it wants to do in the overall.[54]

Pitfield here reflects the retrospective agency philosophy of the Priorities and Planning Secretariat of the Plans Division of the Privy Council Office, which, one is asked to believe, did not so much attempt to plan as simply "to help ministers to know what they were doing". Perhaps such a construction of events is not ill-placed, but it is no service to obscure the planning premises which underlay the attempt "to help ministers to know what they were doing". For these Cabinet Planning premises—the notion of anticipating future challenges by comprehensive analysis and establishment of objectives, the insistence on a systems view of policy and program interconnections, which even its proponents now recognize led inevitably to analysis infinitely regressing through countless interactions and subeffects[55]—proved extraordinarily fertile ground for the PCO critique of departmental and ministerial attempts to develop policy for the consideration of cabinet. These critiques simply did not make sense in a context as simple as "helping ministers to know what they were doing" unless one shared the confidence of the Cabinet Planning System in the possibility of a fully comprehensive longitudinal and cross-sectional analysis, beginning from overall government objectives, and ending with a policy or program sufficiently tangible to meet the needs of ministers and citizens.

Hartle and the Treasury Planning System, lacking a power base, had to do their own sophisticated analysis. Reisman and the Finance Planning System, custodians of many of the significant economic policy instruments, had to defend their own autonomy and prerogatives. Pitfield and the Cabinet Planning System, given their access to the cabinet and the Prime Minister, wrote and rewrote the rules, refereed the game, and played only when they chose to. They were threatened by the Treasury Planning System's analysis and envied Finance's traditional independence, but integrated with neither in the central decision-making game.

What was the Cabinet Planning System? How was it supposed "to help ministers to know what they were doing"? In the narrowest sense, the instruments of the System were planning documents whose function was to catalogue, define, schedule, monitor and update various categories of issues facing the government. While the other planning systems were based in formal academic disciplines, the Cabinet Planning System created its own abstruse "discipline" out of the experience of a cabinet secretariat. It used a network of interrelated concepts and categories to structure ministers' views at a governmental, rather than departmental, level of aggregation. The categories and concepts of the Cabinet Planning System were not broadly understood in the bureaucracy or even in the cabinet or the PCO. They were accessible mainly by apprenticeship within the prime ministerial bureaucracy, and they changed considerably over time. Indeed, by 1975, when the Cabinet Planning System had reached its most elaborate incarnation, two major attempts were launched within the Plans Division of the PCO simply to describe the system as it had developed (they differed significantly!).

A comprehensive examination of the Cabinet Planning System will have to await the passage of time, or of legislation to improve public access to government documents. It should be possible, however, to convey the central features of the System. Like Pitfield, one can see it as an attempt to control and display the development of key issues demanding ministerial attention, to categorize them as to stage of evolution and to the nature of treatment required, and to present them to ministers to elicit their views.

The initial phase of development of the Cabinet Planning System, during the first Trudeau administration, 1968–72, was filled with optimism, excitement and a sense of breaking new ground. Although the later Pearson years had seen the origins of some first phase initiatives, the arrival of Pierre Trudeau as Prime Minister, with his antecedent commitments to rational government, seemed to promise the opportunity to turn the form of priority choice into substance.

Michael Pitfield, who had had a spectacular career in Ottawa through the Sixties, joined the Privy Council Office in 1965. He became an Assistant Secretary to the Cabinet in 1967 and Deputy Secretary of the Plans Division of the PCO when it was established in 1969. Pitfield had a decisive role in the development of both the cabinet committee system and the Cabinet Planning System. His knowledge of government and the public service, his single-minded devotion to their functioning, his extensive acquaintance in Ottawa and his subtle intellect, made him the confidant of a Prime Minister impressed by the capacity for abstraction and wary of being captured by a mandarinate which was years Pitfield's senior. It was Pitfield who built the Priorities and Planning Secretariat of the PCO into the cabinet counterpart to Hartle's ginger group in the Planning Branch of TBS, and who oversaw that Secretariat's design of the Cabinet Planning System.

The Priorities and Planning Committee's functions in 1972 were to report to cabinet on:

- the overall thrust of government policy, including the initiation and consideration of major policy reviews;
- the priorities to be assigned among the scarce resources of manpower, money and the time of ministers;
- the identification of priority problems and assignments of responsibility for their solution; and
- the consideration of specific important issues that need to be dealt with quickly and for the handling of which there is no established machinery.[56]

The Cabinet Planning System may be considered in summary fashion under three themes: *priority choice, priority problems* and *policy reviews*. Each has particular meanings within the Cabinet Planning System and for each the period 1968–72 was formative.

The first explicit cabinet involvement in the identification of *priorities* for the government as a whole occurred as early as 1966–67. With the implementation of the Planning, Programming, Budgeting System, and the increasing sophistication of the expenditure budget process, the pressure on cabinet to express its priorities increased apace. According to Phidd and Doern,

> ... in 1968–69 and 1969–70 the priority-setting exercise was characterized by the development of a short list of general but tough priorities including language policies and the removal of regional disparities. Most other programs were held constant in budgetary terms. The priorities reflected the initial flowering of the Trudeau "rational" priority-setting process, and were aided by the newness and hence the power of the 1968 Trudeau mandate. The toughness and shortness of the priority list were

also aided by the 1969 fight against inflation which included an effort to curtail government expenditure growth.[57]

In these early years, the results of such priority-setting exercises were literally lists of policy areas numerically ranked in order of priority. What it meant for either area when, say, constitutional reform was ranked above or below regional development was not entirely clear; there were inevitable problems implementing the priorities. However, they must have had some early impact on the resource allocation process, for some ministers and departments apparently saw themselves as losers in the exercise. Consider Phidd and Doern on priority choice during the latter part of the first Trudeau administration:

> By 1970, however, both the general political environment and the pressure of ministers and bureaucratic departments made the priority exercise less formally "rational" in the abstract sense of that word, but quite politically rational. Thus the October Crisis of 1970 converted the priority-setting exercise into a vague search for programs that would aid "national unity". In addition the pressure from ministers and departments that had been "ranked" low for two or three years in a row increased greatly. They increasingly demanded fairer treatment and e-quity in the budgetary and priority-setting process. These internal arguments and the need to maintain bureaucratic and ministerial peace and tranquility were aided by, and reflected in, the declining political strength of the Trudeau government in 1971 and 1972 and by growing unemployment. By the 1972 election, the priority-setting process generated a veritable "wish-list" of priorities.[58]

The failure of Finance Minister Edgar Benson's White Paper, *Proposals for Tax Reform*, severely shook the nerve of a government which had been determined and confident that it could make public decisions in a new way. By early 1971, the aggressive approach to planning and decision-making had given way to both fatigue and prudence. An election loomed and its result, a Liberal minority, chastened the government.

The electorate's failure in 1972 to appreciate the policy products of the Cabinet Planning System seemed to many observers, including a number of Liberal backbenchers and ministers, a clear indication that the Prime Minister's closest advisors in the PCO and Prime Minister's Office had isolated him from the political realities in a cocoon of technocratic structure and process. This diagnosis was implicitly accepted by the Prime Minister when, during the minority period, he moved Michael Pitfield from PCO to be the deputy minister of Consumer and Corporate Affairs and James Davey from Program Secretary in the Prime Minister's Office to senior advisor in the office of the Minister of Transport.[59] Since the election itself had moved others who personified the rational style of the first Trudeau administration out of the Prime Minister's Office, the new prime ministerial bureaucracy appeared to presage a greater sensitivity to both departments and the political grass roots.

During the minority period of 1972–74, the Cabinet Planning System was less concerned with "what kind of Canada do we want in the year 2000?". The prospect of a vote of no confidence concentrated ministerial minds and reduced their tolerance for the abstract planning exercises which had characterized the Cabinet Planning System between 1968 and 1972. Instead, Priorities and Planning served as a co-ordinating and general management committee, ensuring the cohesion necessary for survival in a minority situation. During this period, priorities came to be expressed as "major objectives" and "policy thrusts". Major objectives, such as "rationalize the social security system", "increase institutional bilingualism", or "secure national economic independence" reflected the objectives ministers believed fundamental to the modification of ongoing activities to move the country in the desired direction. Policy thrusts were more specific and implied more immediate implementation through policies and programs in, say, the urban environment or industrial development. According to Kirby and Kroeker, the Cabinet Planning System during the minority period "clarified for government the principles for which it stood and the actions on which it was prepared to stand or [as happened in 1974] fall".[60]

The original impetus for priorities had grown naturally out of the implementation of the Planning, Programming, Budgeting System in the latter half of the Sixties. A systematic expression of ministerial preferences, ultimately embodied in Expenditure Guidelines, was required to guide the management of the budgetary process by the Treasury Board Secretariat. The Cabinet Planning System as it developed during the first Trudeau administration implied a priorities framework much more ambitious and exhaustive in scope than simple guidance for resource allocation. The priorities developed by the Cabinet Planning System were to:

(i) assist cabinet in considering the multitude of items in its work program, in identifying gaps and in relating the government's activities to ministers' political concerns;
(ii) assist cabinet in establishing Expenditure Guidelines;
(iii) guide the activities of departments with respect to their work, both day-to-day and flowing from the Speech from the Throne;
(iv) guide federal-provincial consultations;
(v) provide a means of assessing existing programs and new proposals coming forward;

(vi) assist in policy development generally, particularly for initiatives which may form part of future Speeches from the Throne;
(vii) assist in communicating the government's concerns;
(viii) guide the review of the legislative program;
(ix) help ministers focus on the new policy thrusts of government.

Given these major aspirations, the process for developing the government's priorities had perforce to be no less thorough than its purposes. The only "official" account of this process, written in 1975 in the midst of its most extensive operation, describes it as follows:

> The planning procedures help in translating Ministers' views on the longer term objectives and priorities of the Government as well as on current issues and problems into concrete policies and proposals. This is easier said than done. The collective development by Ministers of an agreed overall appreciation of their concerns is a difficult undertaking, as is the organization and selection of areas or sectors where major significant change is desired—i.e., setting the Government's priorities. The priorities serve as a guide for the activities of the Government and as a means of responding to the requirements of particular problems, although they must themselves be changed as the political, social, or economic climate alters.
>
> Ministers collectively are assisted by the Plans Division of the Privy Council Office in formulating a general orientation, and in identifying future concerns and considering the importance and priority of such concerns. Each year an attempt is made to bring together in a single memorandum proposed priorities for the Government. The sources for this paper include the following:
>
> —individual interviews with all Ministers in order to gather their views as to the desired direction in which the Government should be moving, and to gather their perceptions of pending issues and concerns;
> —concerns and issues identified by Ministers in Cabinet and Cabinet Committee meetings, and by general contact and liaison with the advisory staffs of the Prime Minister and Ministers;
> —the proposals of the Party holding office (made in an election or resolutions passed at a Party policy convention); and,
> —legislative items of an essential, urgent nature and those carried over from previous sessions of Parliament.
>
> An additional means of gathering Ministers' perceptions of this sort has been to hold an informal, day-long meeting of Ministers. No background papers or formal agenda are prepared. The meeting provides Ministers with an opportunity to discuss their political program and identify issues of future concern. The conclusions reached at such meetings are recorded and form part of the process of arriving at an agreed program for the development and implementation of policy proposals.[61]

The results of the process to this point were then "summarized and synthesized" by the PCO and the Prime Minister's Office in a Memorandum to Cabinet. The document went to ministers after it had the Prime Minister's approval.

> After discussion in Cabinet the document together with any additional changes is presented to Deputy Ministers, who are asked to respond by describing how existing programs, or variations of such programs, might contribute towards the Government's priorities, and by proposing new programs. Following further detailed consideration by Cabinet of the responses of Deputy Ministers, Ministers will usually agree to a set of priorities to extend over the next two to four year period. In this way it is hoped to ensure (i) that departments are aware of the Government's priorities, and (ii) that the Government's priorities can be given practical expression in the form of new programs or alterations to existing ones. The priorities are reviewed every six months to determine whether they continue to reflect Ministers' concerns and are adapted to changing circumstances. At the same time progress in achieving the priorities is reviewed.[62]

The foregoing passages reveal the absolutely key role in the process played by officers of the Priorities and Planning Secretariat of the Plans Division of the Privy Council Office, and by the one or two members of the Prime Minister's Office who worked with them. They were the interviewers, the synthesizers, the schedulers and the packagers. They elicited the ministerial musings, transformed them into language suitable to the Cabinet Planning System and combined them in a Cabinet Memorandum for the approval of the Prime Minister. They drafted the resulting Records of Decision, and interpreted them for departments. Unlike the Department of Finance, unlike the Planning Branch of the Treasury Board Secretariat, the Privy Council Office minimized its role in analysis and the substance of policy. It portrayed itself as a neutral vehicle for ministerial and prime ministerial views, but the comprehensiveness of the premises of the Cabinet Planning System permitted, even required, the expression of some sort of agency philosophy, lest the exercise of priority choice become completely unmanageable. And those premises, from the cybernetics/ systems approach, likewise supplied much of the motif of the PCO planners' philosophy when faced with the initiatives or responses of departments or other central agencies: emphasis on dealing with longer term problems, establishment of goals and objectives, systematic canvassing of policy interrelationships and alternatives. If the perfect analysis seemed elusive, that was not the PCO's problem; far be it from them to usurp departmental responsibilities to carry out policy analysis in substantive areas! Their role was to transmit ministerial views to departments and to apply the standards of the Cabinet Planning System to the results.

50

A second major theme of the Cabinet Planning System was the identification of *priority problems*. "Priority problems" are not to be confused with "the government's priorities".[63] They were problems which required analysis and perhaps action, but which might fail to receive them, usually because they did not fall clearly within the responsibilities of any single portfolio. The PCO developed the concept of the priority problem to ensure that issues which might otherwise "fall between the stools" would receive the attention they needed. Donald Gow has described how priority problems were supposed to be dealt with:

> The general approach for the Committee on Priorities and Planning is to prepare a list of priority problems, with a brief description of each that attempts to get at the main issue. The Committee goes on to identify one Minister who will be responsible for a further definition of each problem and proposals for its solution. In a ways-and-means paper, the Minister indicates how he intends to take on its examination. He may also refine the definition of the problem. Once the Committee on Priorities and Planning has reached agreement on ways and means, a schedule is drawn up, and the Minister usually assembles a special staff, drawing on a special fund of the Privy Council Office or seeking appropriate funding from the Treasury Board. After his study of the matter, he presents a planning paper to the appropriate functional committee of Cabinet, giving an account of the likely results of alternative ways of solving the problem and a proposal for action. After consideration by the functional committee, the proposed solution is passed on to the Committee on Priorities and Planning and then to Cabinet. Along the way, plans are made for its possible implementation through the devices of legislation, budgetary provision and organizational change.[64]

Although Gow's description represents an idealized version of the development of a priority problem, it captures the PCO thinking behind the concept during 1968–1972.

In 1970, the list of priority problems (fourteen in all) included inflation, pollution, national unity, information, the public service, participatory democracy, education, social justice, urban growth and housing, tax reform and the ownership and control of Canadian resources.[65] Later lists included such subjects as regional economic expansion, bilingualism, foreign investment, cartels, guilds, labour unions and professional associations, freedom within the law, energy, science policy and industrial development policy.

The fate of priority problems was as varied as the lists themselves. Some culminated with the establishment of organizations, often full cabinet portfolios, which were given responsibility to deal with them. Science policy and urban growth and housing produced, in 1971, the Ministries of State for Science and Technology, and Urban Affairs

51

(dismantled in 1978), respectively. Regional economic expansion and "pollution" engendered full-fledged line departments with major program capacity. Some priority problems—such as participatory democracy and social justice—were simply too amorphous to produce tangible results, despite their fashionable political overtones. Others turned out to be non-problems either because, like education or urban affairs, the federal government lacked the constitutional jurisdiction to play a sufficient role, or because, like science policy or the public service, they represented problems which lay within the more or less unrelenting grasp of other entrenched and powerful bureaucratic interests. Still other priority problems, like foreign investment, launched major policy exercises which resulted in significant legislative and organizational change.

A degree of wastage was inevitable in an approach as ambitious as that of the Cabinet Planning System. Both priorities and priority problems were nevertheless intended "to prod departments into making new policy proposals and to initiate inter-departmental committees where no clear departmental interest had been established or where more than one department could claim an expertise".[66]

Much the same purposes were served by a third central aspect of the Cabinet Planning System, the plans document, or departmental *policy review*. In this case, the purpose was to stimulate a particular department to reflect on its plans for a policy sector for which it was responsible, and to share the product of those reflections with cabinet. Such an overall policy sector review might or might not coincide with a government priority, and unlike a priority problem, it would imply that planning be conceived within the horizons of a single portfolio. Among the major policy reviews initiated during 1968–71 were those on constitutional reform, foreign policy,[67] defence policy,[68] northern development and others.[69] A number of these reviews were published, and some are earmarked with the premises of the Cabinet Planning System. Again, some were more successful (and realistic) than others. They all reflected the attempt to use cabinet and the Committee on Priorities and Planning to elicit proposals from ministers which would consider the ensemble of departmental policies and programs, rather than any single one, and within a context of overall government priorities and objectives into the medium and longer term. All of them manifested the enormous faith in the power and persuasiveness of rational analysis that underlay the Cabinet Planning System.

The choice of the government's priorities evolved after 1972 into the establishment of major objectives and policy thrusts, and after 1974, into the Priorities Exercise of 1974–75. Likewise, priority problems and the overall policy reviews, or plans documents, together metamorphosed by 1973–74 into "cabinet planning studies". The theory of cabinet planning studies was less limited as to the kinds of policy problems which could qualify. It combined in this respect issues which a few years earlier could have been either priority problems or policy reviews.[70] This is clearly demonstrated by some of the cabinet planning studies open in 1974: demographic objectives, energy, mineral policy, communications, municipal finance, decentralization and responsiveness of the public service, participation, education; cartels, guilds, labour unions and professional associations; freedom within the law, labour relations, ethnic tensions and real income distribution. Comparison of these cabinet planning studies with the list of priority problems of four years earlier demonstrates that all of the initiatives of the Cabinet Planning System did not bear fruit immediately. Many of the 1974 studies had been designated as early as 1970.

Shortly after the introduction of cabinet planning studies, an attempt was made in the PCO to revive the enterprise of evaluation in the wake of Douglas Hartle's departure from the Treasury Board Secretariat. Cabinet evaluation studies were meant to bring the weight of cabinet behind the designation of particular policies or programs for evaluation. Five or ten cabinet evaluation studies were to be designated annually, with the department sponsoring each program to be responsible for the evaluation. Terms of reference were to be established by cabinet and monitored interdepartmentally. However, cabinet evaluation studies were launched in the fall of 1974, just as the Priorities Exercise of 1974–75 was getting under way, and they vanished without a trace in the midst of that larger and more elaborate enterprise. Deputy ministers had only so much time to devote to the demands of the Cabinet Planning System, and those of the Priorities Exercise were by far the most visible and urgently pressed.

At this point, mind whirling with the lexicon of the Cabinet Planning System, one is likely to cry—as did many a confused or frustrated deputy minister at the time—"Enough"! The appetite for minutiae more than satisfied, one wonders what it all meant. The PCO itself launched a couple of attempts simply to describe the Cabinet Planning System in 1974. Earlier and much more important than these was a major effort to provide an overall framework, current appreciation and blueprint for future development of central planning, which was undertaken within the Plans Division of PCO in 1971–72.

Planning Phase II, as this effort was called, was to be set in motion immediately after the election of 1972. The election result, a minority Liberal government, left Planning Phase II to gather dust in PCO files. The project is nevertheless of considerable interest, for its systematic attempt at metapolicy (policy on how to make policy) represented at once the characteristic preoccupations of the individuals who developed the Cabinet Planning System and their recognition that the System had overloaded the existing capacity of ministers and the bureaucracy to respond. In the end, however, Planning Phase II was not to question the basic premises of the Cabinet Planning System, nor to recognize that that system was in practice not the sole planning system. Thus, Planning Phase II sought to reinforce the reliance on the establishment of objectives, rational analysis in their pursuit and the other sacred assumptions of the Cabinet Planning System. Likewise, Planning Phase II never broached the relative dominance of the Cabinet Planning System. Accordingly, it never saw the Department of Finance as in fact more than a reluctant but necessary supporting player and it never faced the incompatibility of the Treasury Planning System, as it had developed under Hartle, with the Cabinet Planning System.

Planning Phase II began by retroactively defining Planning Phase I, that is, the reforms in central decision-making and planning which had been undertaken particularly during 1968–71. The most important of these were described earlier under the cabinet committee system, the Treasury Board and the expenditure budget process. The major accomplishments of Planning Phase I were seen as the creation of the Priorities and Planning Committee of cabinet, which was the focus of the Cabinet Planning System as it had developed to that point; the development of the priority problems approach; and the extensive government organization legislation passed during the first Trudeau administration, notably the establishment of two Ministries of State to deal with the priority problems of science and urban affairs.[71]

Planning Phase II sought to improve on previous performance by developing a more comprehensive and sophisticated planning system. By 1969–70, the planning theorists in the Privy Council Office had become seriously concerned at the relative failure of departments and agencies to respond adequately to the signals they were being sent by the Cabinet Planning System. Records of Decision seeking action on priorities, priority problems or policy reviews seemed to slip ever lower on ministerial and deputy ministerial agenda in the face of shorter term but more tangible political and administrative issues. Alternatively, a response would come forward which would be analytically incomplete or worse, by the standards built into the Cabinet Planning System, and/or which would represent no more than a ritualistic conformity with PCO demands on the part of ministers and departments. Time and again the Prime Minister would receive briefing notes from the Priorities and Planning Secretariat on departmental responses to initiatives launched by the Cabinet Planning System.

54

Time and again he would read in the distressed tones of the PCO officer of the department's apparently inexplicable failure to ask the fundamental questions and to establish broad objectives in a philosophical framework ("What is culture? What are Canada's cultural objectives? How do they relate to other federal objectives?") Time and again the Priorities and Planning Secretariat would recommend regretfully that the analysts be sent back to the drawing board to take another, broader look at the problem.

Departmental incapacity to execute in timely fashion the kind of analysis on which the Cabinet Planning System was predicated had been recognized in PCO before Planning Phase II. This recognition led to a distinctive redirection of PCO planning interest toward the restructuring of the machinery of government, beginning in about 1970, and exemplified by the *Government Organization Act of 1971*, which created the Department of the Environment and Ministries of State. Planning Phase II represented an imaginative and aggressive PCO interest in governmental structure, personnel and process, within a philosophical context entirely typical of the Cabinet Planning System. Although Planning Phase II contained thumbnail sketches of virtually all policy sectors, these consisted not of substantive analysis but simply a current status report and a reiteration of the demands of the Cabinet Planning System on the departments and agencies in the policy sector in question. The document's principal focus was an heroic attempt to knit together a series of major structural and procedural reforms, tortuously interlinked and rationalized within the framework of a bigger and better planning system. Some of these reforms have been instituted piecemeal; others may yet be, but it is symbolic that the most elaborate and complete blueprint for planning ever developed in the Government of Canada was to remain unimplemented, and almost unread. In a way, Planning Phase II shared the fate of the Cabinet Planning System more generally: enormous effort expended, prodigious accomplishments conceived, forms and targets established, all at a frustrating and seemingly insurmountable remove from the delivery of specific programs to citizens.

What can be made, then, of the Cabinet Planning System as it operated during 1968 to 1974? It was distinct from the Finance and Treasury Planning Systems, and it did not in fact subsume them. Furthermore, it was just as clearly a failure on its own ambitious terms as they were on theirs. On the other hand, it did force ministers to reflect on the overall directions of government more than they had ever been required to do before 1968. In this sense, the retrospective claim of its sponsors to have attempted "to help ministers to understand what they were doing" is a real and legitimate one. Furthermore, the momentum of the Cabinet and Treasury Planning Systems, reflected in the creation of policy and planning units throughout the bureaucracy in 1969–75, raised the standards of policy analysis and increased the breadth and quality of interdepartmental and cabinet discussion. The claim to have fostered "a degree of countervailance in the advice Ministers receive and the debate given to ideas before they are accepted"[72] has substance, although these benefits must be measured against the degree to which they slowed or even paralysed the decision-making process.[73]

The summary judgment of Phidd and Doern is most apt:

> ... while considerable effort has been expended to rationalize, in a formal way, the priority-setting process, and ... the economic-policy and budgetary process is tied to these more rationalized processes, the political processes imposed by the economy as well as the internal dynamics of the Cabinet and bureaucracy exert their own "rationality".[74]

Jackson and Atkinson drew the same kind of conclusion: "In Canada we have created the structures of rational policy-making, but incrementalism predominates within them".[75]

The Cabinet Planning System lost its focus and its legitimacy in the eyes of many ministers and officials because it attempted too much, altered direction too often and swelled the very notion of "priority" to a point where it no longer implied a paramount claim for any policy area over any other. There were entirely too many priorities, objectives, policy thrusts, priority problems and so forth, for any single, stable and coherent picture to emerge. Even where a priority set could be said to exist, it was often, technocratic assumptions notwithstanding, extraordinarily difficult to implement. Jackson and Atkinson noted that " ... policies cannot be extracted from ringing phrases".[76] Here is their account of the relationship between the legislative program and the government's goals:

> When the legislative program is being developed, each item is categorized under one of cabinet's goals or priorities. The relationship between the goals, the priorities, and the legislation is broadly intuitive. Ministers do not develop their legislation in response to the government's goals, but use the goals as rhetorical categories to justify their legislation. The relationship between goals and bills is sometimes so tenuous that when legislative proposals arrive at the PCO, officials merely group bills under one of the government's goals or priorities. Many senior politicians, skeptical of the so-called rational structures, do not believe it would be advisable to do otherwise.[77]

Likewise, Douglas Hartle, writing in 1973 while he was still Deputy Secretary of the Planning Branch of the Treasury Board, reflected on the utility for purposes of evaluation of the goals produced by the

Cabinet Planning System. Noting that the Cabinet Planning System was "following a related but slightly different course" to that of (what has been here called) the Treasury Planning System, he went on to observe:

> These two courses of action are obviously complementary and there is need to integrate them more closely. The criteria used to assess individual programs clearly should be consistent with the government's overall objectives. However, this requires that the government's overall objectives be defined, insofar as possible, in operational terms so that as much analysis as possible can proceed on an empirical basis. The strategic planning process that begins with the identification of priority problems [meaning: priorities] would be strengthened by bringing to bear the results of the evaluation of the effect of past changes in particular policy instruments. Without this information about the effectiveness of earlier decisions there is a danger that mistakes will be repeated and opportunities missed.[78]

Stripped of its diplomatic nuance, Hartle's message was that the priorities and objectives produced by the Cabinet Planning System were simply too nebulous to permit any rigorous evaluation, and that planning without evaluation was incomplete.

Furthermore, the Cabinet Planning System placed a broad and rapidly shifting set of demands on departments and agencies, even as its dogma emphasized thorough and far-reaching analysis of problems within a long term context. Departmental officials were caught between the shorter term political contingencies pressing on the minister, the multiple requirements of the Cabinet Planning System, and the unrealistically high expectations of the Priorities and Planning Secretariat as to what constituted adequate policy analysis. As Hartle noted in 1978:

> PCO prides itself upon its breadth of perspective, its perspicacity, its intimate knowledge of political realities in the Cabinet, the party and the country. It prides itself on its capacity to set in motion, through memoranda to Cabinet, studies, task forces, organizational changes, forces that will head off impending disaster. Although its efforts have been laudable in many ways, because other departments and agencies often become too narrow and/or rigid in their views and/or too embroiled in jurisdictional disputes to be able to cooperate in the resolution of a common problem, *the PCO has tended to initiate far more than it could successfully pursue to a conclusion.* Too frequently the attention of PCO has shifted from one problem to another so rapidly that those working on the problem (usually staff drawn principally from other departments and agencies) at its instigation found themselves rudderless and powerless. This is particularly galling to those from other departments, who are usually less than completely enthusiastic in the first instance.[79]

What was ultimately at stake in the development of the Cabinet Planning System was the distribution of power and influence within the central decision-making process. As that process became more complex after 1968, as the substantive policy input became more sophisticated, and as the planning ambitions of the government as a whole and the central agencies in particular grew, the designers, gate-keepers and critics in the PCO seemed to ministers and departments more and more powerful. Never mind that the Cabinet Planning System aimed at cohesion and foresight for cabinet and the government collectively. Never mind the ritual professions of central agency neutrality and the deferential references to "the views of ministers". Frustrated ministers saw the Cabinet Planning System as an essentially peripheral, but enormously time-consuming distraction from the essential concerns of political life. It was a barrier to be surmounted and a forum for administrative gamesmanship. While an ambitious younger cohort of bureaucrats found the Treasury and Cabinet Planning Systems a careerist's dream come true, an entire generation of their elders felt threatened and provoked by the rapidity with which the norms and expectations of life in the senior public service were changed before their eyes. Some ultimately prospered, some resisted, some resigned or retired.

The Cabinet Planning System, supported as it was by the Prime Minister, placed substantial influence within the hands of a small group of senior planning personnel within the PCO and centred during 1968–1972 and 1975–79 on Michael Pitfield. But this focus of influence, however visible within the bureaucracy and however common a target for disillusioned ministers and officials, was never strong enough to subsume the Finance and Treasury Planning Systems—indeed, its agency philosophy of countervailing ideas in the policy process in theory supported them—before the pressure of events in 1975–76 brought about the beginning of the end for all three.

Resource Allocation and Fiscal Policy

3

Resource allocation and fiscal policy are essential elements in the central decision-making process. They are fundamental to the attempt to plan in government. Despite the tidy symmetry of the expenditure budget process, however, resource allocation escaped the control of all three of the planning systems which coexisted during the first half of the Seventies. Indeed, it was this very loss of control, grounded ultimately in ministerial attitudes, and manifested in the persistence of three separate planning systems, which provided the roots of the manifold maladies of federal financial administration, which have so preoccupied the Auditor General, the Controller General, and the Lambert Royal Commission. Middle managers and financial clerks took their cues from cabinet and senior public servants. An examination of the interaction of the planning systems around resource allocation and fiscal policy illuminates the background to growth in public expenditure during the Seventies. Canadians will be contending with the implications of that growth for some time to come.

Fine Tuning and the Fiscal Framework
The Fiscal Framework is the Department of Finance's assessment of the economic picture for the forthcoming fiscal year. Among other things, the Fiscal Framework forecasts the government's revenues and recommends a target level of government expenditure, predicated on stabilization of the business cycle. A number of severe and interrelated problems plagued the Fiscal Framework during the Seventies.

The first and most general of these involved the inevitable conflicts between the time frames and the purposes of stabilization policy, on the one hand, and expenditure management, on the other. As Hartle points out, no univocal set of criteria emerged to guide us in the stagflationary Seventies:

> The balanced budget pre-1930 was a disciplinary device that kept government honest. Keynesian economics plus World War II ended the

59

unemployment problem for decades, but the discipline of the balanced budget was not replaced in the post-war period by a more rational and appropriate yard-stick, unfortunately.[1]

Thus, while stabilization policy operates within a twelve to eighteen month time frame, the control of overall growth in government expenditure is unlikely to be effective unless it is undertaken within a time frame two or three times that length.[2] Neither is there any necessary compatibility between the goals underlying stabilization and expenditure policies in any given time and place. Phidd and Doern express this clearly:

> Budgetary principles, on the one hand, require expenditures to be determined by program needs and tax levels to be set so as to cover expenditures, irrespective of the state of the economy. Countercyclical fiscal policy, on the other hand, requires a net budget surplus of revenues over expenditures when economic conditions are inflationary and a net deficit when the economy is sluggish. These two standards often conflict with each other, and this conflict gives rise to the intense political battles every year within the Cabinet, the bureaucracy, and the House of Commons.[3]

The second major problem relating to the Fiscal Framework focussed upon the analytical tools available for its development. Economics could not provide the instruments of analysis necessary to forecast government revenues accurately the many months in advance theoretically required for the role of the Fiscal Framework within the expenditure budget process.[4] Before the indexing of personal income tax to the rate of inflation in 1975, economic growth, inflation and consequent buoyant revenues rendered Fiscal Frameworks obsolete even before the beginning of the fiscal year to which they were meant to apply.

The Finance Planning System coped with these problems in a characteristic way. Confident in its own ability to "fine tune" demand in the economy, Finance attempted to operate a flexible fiscal policy. Neither the external deficit nor the absolute size of the government deficit represented serious constraints on the manoeuvrability of such a policy until 1975. In developing the Fiscal Framework the Department tended simply to assume the worst of the economy and of the capacity for self-control by ministers and departments.

Faithful to its agency philosophy, fearful above all of the economic distortions created by excess public spending, the Finance Planning System knowingly attempted to "counter-bias" a decision-making process weighted in favour of expenditure. Public spending and the raising of revenue are the two crucial elements for fiscal policy. By holding the line on spending, the Finance strategy went, the raising of revenue, principally through taxation, would play the major role in demand management. Tax policy happened to belong to the Department of Finance.

The Finance Planning System therefore produced consistently restrictive and conservative Fiscal Frameworks. These frameworks in some years underestimated revenues by a margin of more than a billion dollars. Since the expenditure ceilings established in the Fiscal Framework governed the cuts in departmental forecasts undertaken by the Program Branch of the Treasury Board Secretariat during the expenditure budget process, the appearance of "new" revenues during the fiscal year undermined seriously the credibility of the process in the eyes of the departments. If, for example, the purpose of the "B" budget was to array all new initiatives together within the ultimate constraint of the amount of new resources available, in order to determine their relative claim on these resources, what became of such a purpose if the constraint turned out to be too restrictive by an extent many times larger than the cost of any single initiative? On the credibility of the Fiscal Framework rested the credibility of the entire expenditure management process.

It is at this point that the Finance Planning System, the Treasury Planning System and the Cabinet Planning System failed to link with one another. This left the resource allocation process falling "between the stools", when in fact only united action by the three central agencies could have protected it from ministerial and departmental ambitions. The third major problem regarding the Fiscal Framework was the process by which it was developed and, equally important, revised. From at least as early as 1970, the Cabinet Planning System fought a continuing campaign to bring the final approval of the Fiscal Framework within the purview of the Cabinet Committee on Priorities and Planning. The secretariat to that committee constantly urged the Prime Minister to press the Minister of Finance to come forward with fiscal plans articulated within a longer term economic framework, and offering definite alternatives for collective choice by ministers. The secretariat further criticized Finance for altering the Fiscal Framework as new revenues appeared, without consulting cabinet and only in favour of policies and programs which coincided with Finance's economic philosophy. As the decade wore on, Finance felt increasingly threatened:

> In the old days, Finance, through the national budget, acted almost unilaterally. Now, in the Trudeau era, PCO has tried to appropriate ultimate responsibility for the budget, which must, of course, be reviewed by the Economic Policy and the Priorities and Planning Committees of the Cabinet. We are getting to the point where the budget is going to

61

have to be negotiated through the entire cabinet. Much of this is PCO's doing.[5]

The Priorities and Planning Secretariat emphasized in particular Finance's failure to go beyond the basic goals of demand management to address increasingly important structural issues, for example, regional development. The Secretariat went so far as to have "Regional Economic Instruments and Techniques" designated as a priority problem, aimed at forcing Finance to consider the possibility of regionally differentiated fiscal and monetary policy.

The Finance Planning System's response was predictable. Ministers of Finance brought to cabinet papers without options for choice, but rather with a single set of recommendations, developed within a conservative and relatively short term stabilization framework. Finance only grudgingly conceded the Cabinet Planning System's insistence on more sophisticated Quarterly Expenditure Reviews during the course of the fiscal year. The Department briefed the Minister to emphasize his periodic meetings with the Prime Minister and the Governor of the Bank of Canada as the crucial forum for collective decision-making on economic management, not so much to protect the Minister from his cabinet colleagues as to protect economic policy from the officials operating the Cabinet Planning System. And the Finance response to the priority problem "Regional Economic Instruments and Techniques" was strictly ritualistic and defensive in tone and content. The Cabinet Planning System's contention had been that the only way to harmonize economic policy with expenditure control was to undertake both in a long term framework and in a collective decision-making mode. In the end, the contention was never tested. What the Cabinet Planning System saw as the only hope for effective reallocation of resources within existing levels of expenditure, and the only hope for legitimacy for the Fiscal Framework in the eyes of ministers, the Finance Planning System saw as the ultimate concession, the ultimate loss of economic and fiscal control to the irresponsible fantasies of the PCO planners.

The Frustration of Treasury Control

Why wasn't the Treasury Planning System, or the Treasury Board and its Secretariat, minding the store? An essential point is the distinction between the former and the latter. The Treasury Planning System was based in the Planning Branch of the Treasury Board Secretariat, and its *raison d'être* was to develop the practice of the evaluation of efficiency and effectiveness of government programs, as a major contribution to resource allocation decisions taken within the expenditure budget process. Its mission was, as already suggested, one of those eminently sensible propositions which turn out to be pre-eminently difficult. In practice, the Treasury Planning System had by far the weakest power base of the three planning systems. For Douglas Hartle and the Planning Branch never succeeded in working in full co-operation with the Program Branch in its central role in the expenditure budget process, much less with the Finance and Cabinet Planning Systems.

For example, Hartle and the Secretary to the Treasury Board, Al Johnson, foreclosed the possibility of co-operation with Finance by arguing economic policy, as well as the efficiency and effectiveness of programs, before cabinet committees in the early Seventies. Finance felt threatened enough by the array of high-powered economic talent which Hartle recruited into the Planning Branch of the Treasury Board. When major program proposals brought briefings from the Treasury Planning System which focussed not only on expenditure impact but on the economic implications of the type of expenditure proposed, Finance's suspicions were confirmed. Indeed, this history is essential to an understanding of the intensity of Finance opposition to the Social Security Review proposals of 1975, in whose development Al Johnson, by then Deputy Minister of Welfare, played a major role.[6]

The quality and complexity of Treasury Planning analysis, as well as the aggressiveness with which it was promoted, threatened too many bureaucratic interests and hard-won compromises. Not the least of these were in the Program Branch of the Treasury Board. Given the lack of credibility of the Fiscal Framework, given the low status and high work volume of the Treasury Board as a committee of ministers, and given what we shall see to be a substantial separation of policy and resource decision-making within the cabinet committee system, the role of the Program Branch was not an easy one. The typical officer in the Branch will always find himself in a somewhat schizophrenic role. In order to maintain access to critical information held by the departments and agencies in whose budgets he specializes, he must maintain reasonably good relations with them, even as he must be the bearer of sad tidings more often than not. Inside the Program Branch, he must demonstrate tough-minded realism even as he endeavours to ensure that the more reasonable of his sector's proposals receives a fair hearing. The solution to these role conflicts, stemming from lack of both analytical conviction and collective ministerial support, was that the Program Branch was forced to manage the expenditure budget in a political style. We refer here to bureaucratic, not partisan, politics: departments and agencies must constantly be kept off balance, lest they pillage the public purse to even greater effect. This political element of Program Branch-departmental relationships is precisely

63

what the Lambert Commission referred to when it spoke of "the distrust which prevails in so many cases today between departments and the Treasury Board" and suggested "complete openness on both sides" as the answer.[7] One of the Program Branch's major tactical advantages in this political management process was the Planning, Programming, Budgeting framework, which provided a rich fund of counter-arguments to departmental initiatives; departments could be told that they had not adequately specified their objectives, had not developed criteria to measure effectiveness, or were not carrying out appropriate evaluations of their programs.

In short, the Program Branch felt embattled in much the same way, and for many of the same reasons, as the Department of Finance, and both adopted the same type of defensive, anti-spending strategies. Neither was able to adopt all of the products of the Treasury Planning System nor to co-operate fully with it. The political skills of Program officers were threatened by the depth and apparent conviction of Treasury Planning System evaluations. There was nothing less welcome in the Program Branch than a departmental proposal backed up by a thoroughgoing evaluation with the endorsement of the TBS Planning Branch. To the extent that Treasury Planning System evaluations showed significant returns for major social expenditures such as job creation programs, they were anathema to the Program Branch and the Finance Planning System alike. Simon Reisman refused on occasion to consider such evaluations, knowing only that they gave aid and comfort to the enemy, that is, to ministerial ambitions for expensive social programs.

This left the Treasury Planning System with one other avenue of recourse: the Cabinet Planning System. Douglas Hartle had explicitly referred in a paper written in the early Seventies while he was still Deputy Secretary—Plans, to the need to integrate the Treasury and Cabinet Planning Systems and, in particular, to develop government objectives sufficiently precise to be used to evaluate the effectiveness of specific programs in achieving those objectives. In March of 1972, in the context of development of the Expenditure Guidelines for the fiscal year 1973–74, the Treasury Planning System made an attempt to do just that. The Priorities and Planning Secretariat was surprised to find that both the Treasury Board Memorandum to Cabinet and the PCO Memorandum proposed sets of government goals and priorities to guide the allocation of "B" budget resources. The Treasury Board Memorandum proposed goals which had been developed from earlier efforts by the prime ministerial bureaucracy, but refined specifically with a view to guiding expenditure decision-making. The PCO document proposed goals which it saw as resulting from its further and broader exposure to ministerial preferences. The Cabinet Planning System defended its own proposals as broader than the Treasury Board's, and as conceived to guide not only expenditures, but also the allocation of other kinds of resources, such as legislative time, political attention, and so forth. In particular, the Priorities and Planning Secretariat was concerned to beat back the Treasury Board initiative and to protect its own franchise on the interpretation of ministerial views. Using tactics that recalled the suspicions of other departments as to the legitimacy of the PCO's management of the cabinet committee system, the Secretariat placed in the Record of Decision a proviso that the responsibility for the definition of government goals would be that of the Prime Minister's and Privy Council Offices. The frustration of the Treasury Planning System was complete. Within a year, Hartle had submitted his resignation.

In the face of all this, the Program Branch of the Treasury Board found itself in the position of the little Dutch boy eagerly poking fingers and thumbs into an ever-widening breach in the dike of the expenditure budget process. In the first place, as on the revenue side, there was no coherent medium term appreciation of the aggregate growth of current expenditure commitments. The Treasury Board and Finance constantly found themselves on the receiving end of nasty surprises as the full implications of program initiatives undertaken two to three years earlier became evident. Furthermore, without the medium or longer term picture, it proved virtually impossible to effect any reallocation or control within the "A" budget, which represented some 90% of the overall budget, and consisted of statutory obligations, federal-provincial obligations, and maintenance of existing levels of service in current programs. The "A" budget grew inexorably. Such commitments provided little scope for political choice until the federal government began to restructure its fiscal policy toward the provinces in the later Seventies.

This is not to say, however, that the 10% of each budget which represented new initiatives or expansions of existing programs was arrived at and allocated through the conscious and controlled exercise of ministerial discretion. To the contrary. While Finance and the Treasury Board felt that much of this "new money" should not have been spent at all, the weakness of the Fiscal Framework, combined with the cabinet committee system, encouraged a ministerial free-for-all in pursuit of resources, at a time when only united action by the three central agencies and their ministers could have controlled such behaviour.

As each fiscal year neared, and revenues above and beyond those forecast in the Fiscal Framework arrived in the public treasury, the laborious exercise of cutting the "B" budget down to the Framework's constraints seemed more and more irrelevant. The most ambitious ministers and departments wondered why they should "play ball" with the Treasury Board by submitting their proposals in the "B" budget forecast, when prospects seemed far better after Main Estimates had been finalized, and the fiscal year approached. The avenue to the new money was not the systematic comparison with alternative proposals sponsored by other departments on which the "B" budget and Expenditure Guidelines exercises were based. Rather it was a later blitz on the cabinet committee system, featuring a determined minister and a politically attractive initiative, embodied in a persuasive Memorandum to Cabinet. In this way, the proposal would be considered in a cabinet committee as a single item just before or during the fiscal year, with the Fiscal Framework inevitably in a vague and fluid state of "revision" owing to the arrival of "unexpected" revenues. While Treasury Board Program officials and their Finance colleagues might struggle manfully in cabinet committee against these proposals, ministers usually found it impossible to say no to a colleague, and impossible to resist a positive recommendation to full cabinet. Nor did the buck stop at cabinet, which typically would approve the proposal "in principle, subject to Treasury Board review". This *caveat* meant little, indeed it was on occasion entirely ignored by ministers, who would take the Record of Decision as a license for a public announcement. This announcement in turn would commit the government irrevocably in the eyes of the clientele who were to benefit from the program. By the time the proposal arrived at the Treasury Board, the Board was in no position to question the advisability of the program as such, no matter how meagre, unrealistic or downright misleading was the financial analysis in the Memorandum to Cabinet developed by the sponsor. As a result, the Treasury Board was reduced to quibbling over the timing of the funding or the details of program design, and the government's commitments would appear in one of the two Supplementary Estimates submitted to Parliament during the fiscal year. Henceforward, of course, the program would have to be included in the expenditure cycle, but within the effective security of the "A" budget.[8]

In summary, then, departments and ministers discounted the accuracy and thus the significance of the revenue forecasts in the Fiscal Framework. Perceiving the success of the strategy, and understandably ambitious to make a mark in their portfolios, departmental ministers systematically "end-ran" the expenditure budget process, through the cabinet committee system and Supplementary Estimates. The cabinet committee system as it was managed by the PCO was biased toward policy initiation and insufficiently sensitive to the expenditure considerations which Treasury and Finance officials sought to introduce into committee consideration of departmental proposals. In any case, these officials were typically operating not only without a credible Fiscal Framework but also without sufficient time and information to critique departmental proposals adequately. In consequence, ministers regularly took decisions involving expenditure without accurate knowledge of the amount and schedule for that expenditure, without knowledge of the government's current fiscal situation and the impact of the proposed expenditure on it, and without being able to evaluate competing claims for the funds within the context of a set of government priorities. The Treasury Board's weakness as a committee of ministers left it entirely unable to cope with this separation of policy and program from resource decision-making, which resulted in *de facto* abdication of responsibility for the latter.

The Demise of Fine Tuning

In the mid-Seventies a series of major events jarred the basic assumptions of the Finance Planning System and forced the Department into joining the search for an alternative to "fine tuning". First, the oil crisis of 1973–74 showed that supply management and the resolution of structural problems could not indefinitely be factored out of the stabilization framework. Their effects were too pervasive. Second, the arrival of monetarism in the Bank of Canada in 1975 put Finance on notice that, in future, monetary policy would not necessarily play its accustomed "accommodative role". Henceforward, targets for the money supply would be set and pursued, while adjustment to shocks in the economy would occur through exchange rate flexibility rather than through "fine tuning". The Department was left with a relatively reduced role in the quarter-by-quarter management of the economy.

Third, the dizzy wage-price spiral of 1974–75 pushed Finance to recommend to a dumbfounded cabinet a policy of controls. The controls period was supposed to create a "window" for major structural adjustments, after which, many in the Department still hoped, a return to the traditional reliance on demand management would be possible. Nevertheless, these structural initiatives would have to be left to others. Finance might show sympathy, but rarely leadership. The classic isolation of the Finance Planning System disappeared with the retirement of Simon Reisman at the end of 1974, and with the Department's involvement in the DM-10 committee of deputy ministers formed for purposes of economic co-ordination during the controls period. Personalities and the underlying agency philosophy remained important, however. Finance was diffident about infringing upon the responsibilities of other economic departments. It hesitated to convert its many "watching briefs" to active policy development, and other departments seemed unable to move immediately forward into the leadership role.

Canada was not the only country experiencing a malaise in economic performance and policy. The so-called McCracken Report for the Organization for Economic Co-operation and Development (OECD), circulated in draft in the middle of the Canadian controls period, explored many of the issues which were bedevilling Ottawa. The McCracken Report was a counsel against panic and a reiteration of faith in Western economics and its institutions:

> ... our reading of recent history is that the most important feature was an unusual bunching of unfortunate disturbances unlikely to be repeated on the same scale, the impact of which was compounded by some avoidable errors in economic policy. The continuing legacy of 1971 –75 makes for unusual difficulties in framing policies for the years immediately ahead. We reject, however, the view that existing market-oriented economic systems and democratic political institutions have failed. What is needed is better use of existing instruments of economic policy, and better functioning and management of existing market mechanisms.[9]

The report defined a policy which came to be known as "gradualism", calling for "a moderate but sustained expansion initially less rapid than would otherwise be desirable, during which memories of recent inflation fade, and confidence in rising sales and employment is restored".[10] McCracken therefore rejected "a strong front-loaded recovery" or any accommodation by governments to high rates of inflation. Monetary and fiscal policy were to be framed in the medium term, with governments undertaking public commitments to achieve appropriate targets.[11] Better guidelines were to be framed for public expenditure, and the efficiency and effectiveness of such expenditure was to be increased.[12]

In Canada, the implications of gradualism took the distinctive form of a search for a better balance between social and economic goals and, in particular, for a grasp on the trade-offs between expensive social programs and economic efficiency. With the eclipse of all three planning systems complete by 1975, the leadership in this exercise fell to two PCO officials who had not been part of the Cabinet Planning System during its heyday: Ian Stewart, Senior Economic Advisor, and Fred Gorbet, Assistant Secretary for Economic Policy. Stewart and Gorbet worked closely with the economic deputies on the DM-10 committee during the controls period. The result was *The Way Ahead*, a discussion paper published in 1976, "outlining the economic and social directions the government intends to take after controls end."[13]

The Way Ahead expressed the government's commitment to the market *and* to "fundamental social goals".[14] In seeking a middle road between a conservative economic philosophy with a complete emphasis on efficiency, and a pursuit of social equality on a scale like that of 1965–75, *The Way Ahead* emphasized public consultation and consensus formation. From the perspective adopted here, it represented an attempt to synthesize the agency philosophies of all three planning systems. Perhaps its most important contribution to economic dialogue was its reinterpretation of the inflation/unemployment trade-off, with all the technicalities that issue implies, into the need for a better *integration* of economic and social goals, a notion more easily grasped by the man on the street. The recognition of the primacy of this need to do less but to do it better, in a document launched with considerable fanfare by the government, represented a considerable departure for an administration whose central decision-making process had hitherto operated to isolate, rather than integrate, economic and social policies. The compromise suggested by *The Way Ahead*, then, was to pose the question, not *whether* to continue to pursue social goals, but *how* to do so more efficiently from the viewpoint of the economy as a whole.

The problem was, as the next two years were to show, that recognition of these objectives was by no means equivalent to achieving them and that technical limitations remained central to the capacity to manage the economy, despite the relative confidence of the McCracken Report. The unexpected persistence of stagflation through 1978 cast further doubt on the efficacy of the traditional instruments of demand management. The impact of inflation, increased oil prices and slow growth greatly reduced the manoeuvrability of fiscal policy. The absolute size of the government's deficit, and its relation to the size of the GNP, became key issues.

While the Treasury Board had always argued from a microeconomic perspective that the deficit was too big, Finance now had to consider the possibility that deficits were no longer effective stabilizers, and that the economy might no longer be able to sustain large deficits. The heretical possibility had to be faced: deficit reduction during a time of economic stagnation might be necessary, the fundamental principles of macroeconomics notwithstanding. The era of "fiscally neutral" budgets had arrived, and the Prime Minister, under prodding from certain advisors, was becoming convinced that stringent restraint was necessary. In addition, however, there was a growing imbalance in the fiscal policy of the federation as a whole; certain provinces were saving money from resource sales to the extent of a considerable macroeconomic impact, while the federal government was in no position to spend in order to compensate. Thus, economic policy would more than ever require effective federal-provincial co-ordination, and the provinces would have a proportionately larger role to play.

These issues came to a head at the First Ministers' Conference of February 1978, at which agreement on a series of economic directions was achieved. The Prime Minister specifically rejected the full implications of the conservative attack on social spending. In pursuing social goals,

> We may have moved too quickly at times, but I could not agree that we have moved in the wrong direction nor could I be a member of a partnership that would destroy these fundamental support systems that have so enhanced the lives of Canadians in every region of the country.[15]

However, the Conference agreed that "private citizens and private markets have the major task in ensuring economic performance in Canada", and governments "cannot and should not manage all the details of economic activity".[16] Furthermore, "government expenditure growth should be held lower than the average rate of growth in real output",[17] this, "to reduce the role of government in the economy".[18] The Economic Council of Canada was asked to study the impact of government regulation of business. A "Shop Canadian" program to encourage the purchase of Canadian goods was to be launched. Provinces were to be fully consulted on the multilateral trade negotiations, then in progress, and would be involved in the federal government's exhaustive private sector consultation efforts, to be launched later that year.[19]

In the aftermath of the First Ministers' Conference, the Prime Minister's personal conviction as to the need for restraint had become a public, intergovernmental commitment to keep the growth of public expenditure below that of the GNP. The Treasury Board was given the mandate to deliver the federal part of this commitment.

As early as 1975–76, the first formal recognition of the Treasury Board's problematic role in resource allocation had occurred. From that point—one not only of increasing economic difficulties, but also of government revenues dampened by indexing of the personal income tax, and of the beginnings of over- rather than under-estimation of revenues in the Fiscal Framework—the Treasury Board was somewhat better integrated into the Trudeau cabinet committee system. After cabinet committee consideration, any Memorandum with expenditure or revenue implications had to be considered by the Treasury Board before it went on the full cabinet Agenda for final decision. Thus, the Program Branch of TBS would get an opportunity for a more detailed analysis of the proposal, which analysis provided a basis for briefing the Treasury Board as to the cost of the proposal, its impact on the expenditure framework, its relationship to other initiatives and similar issues. This briefing in turn suggested recommendations which the Treasury Board could submit when the Memorandum was subsequently considered by full cabinet. Efforts were also made to strengthen the membership of the Treasury Board by tightening the links between the Board and the other committees of cabinet, but it is doubtful that the Board ever recovered much prestige within the Trudeau committee system.[20]

Faced with the stringent requirements of the spring of 1978, the Prime Minister wrote in support of the Treasury Board to all ministers, seeking suggestions as to expenditures which could be cut in order to meet the commitments undertaken at the First Ministers' Conference. Despite the urgency and the momentum behind the drive for restraint, the letter was no more successful in locating volunteers to walk the plank than had been previous "X" budget exercises. The Prime Minister seemed to have the collective, but not the individual, support of his ministers.

Shortly after this abortive attempt to cut, in July 1978, the Prime Minister attended the economic summit in Bonn, West Germany. Although reports of the death of gradualism were greatly exaggerated, it had become evident that the industrial democracies could not continue to finance mounting internal and external deficits. They would have to force the pace of adjustment. Again, Trudeau found himself making a commitment to show leadership in this enterprise, this time before Western leaders of government rather than provincial first ministers.

On his return, the Prime Minister began the process of negotiating increases in oil prices, recognizing that Canada could not continue to cushion prices indefinitely. Equally important, Trudeau recognized that the federal resource allocation process was wholly inadequate to the challenge of restraint. Furthermore, his government was in serious political trouble. Public opinion polls showed a major decline in Liberal Party support in the pivotal region of Southern Ontario, and this decline was generally analysed as the product of middle class disenchantment with the Trudeau government's tax and fiscal policies. A group of relatively affluent voters seemed to be rebelling against high levels of taxation and government spending. The summit meeting itself had highlighted the role of public spending in causing inflation and international monetary instability. It therefore seemed both good politics and good economics when the Prime Minister announced, in a nationally televised address on August 1, 1978, a cut in planned expenditures of $2.5 billion. Some of this money, Trudeau went on, was

71

to be reallocated toward industrial development. The Prime Minister rationalized the budget cuts in the context of his commitments to other Western leaders, undertaken at Bonn.

The Prime Minister's initiative was interpreted by the pundits as a desperate attempt to shore up sagging Liberal fortunes among a fiscally conservative middle class constituency, especially among the small businessmen, managers and professionals of Southern Ontario. Politically, it was a failure. The rediscovery of economic growth as a popular issue, and the self-denying ordinance of public sector restraint, had about them the air of an unconvincing deathbed conversion, as the results of the by-elections of October 1978 demonstrated.

Perhaps the most significant feature of the August cuts was their unilateral nature. The Prime Minister's decision on the budget was essentially his alone. In a spectacular departure from the collegial style, cabinet had no opportunity to discuss the size and nature of the cuts and most ministers were informed of them by telephone, a matter of hours before the Prime Minister made the public announcement. The cuts were an admission of administrative failure, at least to the extent that the need for them, and the way in which they were carried out, constituted the final demonstration of the inefficacy of the resource allocation process. Furthermore, the money released by the cuts for the purposes of industrial development became the only game in town for ministers in economic portfolios. There was a free-for-all in pursuit of this "new money" and it was conducted in a vacuum created by the Prime Minister's *coup de grace* to the tattered remnants of the expenditure control system.[21] Chapters 6 and 7 will describe the structural innovations which grew out of the consequences of the initiative of August 1978.

Conclusion

It would be a mistake to see the Department of Finance's role in the last half of the Seventies as one constantly trailing behind or being forced by events. At least, to the extent this image is accurate, it was one which applied equally to most of the exchequers or treasuries of the industrialized democracies. Finance showed a kind of cautious flexibility of policy direction which was very much in the mainstream of the best of national economic management practice. It was a time of frustration for economic policy-makers, who ransacked theory in a continuing search for a better handle on events. The Department of Finance was, and remains, very much a part of this search, which is common to all of the OECD countries.

The Eighties promise more of the same. The complementary/competing philosophies of demand management, supply management and monetarism jostle for dominance, but a principal issue surrounding each would appear to be doubt as to its adequacy to the tasks at hand. The new decade may see a more determined and concerted attack on structural problems, particularly should monetarism, now undergoing its *experimentum crucis* in many Western countries, fail to arrest the pattern of stagflation.

As for the Department itself, 1980 finds it in the midst of a critical change of generations in the senior management group, potentially the most important since the Bryce era which ended ten years ago. The new leadership in Finance must be composed of policy-makers rather than technicians, as the Cabinet Planning System had been insisting since at least 1970, albeit in an idiosyncratic and, to the technicians, threatening way. Of course economic literacy and insight will remain prerequisites, but they must be combined with the analytical and political skills necessary to carry the Finance position in forums which demand co-operation and leadership rather than readings from the sacred texts of economics. There is a hoary Ottawa cliché that there are no problems without opportunities. Economic problems present Finance with the opportunity to come to advantageous terms with a process of economic policy formulation which *will* be increasingly collective in nature. The new generation in Finance must have the imagination, the flexibility and the confidence to grasp that opportunity. No other department can play the leadership role. If Finance fails, however, the vacuum will have to be filled, and it is likely to be filled by narrower interests.

What of the expenditure budget process? Overall resource allocation performance during the Trudeau era was a fundamental preoccupation of the Lambert Commission. The situation outlined in this chapter drew some extremely pungent comment from the Commission:

> The deficiencies in central management of government today relate in no small measure to a failure to plan thoroughly at the top. Accepted, instead, is a planning process too often dependent on trying too many unco-ordinated proposals coming up from the bottom . . . we cannot accept that priorities and objectives can continue to be set without a full awareness of the financial implications of attempting to achieve them . . . co-ordination and discipline are absent. This has led to incremental budgeting, crisis planning, poorly conceived ad hoc solutions to problems, and excessive flexibility in program management . . . planning is a misnomer for a process that focusses principally on new initiatives and how they might be realized. It is not planning if it does not require choices among new initiatives, and encourage the review and evaluation of ongoing activities and the identification of cost-reduction potential.[22]

The argument for planning, and for control of expenditure, need not necessarily be an argument for limitation of expenditure, although this was how Lambert construed it. It refers simply to the making of expenditure decisions in the fullest possible knowledge of their relative claims and implications. Expenditure decisions could ideally be characterized as the synthesis resulting from a kind of dialectic between the Fiscal Framework and the government's priorities. This means not only that the Fiscal Framework could have been conceived as more than simply a static governor on expenditure, but also that its dynamism ought to have derived, in part, from the impact of the priorities themselves. That is, only priorities developed within a five- to ten-year framework could be such as to alter the government's "degrees of freedom", within the Fiscal Framework, by permitting significant reallocation within the "A" base.

In this section, much has been made of the technicalities of expenditure decision-making. If there were substantial technical weaknesses, they were nevertheless only part of the story. If the expenditure control system was feeble, if expenditure mounted at dizzying rates over the first half of the Seventies, it was ultimately because ministers wished it to be thus. Although there was a sense in which the clash of agency philosophies resulted in a system which failed dramatically "to help ministers to understand what it was they were doing", and penalized politically the fiscally responsible departmental minister, the political will to control expenditure simply wasn't there. A substantial majority of the incremental growth in government spending during the first six or seven years of the Trudeau administration stemmed from a relatively few (less than twenty per year) major policy and program decisions, where the amounts of money involved were so great that it is unreasonable to assume that cabinet could have been unaware of their significance, if not of the precise magnitude of their aggregate impact. All of the integrated planning systems, all of the technical improvements in the world, will hardly function effectively where political conviction is lacking.

Finally, it is worth noting that the image of the federal deficit as a future mortgaged by an irresponsible indulgence in non-productive social programs is misleading, to say the least. Among the most important sources of the deficit were decisions to index personal income tax, increase transfers to provinces, and institute tax expenditures targeted on the corporate sector in the name of growth, jobs and competitiveness. It is unrealistic, therefore, to see the early Eighties as likely to witness a mere playing out of the implications of the conservative diagnosis of government spending. On the contrary, policy-makers will be under intense pressure to reconsider indexation and to examine sceptically the cost/benefit justification of tax expenditures.

The Priorities Exercise of 1974-75

The description of the Cabinet Planning System in Chapter 2 focussed on the experience of the first two Trudeau administrations, 1968-72 and 1972-74. This chapter examines the Priorities Exercise which followed the return of a Liberal majority in the election of July 1974. The Priorities Exercise may now be seen as a monument to the Cabinet Planning System, as well as yet another illustration of the failure of that system to integrate with the Finance Planning System. Although the remnants of the post-Hartle Treasury Planning System were co-opted into the Priorities Exercise, the Finance Planning System, despite the departure of Simon Reisman, held aloof from the Exercise. Given the economic circumstances of 1974-75, however, this schism could not endure. It began to dissolve with the arrival of wage and price controls in the fall of 1975, which at the same time signalled the demise of the Cabinet Planning System. The Priorities Exercise of 1974-75 was thus a perverse sort of prehistory to the arrival of controls. The controls program was the most important policy never to have been planned by the Cabinet Planning System.

The election result of 1974 was generally interpreted as a response to Pierre Trudeau's definitive and popular rejection of the policy of wage and price controls advocated by Robert Stanfield, leader of the Progressive Conservative Party. If the election result constituted a mandate of a substantive kind, it was that the new government *not* implement this kind of policy to combat the problems of serious inflation and astronomical wage settlements which characterized the economy of 1974. This kind of ambiguous and negative mandate was fine as far as it went, but that was hardly far enough. The brief embarrassment of the minority period over, the Liberal Party returned to its accustomed position with a solid majority in power. What to do?

When the Canadian electoral process fails to produce policy ideas— and that is often—it is the bureaucracy which is called upon to generate them. The architects of the Cabinet Planning System were, in the summer of 1974, nothing loath to try. Although proud of the co-ordinating function which the Cabinet Planning System had played during the minority period, they were anxious to continue the development of the longer term, government-wide planning function of their system, a development which had been rudely interrupted by the results of the 1972 election. That the Prime Minister shared these ambitions was obvious in his choice, as Secretary to the Cabinet, of Michael Pitfield, who had spent the minority period as deputy minister of Consumer and Corporate Affairs and then on leave at Harvard University. Pitfield had had a decisive role in the development of the cabinet committee and Cabinet Planning Systems during his years in the PCO from the mid-Sixties to 1972. His return to the most senior position in the PCO, and indeed in the public service, made the minority period look like a mere interregnum. The Priorities Exercise as such, however, was not Pitfield's doing; he did not return to the PCO until the beginning of 1975, in the midst of the Exercise.

Despite the secure position of the new government, and ambitions in the PCO to take up where the Cabinet Planning System had left off in 1972, the blueprint for 1974 did not include Planning Phase II, as had been intended prior to the 1972 election. Although personalities and responsibilities within the Plans Division of PCO had changed somewhat, the principal reason why Planning Phase II was not dusted off and reintroduced in 1974 was greater scepticism about the workability of its major and extensive structural recommendations. Planning Phase II had been conceived in 1972, when faith abounded in changes in machinery of government to revitalize the attack on policy problems. By 1974, the full cost of the enormous organizational changes of 1965–72 was becoming evident to all, and in particular to the central agencies responsible for these reforms, PCO and TBS. The indifferent performance of initiatives like Information Canada, the Ministries of State for Science and Technology and Urban Affairs and the Department of the Environment refuted structural change as a panacea for policy problems. Confidence had waned in the ability to transfer the rationality and symmetry of organizational redesign from paper to reality. The watchword in machinery of government was no longer innovation, but consolidation. If Planning Phase II was the victim of electoral results in the fall of 1972, it was the victim of a disillusioned realism about bureaucratic reorganization in the summer of 1974.

The government's need for a program was to be answered by a bigger and better planning process, a bigger and better Cabinet Planning System which would not necessitate permanent organizational change. This was the Priorities Exercise of 1974–75 which was developed, as Planning Phase II had been, within the Priorities and Plan-

76

ning Secretariat of the Plans Division of the PCO. Two cardinal factors underlay the Secretariat's conception of the Priorities Exercise. One, the Exercise would be the first to apply to the entire four year period at the disposal of a majority government. Thus the Secretariat hoped to adapt the framework of major objectives and policy thrusts, which it had developed for the government's priorities during 1972–74, in order to plan the full mandate of the new government. The planning framework was to guide allocation of resources such as money, personnel, cabinet committee time and legislative time. The Secretariat expected that this more extensive and detailed "plan" would generate more tangible results in the way of policies and programs than had previous priority sets. This intention related directly to the second factor crucial to the conception of the Priorities Exercise, the attempt to involve departments far more thoroughly in the development of priorities than had been the case thus far. PCO officials were well aware that some ministers and senior officials had been frustrated and impatient with the Cabinet Planning System, especially in 1970–72, and Planning Phase II had dealt explicitly with that problem. As the Priorities Exercise was conceived, departmental contributions were to be critical to the fleshing out of specific priorities as the Exercise proceeded, and this, it was hoped, would in turn communicate the priorities effectively to departments and generate commitment from them. Thus, the need for, and to a degree, the character of the Priorities Exercise was a product of the election of 1974. The process itself, however, evolved logically from the Cabinet Planning System, especially its functioning from 1970–72.

The Idea

The Priorities Exercise was carefully planned. In the early fall of 1974, senior people from the Priorities and Planning Secretariat and from the small policy group in the Prime Minister's Office would jointly interview each minister in the new cabinet. The interview would revolve around two questions posed to the minister: "what does the government have to do during its mandate in order to win the next election?" and "what do you want to be remembered for having done, should the government lose the next election?". These interviews were to result in a list of desired accomplishments. From the list, from existing major objectives and policy thrusts and from cabinet planning studies, a set of five to ten priorities were to be identified by cabinet at a meeting at the government's Meach Lake retreat in late November.

Following the Meach Lake meeting, the set of priorities was to be articulated for discussion by the Liberal caucus and for final approval by the Priorities and Planning Committee and cabinet. This was to have taken place by January 1, 1975, at which time the Memorandum to Cabinet and the Record of Decision resulting from it were to be circulated to departments. Each department was to be requested to provide a summary response to the priorities by March 1, 1975, in the form of a letter of less than eight pages to the Secretary to the Cabinet. (The Prime Minister also held a luncheon meeting during the month of February 1975, with some thirty-five deputy heads, in order to impress upon them the importance of the Exercise and outline his expectations for their participation.)

Departmental responses to the priorities were specifically to include an assessment of how the department's existing policies and programs contributed to the government's priorities, and how new departmental initiatives could do so. Departments were also asked to express their own priorities, so that cabinet could review them and relate them to the government's priorities. The PCO, through the Prime Minister, explicitly requested that departments be innovative in their responses, and that they emphasize reallocation of effort within existing resource levels in light of the priorities. Noting that government spending had risen significantly in recent years, the material circulated to departments cautioned that the Priorities Exercise should not be used as an occasion to plead for new resources. The PCO expected that every department and agency should be able to find ways to contribute to the priorities, even if their substantive responsibilities might seem distant from them. Finally, departments were requested to suggest specific criteria against which the contribution of departmental programs to the achievement of objectives within the priorities could be measured.

At the beginning of March, departmental responses were to be broken down according to their relevance to each priority by a ten member "core group" recruited from the PCO, TBS Planning Branch, Finance and the Federal-Provincial Relations Office, and supervised by the Priorities and Planning Secretariat. A Memorandum to Cabinet summarizing departmental responses overall was to be sent for information to the Committee on Priorities and Planning. More important, a Memorandum to Cabinet for each priority was to be composed of a summary of all the departmental responses relevant to that priority, and to be submitted, under the signature of the minister who was chairman of the committee, to the appropriate cabinet committee. The committee consideration was to take place during April to June 1975.

After the Memorandum to Cabinet for each priority had been considered by the appropriate cabinet committee, the resulting Committee Reports were to be consolidated in a single Memorandum to

Cabinet. This Memorandum was to be considered by full cabinet at another Meach Lake meeting at the end of June. The Record of Decision issuing from this discussion, together with the Memorandum itself, were to constitute a concrete plan embodying the central concerns for the government's mandate from mid-1975 onward. In particular, the results of the Priorities Exercise were to guide the Speech from the Throne for the fall of 1975 and the expenditure budget cycle for the fiscal year 1976–77.

The Execution

The Priorities Exercise represents a rather heroic attempt to plan. No doubt the vicissitudes of politics and of organizational relations would have rendered such an enterprise difficult at any time. As it happened, the Priorities Exercise took place at a time when no elaborate and tortuous planning process, no flood of policy papers, no interminable committee meetings, were really required to identify the government's priorities. But the veneer of technocratic sophistication seemed almost to deny that essential and overriding reality. The more or less fashionable set of issues which surfaced seemed to suggest that it might be possible to find some circuses to divert the citizenry from the issue of bread. Consider the policy framework of five "themes" with no less than sixteen "priority policy areas" which emerged from the ministerial interviews of September and October 1974, and discussion of the resulting Memorandum to Cabinet at the Meach Lake cabinet meeting of late November 1974:

I.   A more just, tolerant, Canadian society including:
- social security
- native rights
- law reform
- bilingualism
- labour-management relations

II. With a greater balance in the distribution of people and the creation and distribution of wealth between and within regions including:
- demographic and growth patterns
- transportation
- national industrial and regional development

III. Which makes more rational use of resources and is sensitive to the natural and human environment including:
- conserving our natural resources, particularly energy resources
- maximizing the use of Canada's agricultural and fisheries resources
- diversity of life styles and mental and physical health

79

IV. Accepting new international responsibilities particularly with regard to assisting developing countries including:
- sharing of resources
- alleviating international crises

V. With an evolving federal state capable of effective national policy as well as sensitive, responsive and competent government at all levels including:
- federal-provincial relations
- communications
- parliamentary reform[1]

In the first phase of the Priorities Exercise certain notable features emerged. First, the Cabinet Planning System's chronic failure to protect the integrity of the notion of "priority" was dramatically underscored by some sixteen priority policy areas, many of them extraordinarily general, even vague, in nature. No wonder it was expected that all departments and agencies would be able to find ways to contribute to the priorities! A priority set of sixteen is in practice an empty set. Second, despite this swollen priority set, there was no mention at all of inflation, and only a backhanded allusion to economic growth in the priority policy area of "national industrial and regional development". Two factors were responsible. The first was the historic gulf separating the Finance and Cabinet Planning Systems, which made the PCO packagers of ministerial preferences wary of designating a priority policy area in Finance's back yard. They had not, of course, hesitated to do so with respect to the jurisdictions of certain line departments such as Transport, Indian Affairs and Northern Development, or Health and Welfare. The second was the negative mandate which was the dubious legacy of the election of July 1974; the commitment not to implement wage and price controls left economic policy in the limbo of "jaw-boning", consultations and references to "international forces beyond Canada's control". Any attempt within the Priorities Exercise to move beyond this impasse was felt to be politically premature and would again have led to confrontation with Finance. These constraints were real, but hardly justified the attempt to plan the government's mandate by ignoring inflation, and hoping it would go away.

A third feature of the Priorities Exercise also emerged early on: an inability to keep to the original schedule. Final approval of the policy framework and the request for departmental responses were to have occurred by January 1, 1975. In fact, this was not accomplished until mid-February and, as a result, departmental responses did not arrive in the PCO until late March and early April. At first, the Priorities and Planning Secretariat was not unduly concerned. After all, the drafting of the Memorandum to Cabinet for each priority policy area was to be essentially an editorial task, one of "cutting and pasting" together the range of departmental responses relevant to each area. The Secretariat issued detailed instructions to the sixteen task forces of central agency personnel charged with carrying out these editorial functions under the "core group". The instructions assumed that the process of summarizing departmental responses, drafting a Memorandum to Cabinet and getting the required approvals from senior PCO personnel and the relevant cabinet committee chairman, could be carried out within ten working days. Then the departmental responses began to arrive in the PCO.

The PCO had intended to limit the number of priorities to between five and ten. It ended up with sixteen. In similar fashion, all of the injunctions that went out to departments along with the policy framework, to the effect that they should be innovative and seek especially to reorient directions within existing resource levels, went for naught. Two or three departments submitted thoughtful and imaginative responses (much longer, incidentally, than the PCO's eight-page limit). The bulk of departmental responses were pedestrian attempts to force existing departmental activities into the conveniently flexible categories provided by the priority policy areas, and to justify additional resources and/or jurisdiction in similar terms. The few successful responses bore the earmarks of detailed attention from the particular deputies who submitted them. The great majority appeared to represent the aggregate ambitions of departmental middle managers, rationalized in the context of the policy framework. There were no bright ideas, no innovative thinking, not one outdated program identified or resource reallocation proposed, no new criteria for measuring program achievement of priority objectives suggested. These self-serving and unimaginative responses were completely inadequate to flesh out the priority policy areas with tangible proposals. They effectively destroyed the Priority and Planning Secretariat's optimistic model of "two weeks to a cabinet document".

There was little time to agonize over departments' lack of vision and their failure to grasp the government-wide perspective of the Cabinet Planning System. The Exercise had created expectations which had to be satisfied. The burden of drafting the Memoranda for each priority policy area fell on the junior and middle level central agency personnel who had been detailed to the sixteen task forces co-ordinated by the core group in the Plans Division of PCO. These task forces, composed principally of staff from the PCO and the Effectiveness Division of the Planning Branch of the Treasury Board Secretariat, began in mid-April 1975 their attempt to make silk purses out of the sow's ears of departmental responses. The task forces varied widely in terms of ability, experience and expertise in their priority policy areas. Nor was there any significant departmental representation on the task forces. These features of the Exercise had not seemed crucial when the drafting process had been conceived as a matter of "editing and packaging" the raw material provided by departments. Since the departmental responses proved all but useless in most priority policy areas, those task forces without significant previous exposure to the area found themselves in very deep water indeed.

The two weeks' drafting model gave way to two months, as most task forces had to develop objectives and propose initiatives in their priority policy area, beginning from ground level. The great bulk of the priority policy area Cabinet Memoranda did not go to cabinet committee until the latter half of June and July 1975. Ministers were increasingly harassed by political pressures as Parliament dragged onward into the summer of 1975, constantly in sight of, but never quite reaching, a recess. And when the long-awaited priority Memoranda finally came to the cabinet committees, ministers were not only distracted but profoundly disappointed. The Memoranda were of varying quality, but there were common characteristics. They were eloquent on the subject of objectives, ambitious in their pursuit of further bureaucratic process in the form of studies, reviews and committees, and largely devoid of politically tangible initiatives which could be announced in the forthcoming months. Nor did there emerge, by the very nature of some sixteen separate Memoranda, any single motif which might provide some character and cohesion to a government now drifting listlessly after a year in office, facing double-digit inflation and unprecedented wage settlements. The priority policy area Memoranda were not drafted under the responsibility of a particular minister, they were written by groups of relatively inexperienced policy analysts for the cabinet as a whole, or rather for the analysts' ideal of a cabinet. As one observer put it, the Memoranda succeeded in "disguising the woods by a too luxuriant display of trees". Hartle's tart judgment is entirely *a propos* in this case:

> ...staff members at the 'working level', to use a common but somewhat ironic phrase, frequently act as though they were serving a congregation of individuals seeking martyrdom. This strange insensitivity of many staff officers to the interests of ministers probably arises in part because of a confusion between the sound idea that bureaucrats should not act in such a way as to make themselves unacceptable to the other party if it were elected to office and the silly idea that information that would be useful in making political decisions is in some way tainted. One

is tempted to say about the prevailing attitudes of many junior advisors that they are truly non-partisan inasmuch as they stand ready to be equally ineffective for any political party.[2]

Some of the committee discussions of late June and July were useful because they provided ministers with an occasion for a wide-ranging discussion of a particular policy area with fewer officials present than in a normal cabinet committee meeting. In general, however, the Committee Reports resulting from the discussions rarely represented anything more concrete than recommendations regarding objectives and more studies, like those contained in the priority Memoranda. Ministers agreed that these Memoranda represented "too little, too late". Ministerial frustration began to filter back to the Press Gallery, whose interest in the Priorities Exercise had first been piqued by the Prime Minister's cryptic insistence on waiting for the results of the process before declaring any general directions. That the Prime Minister had clung to this position while the post-election anti-climax stretched into a long winter of ennui and indirection only underlined the disparity between prime ministerial expectations and the diffuse, uninspired product of the Exercise. Not only had urgent business been set aside while the government waited for the "big picture" to emerge from the Priorities Exercise, but the "big picture" itself turned out to be a mirage. The end was apparent in late July 1975, when a Memorandum to Cabinet which attempted to consolidate the results of the sixteen committee discussions received an unenthusiastic reception from a meeting of the Committee on Priorities and Planning (to which all ministers had been invited).

At the moment which should have been its greatest triumph, the Cabinet Planning System was at the point of collapse. The disparity between the nature of the political pressures bearing upon the government in the House of Commons, in the media and elsewhere, on the one hand, and the abstractions—like "lifestyles" or "demographic patterns"—typical of the Priorities Exercise, on the other, robbed the Exercise of its relevance and credibility. Economic and political events had evolved beyond it. The wage-price spiral continued unabated, John Turner pondered his political options and the Prime Minister's Office, intimately involved in the Priorities Exercise from the beginning, smelled disaster. The PMO commissioned a public opinion survey of the concerns of Canadians. To no one's surprise, inflation and the state of the economy constituted the issue of greatest concern, while violent crime and firearm tragedies were a distant second. In the end, the few thousand dollars invested with the Liberal Party's house pollster to confirm the instincts of political insiders, was to have a far greater influence on the government's priorities than the thousands of bureaucratic manhours invested in the Priorities Exercise.

The second Meach Lake cabinet meeting, which took place in mid-September 1975, was far different from its predecessor ten months earlier. The resignation of John Turner, the conversion of the Deparment of Finance to a policy of wage and price controls, and the PMO's polling results gave the Meach Lake meeting a tangible focus and a sense of urgency.[3] The Memorandum to Cabinet consolidating the results of the Priorities Exercise was ignored. The cabinet adopted the Economy and "Law and Order" (later to become "Peace and Security") as its two priorities. The Economy priority was composed of the program of wage and price controls, to be instituted immediately on announcement in the forthcoming Speech from the Throne. Relevant sectors of the bureaucracy were galvanized into action with urgency unknown since the October Crisis of 1970. The Law and Order package was to be unveiled in the spring of 1976, to coincide with the Progressive Conservative leadership convention. It was to be a potpourri including gun control, abolition of capital punishment and other measures which were to be marketed under a "lock 'em up and throw away the key" theme, since this was what the poll indicated Canadians wanted. (The package later became unravelled when the abolition of capital punishment was rejected by the man on the street, overshadowing the other initiatives entirely, and became a substantial political disadvantage.)

The ambiguous fate of the Priorities Exercise was symbolized by the fact that no Record of Decision, either confirming or rejecting the sixteen Committee Reports embodied in the final consolidation Memorandum, was ever issued. The Priorities Exercise dissolved with the arrival of the controls period, and the Cabinet Planning System as an ambitious developing entity disappeared with it, though its shadow remained to make ghost-like appearances at Expenditure Guidelines time. The Finance Planning System died as a separate entity at precisely the same point, since the requirements of the controls program spelled the end of the splendid isolation of the Department of Finance in its macroeconomic ivory tower. For the remainder of the Seventies, Finance was to begin to assert its leadership in the interdepartmental and cabinet committee arenas, because the penalty for failing to do so, in terms of loss of control over crucial economic policies developed collectively, would become too great to risk.

The principal irony of the choice of the economy and public order in the fall of 1975 was the complete failure of the Priorities Exercise of the previous year to broach either. Whenever ministers, deputy ministers or departments queried the absence of the economic dimension in the priorities, they were assured by the PCO—in accordance with the position adopted by the Prime Minister at his luncheon with deputy ministers in February 1975—that this would be dealt with separately. The architects of the Priorities Exercise found themselves trying to show how the economy related to the priorities, since they were unwilling or unable to face the fact known to every Canadian on a limited income: that the economy had to be *the* priority. As for public order, the Exercise's priority of law reform was precisely the obverse of the hard-line approach deemed desirable by the analysis of the polls.

The full political implications of the failure of the Priorities Exercise will be difficult to assess for some time to come, but it certainly constituted a most uncertain beginning for the new government. The journalists were devastating. Hugh Winsor referred to "the failure of the extensive PCO exercise to establish Government priorities":

> The exercise was supposed to chart the new Camelot for the remainder of the Trudeau mandate. But because it was conducted in secret and out of touch with reality, it had ignored the mundane concerns of soaring food prices, deteriorating labour-management-government relations and the public's lack of confidence in the Government's economic policies. The whole exercise died a silent death one September afternoon at [the] Meach Lake country hideaway while the Cabinet prepared for wage and price controls.[4]

According to George Radwanski,

> After the 1974 election, Mr. Trudeau decided that Canada could benefit from a year of deliberate undergovernment to wind down from the intensity of the minority period and the campaign. That was a blunder. The Prime Minister's aggressive campaign created expectations of leadership. These were left unfulfilled when his government became almost invisible. And since little positive activity was visible, relatively minor missteps and misfortunes dominated public attention enough to undermine the government's credibility.
>
> At the policy level, meanwhile, the government spent that first year drawing up an elaborate list of priorities which was promptly scuttled by the decision to impose controls and cut spending.[5]

Radwanski later summed up the fate of the government after the imposition of controls: "From that point on, Trudeau and his government found themselves doing exactly what the ill-fated and politically costly priorities exercise had been designed to avoid: they were reduced to stumbling along without a plan, racing to catch up to events, improvising desperately".[6]

The Idea of Industrial Strategy

5

The issues raised by the expression "industrial strategy" are about as important as any facing Canada in the closing decades of the twentieth century. At stake is Canada's economic strength in an era of resource scarcity, monetary imbalance and inflation without growth, where effective trading in finished goods depends upon high productivity, sophisticated technology, favourable exchange rates and/or low labour costs. To many, the nation's economic prospects appear uncertain, but there is considerable disagreement as to the causes of the current situation, and as to what measures might be adopted to improve it. The expression "industrial strategy" encompasses many of these issues, although some participants in the discussion are reluctant to use the term at all.

After a boom in the early Seventies, "industrial strategy" all but disappeared from official pronouncements during the controls period. At about the same time as the term "planning", it became more or less taboo in the same quarters, and for parallel reasons. The idea never quite disappeared, however. It was sustained by various political forces outside the centres of power, such as certain Liberal backbenchers, Conservative critics and especially the NDP. At the end of the decade, it experienced a modest resurrection on the hustings, in the media and at the service club luncheons.

If the issues raised by industrial strategy are important, the concept itself constitutes perhaps the most difficult planning problem brought to the fore by the Cabinet Planning System in the late Sixties and early Seventies. Under the Trudeau administration industrial strategy epitomized the fate of many other planning issues: the pursuit of certain of its objectives through specific policies and programs, combined with an embarrassed attempt to forget the heroic and comprehensive nature of the problem as the Cabinet Planning System had originally conceived it. The industrial strategy debate can thus be seen as a case study in the interaction of the Cabinet and Finance Planning

Systems. The purpose is less to draw conclusions about what the substance of an industrial strategy for Canada ought to look like, than to explore the relationships between planning ideas and the institutional realities.

Before 1972, there was little explicit discussion of "industrial strategy". An examination of the pressures on Canada's implicit industrial strategy of previous decades, accumulating during the late Sixties and Seventies, provides a sense of the context within which the notion of industrial strategy emerged. In this chapter and the next, the major alternatives for industrial strategy are considered, together with an account of the discussion within Cabinet and the bureaucracy of industrial development policy. The resulting governmental approach to industrial strategy can then be located within the context of planning and the central decision-making process.

Industrial strategy, as government spokesmen never tire of pointing out, means different things to different people. "Canada *has had* an industrial policy if one accepts the definition of such a policy as simply a collection of measures directed at industry", says the Science Council of Canada, ". . . however, if the more rigorous definition of industrial policy as *an integrated set of complementary measures embodying both strategic economic and industrial objectives* is taken, then clearly Canada has not had a coherent industrial strategy."[1]

In this sense, then, industrial strategy is clearly a planning problem since planning implies political choice of overriding criteria within which the competing claims of different sectors to the limited resources of government will be rationalized. It also implies the identification by ministers of dominant concerns to which policies and programs conceived within the parochial context of a given sector must be bent. In the case of industrial strategy, the "dominant concerns" in question would be "strategic economic and industrial objectives" and the policies to be "bent" in the light of these concerns would be those of commercial policy—trade and tariff policies, import quotas, antidumping measures, countervailing duties in case of inappropriate subsidy by foreign governments—and of industrial development policy including research and development incentives, procurement policy, regulation of foreign investment, regional development incentives, and so forth. There is, as government spokesmen noted during the euphoric phase of the Trudeau government's approach to industrial strategy, no limit to the policies which are relevant. Aspects of tax, competition, manpower and energy policy are clearly germane. The more ambitious the construction of an industrial strategy, the greater the number of policies which must be bent to its needs: environmental, transportation, communication. . . .

There is general agreement that a significant degree of such policy- and program-bending[2] in the interests of industrial development objectives is overdue. There is even a reasonable consensus as to the kinds of objectives to be sought. There are, however, fundamental differences as to the *causes* of weakness in the structure of Canadian industry, and hence, as to the *direction* in which the policies and programs in question ought to be bent or reformulated. Some of the confusion surrounding the concept of industrial strategy arises from various analysts who, in the process of contention over diagnosis and prescription for an admittedly sick patient, have sought, depending on their point of view, either to appropriate the term for their preferred nostrums, or to stigmatize those of others with it.

Conceptual ambiguities and analytical differences quickly become political and administrative ones. Industrial strategy requires diverse policies and programs, whose use in a "coherent" way, in the service of an "integrated" approach, goes to the heart of some of the most primordial ideological divisions in liberal democratic societies. Not incidentally, these divisions were reflected explicitly in the differences in agency philosophy underlying the Cabinet and Finance Planning Systems. The more ambitious the construction of industrial strategy and the greater the range of policies and programs to be reformulated in its interests, the further these policies and programs lie from the traditional orbit of influence of the Department of Finance, the more coercive and "interventionist" their use appears, and the greater the political polarization which results.[3] The political sensitivities underlying what is now familiar as the issue of "economic freedom" are aroused simply by the notion of "planning" in its public-private dimensions:

> Economic planning in Canada . . . has not until recently been openly espoused in the political arena by either the Liberal or Progressive Conservative parties. We are left rather with a gradual evolution toward economic management which ultimately carries with it enormous planning implications. The evolving mix and complexity of economic goals and processes has generated an increasing concern . . . [4]

The very number and diversity of existing commercial and industrial development policies implies economic planning, but it is discussion of their use in pursuit of a limited and specific group of objectives—such as those of a particular industrial strategy—which touches off a debate largely ideological in nature. The debate turns upon the sanctity of the marketplace and the ways by which the pursuit of private interests may be made to coincide with the pursuit of public ones. There are two overlapping levels of debate, one very crude and general, in which industrial strategy as a species of economic planning is attacked as "socialism" or as a precursor to it, and a second in which the most informed and interested participants—officials, academics, business leaders, economic analysts—discuss the specific substantive alternatives for industrial strategy.

Both of these levels of debate are important in any consideration of the history of, and prospects for, industrial strategy. One of the reasons that industrial strategy is a classic planning problem is that it not only requires a significant degree of concertation within the federal executive but also between the federal and provincial governments and between governments and the private sector. Furthermore, the behaviour of foreign governments, multinational corporations headquartered outside Canada and labour unions are important to the ultimate viability of any industrial strategy. This extraordinary web of institutional power, a network of interdependent private and public interests, provides a very complex context for the debate on industrial strategy. While the primary focus here is the fate of industrial strategy within federal efforts to plan, the implementation of such a strategy inevitably depends upon provincial governments, and upon the private corporations whose contribution to employment and economic growth constitute the *raison d'être* of such a policy in the first place.

The realities of a pluralistic and heterogeneous national political economy, then, create a kind of framework, at once elusive and constraining, for efforts to develop industrial strategy. The lack of a generally compelling analysis of the substantive economic problems at issue creates major political difficulties. Agreement on any given analysis, and mobilization of the policies and programs needed to resolve such problems on the basis of that analysis, become extremely formidable tasks. The Science Council of Canada, which learned the hard way, recently pointed out, " . . . as much attention will have to be paid to the political aspects of implementing an industrial policy (i.e. industry-government relations and federal-provincial relations) as is paid to the technical and economic aspects."[5] Phidd and Doern make the same point:

> . . . planning, as such, can have a disarming and naive simplicity to it unless it is rigorously related to the determinants of governing in a liberal democratic, federal system of government in which formal political power is concentrated within cabinets in a cabinet-parliamentary system, and where great economic power resides in the corporate sector and, to a lesser extent, in the union sector.[6]

According to one of the leading analysts of Canadian federalism, Richard Simeon, "Ottawa has neither the constitutional and fiscal power, nor the political legitimacy to be responsible for industrial strategy on its own". The provincial share of such crucial instruments as fiscal power, regulatory authority and natural resource jurisdiction makes provinces "capable of frustrating or subverting" a national industrial strategy developed by the federal government. Emphasizing the distinction between analytical/conceptual difficulties and political/ administrative ones, Simeon suggests:

> ...We have a clash at two levels. At the level of the *substance* of industrial strategy, the questions are: where development will take place; what sectors will be emphasized; and how the conflict between the desire for regional growth can be reconciled with the desire to promote redistribution and maximization of aggregate growth across the whole country. At the level of *procedure*, there is the question of how such a reconciliation might be brought about and who is to make industrial policy.[7]

Simeon represents the dominant school of thought in Canada as to the need for full federal-provincial collaboration in economic development generally, and industrial strategy in particular.[8] There are two major implications inherent in this position. The first is that federal initiatives must take explicit account of their impact upon regional economies.[9] National economic policies have been interpreted as systematically discriminatory against certain regions, and provinces will not accept any federal policy which implicitly assumes a position contrary to the Simeon view. For example, the kind of theory of economic development common to certain versions of industrial strategy and to those who oppose any "global" industrial strategy whatever —that development policies should promote high growth areas wherever they may be, and count on these areas to carry the remainder of the economic community along with them—is simply anachronistic in a political system of sensitive and sophisticated provincial governments. The other counter-implication is that provincial industrial strategies must be harmonized within a policy context that balances the interests of the various regions of the country. Ontario, Québec, Alberta and Saskatchewan are among the provinces developing their own industrial strategies. Provincial strategies, however, have an inevitable beggar-thy-neighbour quality which renders them more competitive than complementary. Markets served by other Canadian producers are more visible than markets served by producers abroad. Such provincial strategies must, insofar as possible, be targeted against international competition rather than against other provinces with similar sectoral strengths. The Science Council, for example, worries about "ten unco-ordinated and, at times, antagonistic industrial policies within one country", a situation which results in "balkanization".[10]

It is clear that the major source of harmony must derive from federal leadership and federal policy. Any federal industrial strategy, even one strictly co-extensive with the limits of federal jurisdiction and thus relatively restricted in scope, will have to take regional interests and provincial prerogatives into account. The more ambitiously or globally a federal industrial strategy is conceived, the greater the importance of regional and provincial elements to its formulation and substance.

The business community's involvement in the industrial strategy debate is even more crucial than that of the provinces.[11] Without the commitment of certain key private sector decision-makers, an industrial strategy has no prospect of success, since the organizations through which its socio-economic benefits are ultimately to be delivered are, in Canada, largely in private (and often foreign) hands. Attitudes within business about the notion of industrial strategy vary enormously, from reflexive distaste for the "socialist" overtones of government intervention or planning, to substantial enthusiasm for an aggressive government-business partnership in pursuit of an ambitious industrial strategy. Most business opinion lies somewhere in between: instinctive antipathy to an increased role for the public sector, coupled with the conviction that if tax advantages, tariffs, subsidies, or regulatory initiatives are to be deployed as part of an industrial strategy, one's own company ought to make a strong claim to such support, "in the public interest". Executives from weak industry sectors will, of course, be even less doctrinaire, to the point where their industry associations regularly beat down the doors in Ottawa.

Suspicion of a rigid and interventionist industrial strategy, therefore, leads private sector spokesmen to warn that "national industrial policy is not planned—it evolves", and occurs through "the give-and-take of various claimants on resources in the economy...by the democratic bargaining process."[12] When Alastair Gillespie met with the Canadian Manufacturers' Association and the Canadian Chamber of Commerce in 1973, he found out precisely how these "claimants on resources" saw the government's industrial strategy exercise:

> They had been wrestling for a year with the question of an industrial strategy. They put together a summary of what they considered to be a practical approach and they supported it with the individual submissions of . . . 13 supporting [member associations]. In a large part the submissions of the 13 supporting organizations were a special pleading for each of the various industry sectors, trying to point out to the government the special need, as well as the special opportunities, for each of the various major sectors.[13]

The problem is not simply that each industry sector offers its own self-serving (and usually protectionist) redefinition of industrial strategy. It is rather that since explicit debate on the subject emerged, there has been no consensus among the leading participants as to objectives which would constitute criteria for arbitrating these claims. During the Fifties and most of the Sixties, economic growth represented a clear and relatively unambiguous objective which commanded general respect in the relevant political and economic communities. Other objectives—employment, equity in class and regional distribution of wealth, sovereignty, a healthy environment—gained prominence at the close of the Sixties. Consensus as to the relative importance of these goals, and the trade-offs between them, has proven elusive. Nevertheless, given the key role of business decision-makers in the implementation of a global industrial strategy, the absence of such a consensus would severely compromise the strategy.

Another issue is the lack of effective and continuing mechanisms of government-business co-ordination in Canada. The Government of Canada has a tradition of (essentially ritualistic) annual meetings between major economic interest groups and Cabinet. It supports hosts of advisory committees, two large advisory councils on science and economics respectively and other forums for government-business interaction. The essence of such consultation, however, has been *ad hoc*, department-by-department, issue-by-issue.[14] Canada has neither the informal social cohesion of political, bureaucratic and business elites characteristic of Japan, nor the regular exchanges over a fluid public-private interface typical of France, nor the formal government-wide machinery of co-ordination with business which has been created in many European economies. The social, geographic and institutional isolation of government and business in Canada represents an additional complication for the development of an industrial strategy. Foreign ownership is at least partly responsible for this mutual incomprehension.

Background to the Debate

The idea of industrial strategy first appeared in Canada at a distinctive socio-economic conjuncture. During the Sixties, the signs of structural weakness in the Canadian economy, which were to lead to the demand for an industrial strategy, first began to emerge. And it was during the Sixties that the consensus surrounding Canada's implicit industrial strategy began to weaken. The Sixties were far from bad years; the decade outperformed both its predecessor and its successor in economic terms. Through the early Sixties, the supply picture in the economy remained bright. Natural resources appeared to be unlimited; international capital markets were open to Canada, for both debt and equity; immigration and urbanization created an elastic labour supply. Furthermore, there was general support for any and all kinds of economic growth, and relatively little discussion of other goals such as sovereignty or redistribution by class or region. In these halcyon days, economic policy focussed principally on stabilization, commercial and exchange policies. Industrial and regional development policy were largely the preserve of a small circle of progressive thinkers, such as Walter Gordon, Maurice Lamontagne and Tom Kent, who were laying the intellectual foundations of a more concerted approach to structural problems.

By the early Seventies, however, this relatively uncomplicated situation altered rapidly. Certain observers began to feel that Canadian optimism about the country's economic future bordered on complacency. Basic social and economic changes in Canada and in its principal trading partner, the United States, dramatically undermined Canada's traditional approach to economic policy. These changes affected the resource sector and, most significantly, the manufacturing sector.

Supply factors became increasingly inelastic and expensive. Capital began to cost more; interest rates rose but, more important, the costs of foreign investment in terms of economic sovereignty became a major and pressing political issue. As industrial demand increased, higher cost natural resource supplies had to be tapped. Costs were pushed even higher as natural resources were seen to be limited, and as previously "external" costs, like environmental damage, were internalized under the pressure of public opinion. Skilled immigration dropped off and the influx to cities from rural regions of the country slowed. While the labour force continued to grow, new arrivals on the labour market became preponderantly Canadian born, with Canadian expectations as to the nature and location of employment. This led to a concern with the regional distribution of employment opportunities. Likewise, new ideals as to social entitlement led to major social programs, many of them intended to transfer resources among social strata.

As a result of these pressures, the late Sixties and early Seventies saw a general recognition that inelasticity of supply factors, and other costly developments, required a much more careful and considered allocation of resources. New and more complex kinds of decisions were necessary to minimize, for example, foreign debt and foreign investment, to economize on expensive and finite natural resources, and to distribute development to underdeveloped regions. The objectives and criteria informing such choices would, according to some observers, be the essential elements of an industrial strategy. For example, the (Gray) Report on *Foreign Direct Investment in Canada* referred repeatedly to the need for an industrial strategy for Canada, to guide the decisions of the screening agency which it recommended to regulate new foreign investment.[15] Furthermore, commercial and exchange policies would be among the instruments of such a larger strategy, as would additional microeconomic policies focussed on particular supply factors other than foreign capital.

Even without the deteriorating cost position and worsening supply pressures in Canadian industry, commercial and exchange policies were themselves in a state of crisis by the early Seventies. In part because of similar difficulties in the American economy, the basic assumptions of Canadian commercial policy began to erode in the late Sixties, finally to be shattered by the Nixon administration's import restriction initiatives of 1971. Canada had historically treated commercial policy as a species of international diplomacy, rather than as an extension of a largely implicit industrial policy. In any event, no obvious alternative policy to the protectionist National Policy was at hand. The *de facto* strategy behind commercial policy assumed U.S. good will toward Canada, expressed through a "special relationship". Canada exported resources into the U.S. market, as well as limited quantities of Canadian manufactured and processed goods. The special relationship involved tariff protection for Canadian manufacturing, much of it U.S. owned; something close to free trade in the energy, automobile and defence sectors; and something close to a currency union, resulting from the pegging of the Canadian dollar and bilateral commitments as to reserve ceilings.

The facade of the special relationship began to crack as the Seventies dawned, first in the natural resource sector, and then in manufacturing. The U.S. restricted the export of Canadian uranium by enrichment regulations for U.S. plants, it tried to impose quotas on oil imports, and it tried to use its monopsony power to force down the prices of natural gas and sulfur. Then, in August 1971, the Nixon administration moved to redress its balance of payments problems by a series of unprecedented policies. In order to restrict imports, a surtax, and countervailing duties specifically addressed to imports from industries subsidized by their governments, were imposed. The Domestic International Sales Company (DISC) Program, amounting to precisely such an export subsidy for U.S. companies, was established. All of these initiatives were contrary to the spirit of the U.S.'s multilateral commitments under the General Agreement on Trade and Tariffs (GATT), but anguished protests from trading partners were to no avail. In particular, Canadian pleas for exemption due to the "special relationship" between the two countries were futile. In the United States, there was no consensus that Canada had played the trade liberalization game with complete sincerity. Nor would it have been easy to modify American policies in favour of Canada as the exception to all other trading partners. If the "special relationship" cut little ice in Washington, it cut even less in Tokyo or Bonn. For certain Canadian policy makers, however, this revealed an American view of Canada as a "spill chamber/resource trove" rather than a unique trading partner, whose interests ought to transcend any particular economic impasse. Although the actual economic impact on Canada of the American attempts to reduce resource and manufactured imports was limited, the crucial assumption of U.S. good will and good faith was destroyed. The search for a new commercial policy was also to lead some to the notion of an industrial strategy, a strategy which would protect Canada from the whims of its major trading partner.

The turbulence of the Canadian economy and the international environment was reflected in its economic performance, especially in the manufacturing sector: "During 1961–66, the manufacturing industries accounted for slightly more than 25% of new jobs created in the economy. In the period 1966-72, by contrast, manufacturing accounted for just more than five per cent of the new jobs".[16] The record of Canadian manufacturing in research and development and in productivity was revealed, by study after study, as inferior to that of its major competitors. Increasing materials costs, a low rate of innovation, relatively weak productivity increases and high wage gains overflowing from a strong resource sector, combined with a high exchange rate for the Canadian dollar. The result was increasing unit costs, declining competitiveness and a declining share in world trade in finished goods. This was particularly true in certain important and regionally-concentrated sectors in which Canada competes with newly industrialized economies in South America and the Far East. In labour-intensive sectors, such as textiles and footwear, labour factor costs in developing countries are mere fractions of such costs in Canada, and Canada's ability to compete suffered accordingly. The trade deficit in end products progressively worsened, creating balance of payments difficulties. These developments exposed systematic structural weaknesses in the manufacturing sector of the Canadian economy.

Exposure of this weakness highlighted the extent of Canadian dependence upon natural resource exploitation for a degree of economic stability. However, the number and quality of jobs produced by extractive industries, and the fact that supplies of natural resources were increasingly costly and seen as finite, impressed many observers once again that, despite some strength in the secondary sector during the Fifties and Sixties, Canada still had not shaken its historic curse—relegation to an economy of "the hewing of wood and the drawing of water".

Weakness in the manufacturing sector and overreliance on a diminishing resource base had become strikingly evident by the early Seventies. Here again, interest converged on the notion of an industrial strategy which would assure maximum returns for exploitation of natural resources and restructure secondary industry in the interests of effective international competitiveness. From the moment of its appearance then, industrial strategy was invested with a diverse and ambitious range of aspirations, explaining at once its rapid currency in 1971–72, and the frustrations attending subsequent attempts to realize the concept. Most elements in this brief sketch of the Canadian economic conundrum remain valid to this day. Participants in the industrial strategy debate differ primarily on their interpretation of some of the key causal factors underlying the situation, and on the policy measures appropriate to confront it. Two distinct "industrial strategies" emerged from the industrial strategy debate; neither has captured ministers and the bureaucracy.

The Bold Alternatives

The public industrial strategy debate during the Seventies has polarized around two alternatives, two ambitious industrial strategies. The primary participants in this debate were academics, sometimes in the employ of the two major federal policy advisory councils, the Economic Council of Canada and the Science Council of Canada. On the whole, business and labour have remained largely aloof from the debate. Although the sympathies of a few corporate and labour leaders may be well known, there has been little institutional commitment of corporations or unions, as such, to either of the alternatives.

While the two options may reasonably be treated as alternative industrial strategies, insofar as either might constitute "an integrated set of complementary measures embodying both strategic economic and industrial objectives" for Canada,[17] the advocates of one alternative would much more readily accept the designation "industrial strategy" than would those supporting the other.[18] The Science Council of Canada fully accepts the notion of an industrial strategy and advocates one of the two main alternatives, now generally known as "technological sovereignty". The critics of technological sovereignty, often also the proponents of the primary alternative industrial strategy, free trade, regard the term "industrial strategy" with some circumspection: it "still does not have any generally accepted concrete meaning; rather it is an invocation to accept the set of policies the particular spokesman recommends".[19]

The fundamental element dividing the advocates of technological sovereignty from the advocates of free trade is their proposed treatment of the legacy of the National Policy. The National Policy, originating in the 1870s, was intended to foster Canadian unity by breaking the natural north-south patterns of regional trade in North America, and stimulating east-west trade within Canada. The National Policy involved tariff protection to reduce imports from the United States and to encourage the development of "infant industries" in Canada. It also involved a major national commitment to the development of east-west transportation linkages. Thus, the National Policy was Canada's first and most sustained industrial strategy. The policy had a degree of success in keeping out foreign products. By the mid-twentieth century, however, there had occurred massive and systematic direct investment in Canadian industry by foreign interests, in particular those headquartered in the United States. The result is a manufacturing sector which is heavily foreign-owned and largely confined to serving a relatively small Canadian market through a diversity of products with short production runs. The manufacturing sector in Canada appears less successful in research, development and innovation than its counterparts in most other Western countries. Its productivity levels have been inferior, its labour factor costs often higher and its export performance weak. Only heavy exports of diminishing natural resources maintain a semblance of balance in Canada's current account. These structural weaknesses have been a source of concern since the Sixties and their implications have become increasingly severe during the last decade.

Very simply, the advocates of free trade emphasize the negative effects of the tariff as such on competition and efficiency in Canadian manufacturing, while the advocates of technological sovereignty emphasize the negative effects of the foreign ownership which resulted at least in part from the tariff structure.[20] The contrasting approaches lead to different detailed analyses and different policy proposals. Both schools of thought, however, agree on the relevance of small market size to the weakness of the secondary manufacturing sector in Canada, and on the central objective of a more internationally competitive manufacturing sector with access to a larger market. The technological sovereignty school might be said to focus specifically on measures, in the first instance public measures, to improve international competitiveness, believing that this will bring effective access to larger markets. The free trade school focusses upon measures—at bottom, international negotiation for the reduction or elimination of tariffs—which would provide access to a larger market, believing that this will stimulate private measures to increase competitiveness, especially cost-competitiveness. The technological sovereignty school fears the disruptions which it sees emerging from free trade without antecedent initiatives to increase competitiveness[21]; the free trade school argues that only tariff reductions, multi- or bilateral in nature, will generate competitiveness, and fears the degree of government intervention implied by technological sovereignty.[22]

Technological sovereignty, according to the Science Council which has been developing the concept in one form or another since the late Sixties, "means the development and control of the technological capability to support national sovereignty".[23] A Canadian industrial strategy based on technological sovereignty would recognize that technological progress is essential to socio-economic development, that this implies an explicit, aggressive technology policy which must take priority over other policies, and that "Government 'intervention' at all levels is essential to reach the goals implied by technological sovereignty", given that "the market place has proved unable to promote technological development and to ensure its correspondence with social and economic objectives". Since Canada cannot expect to be self-sufficient with respect to technology, "a strategy of selective interdependence" with overseas sources of and markets for technology is required. Such a policy must focus on "both the demand and supply of technology", must "take account of the various industries and regions" and, in order to be sensitive to a dynamic environment, "must be kept flexible and should be implemented gradually".[24]

According to the proponents of technological sovereignty, Canada's declining international competitiveness in the manufacturing sector is an indication that the structural weaknesses in that sector, notably foreign ownership, are having a more and more critical negative impact. Canada is "a nation retreating from industrialism", "on the brink of surrendering any claims it may have possessed to be a major producer of highly manufactured goods, especially those dependent on high technology product development and design excellence".[25] Canada is a hinterland economy composed of "hewers of wood and drawers of water", unduly dependent on a diminishing resource base and highly cyclical world resource markets. Canada will remain in this undesirably exposed situation, according to this analysis, until reluctant elites in government, business and labour are prepared to face the full implications of foreign ownership: a "branch plant economy" of "truncated firms", without the high quality management and research functions which are located at foreign head offices, and without the international market potential that goes with such functions. Tariffs do not really prevent import penetration because foreign-owned multinationals import technology and make sourcing decisions in a context of global integration which discriminates against Canadian suppliers. Multinationals allocate markets in the same fashion, leaving Canadian branch plants only the tiny Canadian market. Canadian firms command such small fragments of even domestic markets that they have little international competitive strength or interests. Canada is stuck in a vicious circle of export failure and import dependence, and only a major public initiative can break the circle.

What kind of initiative? Innovation, and the international competitiveness which innovation brings, must be the centrepiece:

> ... little industrial development will occur without improvement in the technological capability of Canadian manufacturing; failure to bring Canada more into line with other industrialized countries may well result in real contraction of the present modest industrialization ... innovative expertise including marketing capability will be a *sine qua non* of industrial success.[26]

Hence, the notion of technological sovereignty. *Technological*, because the possession of original technology is seen as the overriding factor in access to foreign markets. *Sovereignty*, because foreign ownership is the most important single barrier to the development and possession of such technology.

An industrial strategy based on technological sovereignty leads to four main lines of action:

1. Increasing the demand for Canadian technology.
2. Increasing the capacity to develop technology.
3. Increasing the demand for technology absorption at the level of the production unit.
4. Regulating technology imports.[27]

To increase the demand for Canadian technology, Canadian firms must be restructured and rationalized to a size where they can use and develop sophisticated technology, and government procurement policies must be oriented toward such domestic technology. The government should undertake major programs and joint ventures to give the private sector the financial muscle to compete in selected high technology markets.[28]

To develop the production of technology, existing patterns of industrial organization must be altered through rationalization and specialization to produce core companies, which are to be the chosen instruments for Canadian entry into world markets:

> Rationalization means vertical or horizontal integration created, principally by means of mergers and joint ventures. Its justification, as outlined earlier, is found in the achievement of economies of scale not presently realized in an industry fragmented by too many (therefore weak) producers, or in the economic efficiencies associated with specialization, or both. It almost always involves the restructuring of an industry,

or a complex of industries, in the sense that the number of firms is reduced either through elimination or amalgamation. Specialization means reduction in the range of activities, or concentration on a narrower range of products with a view to achieving the higher levels of efficiency that are associated with greater production-run length.[29]

"Direct involvement of government in the rationalization process can and should be avoided", but "government must accept the responsibility for the creation of an environment which will prove encouraging to private sector initiative [to rationalize]".[30] Commercial policy would have to be adjusted to this core company strategy, rather than the inverse, as the free trade school would have it. Only strong public policy commitment will create "world trading enterprises" or "world scale national corporations" in Canada.[31]

To increase the capacity for technology absorption at the enterprise level, government and industry must establish a "technological infrastructure" to assist small and medium-sized manufacturers with technological information and innovative know-how.[32]

To regulate technological imports, "in order to maximize the realizable social and economic benefits and to minimize the disbenefits", the Foreign Investment Review Agency should add a technology screening function "to provide a defensive perimeter around the work of repair, reconstruction, and enhancement of Canadian manufacturing, keeping out foreign technology and other factors of production in a form harmful to our plans and objectives".[33] The objectives guiding regulation would be

1. Technology interdependence as opposed to technological dependence;
2. Selective development of an indigenous technological capability; allied with
3. Selective development of internationally competitive firms and industries.[34]

According to John Britton and James Gilmour, who have provided the most complete account of technological sovereignty, the four principal lines of action interlock: "remove any one, including control of technology imports, and the industrial development strategy they are capable of supporting will ultimately collapse under the weight of contradictions in the 'real' world of industrial decision making".[35] The crux of their analysis is captured in their conclusion that "the long term, the ultimate and the only solution to Canada's problems from its uniquely high degree of foreign ownership, lies in the successful promotion of competitive Canadian-controlled firms and industries, i.e. positive development of Canadian firms".[36] That analysis, and the notion that its resolution lies in the development and marketing of technology, constitutes the essence of technological sovereignty as an industrial strategy.

In contrast to technological sovereignty, an industrial strategy based on free trade is straightforward. Free trade assumes that it is tariff protection *per se*, and market opportunities severely limited by foreign tariffs (especially those of our leading trading partner, the United States), which are responsible for weakness in the Canadian manufacturing sector. Canadian tariffs shelter inefficiency and foreign tariffs limit Canadian production runs to lengths far below those optimal from the point of view of economies of scale. Hence, employment and real income are being held below potential by existing commercial and industrial policy. The solution is the reduction or elimination of protection; multilateral free trade is the ultimate goal, bilateral free trade with the United States a realistic first step. In the definitive expression of this point of view, the Economic Council of Canada stated in 1975:

> We believe that Canada could prosper in a totally free trade situation, provided the adjustment was eased by means of appropriate transitional arrangements. A move toward free trade entails a transformation of the existing pattern of production to one with greater competitive viability. There is no reason to suppose that a viable economy is not available to Canada, which has immense resources of all kinds—raw materials, capital labour—and a sophisticated and advanced social system well-equipped to cope with change. Thus we have suggested that a free trade policy is not only feasible for Canada but is the best guarantee of its national objectives.[37]

In short, the free trade school is most concerned, not with the degree of foreign ownership, but with another unique feature of the Canadian economic situation: the fact that it is virtually alone among industrialized nations in not having access to a market on the order of 150 million people or more. The trend toward block trading arrangements, extending beyond anything feasible under the General Agreement on Trade and Tariffs, threatens to leave Canada altogether too alone for comfort.

The free trade school is also concerned with the dangers of foreign retaliation against exports by Canadian firms benefitting from various measures of public support. For those who believe in open markets, technological sovereignty rests on an unrealistic assumption that Canadian policies of protection or subsidy for "chosen instruments" will be ignored by our trading partners, who will eschew countervailing measures themselves.

Technological sovereignty and free trade, then, are the two major alternatives which have emerged from the debate on industrial strategy. They are not totally irreconcilable. The technological sovereignty school does not reject free trade as an ultimate objective, while the free trade school agrees that technological superiority could be a powerful competitive advantage in international markets. They differ very significantly, however, in their priorities for policy action. Underlying these different priorities are different ideological positions on the role of the state in economic life. The free trade school, drawing on the ideology of western economic orthodoxy, wishes to confine the role of the state as much as possible to framework policies. The technological sovereignty school, emerging from a more catholic intellectual tradition, which includes economic geography and political economy, insists upon the necessity for a significant degree of operation-by-operation intervention to a successful industrial strategy. Albert Breton distinguishes between framework policies and operation-by-operation intervention as follows:

> Framework policies are designed to alter the constraints [e.g. tariffs] that determine the responses of economic agents to change, while operation-by-operation intervention or, more simply, direct intervention refers to policies [e.g. creation of core companies, regulation of technology imports] aimed at controlling the responses of economic agents directly, one by one as it were. Framework policies, as the phrase implies, modify the context, or environment, or framework of decision-making, without intervening in the decision-making process itself. Thus their purpose is to make it possible for economic agents responding to a different framework to engage in actions deemed by the public to be socially more desirable than those that would be undertaken if the framework were not altered. Direct intervention takes place at the decision-making level itself and, therefore, must occur when and where the economic agents decide to act.[38]

The free trade school foresees, however, a degree of operation-by-operation intervention in the process of adjustment to free trade,[39] and indeed Breton argues that subsidy payments tend to become increasingly direct forms of intervention in response to strategic behaviour by potential beneficiary firms.[40] From this perspective, the pretence that free trade cannot be an industrial strategy, with the interventionist overtones that the term conveys, is less than compelling. Nevertheless, the ideological differences between the two schools of industrial strategy are real, and the choice of primary policy instruments distinctive.

It is equally clear that both industrial strategies constitute major planning problems in the sense that they require

> ...the attempt to place government policies and programs within a suprasectoral or national context to permit political decision-making about their relationships and relative priority.

The free trade option is recognized to have very significant implications, not only for virtually all aspects of economic policy, but also for foreign, social, regional and cultural policies.[41] Without major reorientation in these areas, free trade could well create unacceptable costs in terms of sovereignty, disruption of the social fabric and regional distribution of wealth. Thus, free trade implies a commitment to economic objectives which require significant consequential alterations in non-economic sectors. The technological sovereignty school, of course, regards the instability attendant upon a free trade policy in the immediate future as beyond the effective reach of any range of policy adjustments, no matter how sweeping. The proponents of technological sovereignty do not, on the other hand, hesitate to identify a myriad of "implicit technology policies" or "contextual factors", which have severely limited the effectiveness of "explicit technology policies" hitherto:

> Technology development strategy, concerned with all policies that bear, in one way or another, on technology development, is defined by its objectives, not its instruments. Thus, to a great extent, technology strategy is concerned with ensuring *coherence* between sets of policies of very different origins, which may not be seen by those who propose them as being associated with technology. Financial, fiscal, trade, development, and other policies may have unintended or unconsidered effects upon technological activities. In the future, these impacts must be considered very carefully.[42]

Once again, the objectives of technological sovereignty as an industrial strategy demand planning criteria for a substantial range of policies.

If these alternative industrial strategies constitute major planning issues, it remains to examine their relationship to the planning systems operative within the Trudeau administration. To do so is somewhat ahistorical, for each alternative evolved apace through the mid-Seventies. However, both were clearly emerging as the planning systems were in operation, and it is worthwhile to outline the degree of compatibility between the strategies and assumptions of the Finance and Cabinet Planning Systems.

The Finance Planning System was based on a macroeconomic tradition congenial to the market economics of free trade. By contrast, the priority which technological sovereignty places on operation-by-operation intervention, such as the choice and support of core companies and the regulation of technology imports, was anathema to the Finance Planning System. To the extent that the general idea of industrial strategy carried interventionist overtones, it also created deep suspicion in the Department of Finance. This is not to say, of course, that the Department supported a strong and immediate free trade strategy. To the contrary. Whatever its intellectual sympathy with the free trade concept, Finance has never been able, as a matter of practical policy, to accept the feasibility of the draconian restructuring of the Canadian economy which, say, some kind of continental common market might bring about. While the Department has played the leading role in Canadian efforts to negotiate multilateral tariff reductions, it has never wished to risk the political and economic uncertainties of going further. There is no evidence that the Department's basic philosophy with respect to these issues—the preference for demand management, the suspicion of too much intervention regarding supply and structural factors—has changed in any way.

The Cabinet Planning System, on the other hand, did not espouse a particular economic philosophy, save a commitment to question the conservatism of the Department of Finance. The Cabinet Planning System was one of the main internal sponsors of the idea of an industrial strategy during the early Seventies. This was done, at least in part, to shake Finance and its satellite, Industry, Trade and Commerce, out of what the Priorities and Planning Secretariat saw as complacency in matters of industrial and regional development. Where Finance could not accept either industrial strategy, the Cabinet Planning System may be said to have welcomed both. Indeed, in 1975, after the Economic Council's endorsement of free trade, the Priorities and Planning Secretariat even attempted to bring the Chairman of the Council to meet the Priorities and Planning Committee, in order to break the Finance monopoly on general economic advice to the most powerful ministers. (The pressure of other events forestalled the manoeuvre.)

In fact, the Trudeau government's internal struggles with industrial strategy, an idea it had helped to popularize, never confronted either of the main options to which the public debate gave rise. Instead, the major share of attention and resources went to a more or less uncoordinated series of policies affecting industry: foreign investment, competition, regional development, research and development and export promotion, for example. Had there existed an industrial strategy, these policies could have been framed within it. Although it was fruitless, the search for an industrial strategy is nevertheless of interest.

The Pursuit of Industrial Strategy   6

Everybody wants an industrial strategy,
and they want it explained in two words.

Jack Horner,
Minister of Industry, Trade and Commerce
November 30, 1978.[1]

How has the federal government construed the idea of industrial strategy? What position, or rather positions, has it adopted relative to it? To trace the idea of industrial strategy in official discourse from 1972–79 is to follow a 180° shift in the federal approach. Notwithstanding the qualifiers and evasions inevitable in political discussion, the transition is one from a government anxious to promote industrial strategy, to a government anxious to suppress a notion which it considered to be inflating public expectations beyond the possibility of fulfillment. This chapter analyses the public history of the federal government's interpretation of the idea and examines the political and bureaucratic events underlying it.

Industrial Strategy in Official Discourse

"Industrial strategy" became a part of the economic policy dialogue in 1971–72. In January 1972, the Prime Minister let it be known that cabinet was "working" on an industrial strategy, and Jean-Luc Pépin, then Minister of Industry, Trade and Commerce, announced in March of that year his hope to bring forward "an industrial strategy" in the fall, as a basis for consultation with the provinces, the private sector and labour.[2]

In a speech to the Annual General Meeting of the Canadian Manufacturers' Association in June 1972, Pépin gave the fullest and most positive exposition of industrial strategy which any Canadian minister had ever attempted. Noting that it was "now an 'in' subject of conversation", Pépin was unequivocal about the government's intentions:

> My Department and I are committed to try and produce an "industrial strategy for Canada", that is, a "better" industrial strategy . . . than the one we have at present.

105

Nor was the Minister cautious about the scope of such a policy:

> Indeed there is hardly an economic, social or cultural "issue" which is not in some way related to an industrial strategy, from "women's lib" (e.g., its effects on rates of participation in the labour force) and control of foreign investments to bilingualism and the competition policy!

Pépin defined the enterprise as follows:

> ... a strategy is an ensemble of co-ordinated objectives and instruments, i.e. policies, programs and institutions.
>
> Applied to *industry*, the term means the proper planning by government (federal) for the optimum co-ordination of policies and decisions, on the use of all productive resources, in order to achieve defined (and accepted) social and economic goals.
>
> The strategy must embrace all sectors of economic activity from resources to services but must emphasize manufacturing and processing.

He went on to enumerate the kinds of issues which an industrial strategy would have to address, the reasons why an industrial strategy was required, and the steps the Department was undertaking to develop one.

Despite his positive tone, Pépin recognized that the exercise would not be an easy one. A consensus on the issues would be difficult to find. Canadians would not accept a *dirigiste* policy. There were severe analytical difficulties. Everyone saw "industrial strategy" from a unique perspective and,

> Unfortunately, expectations are sometimes unrealistic: industrial strategy is looked upon by some more or less as the panacea! It would solve all problems, once and for all ... without ever producing uncertainty in the business community! The Prime Minister, the Minister of Finance and myself have done our best to cool these excessive hopes.

Pépin had glimpsed the political risk in industrial strategy, but in the summer of 1972, this was no more than a minor cloud on an otherwise clear horizon. The commitment to an industrial strategy was fundamental. For example, as far as Pépin was concerned, strategies designed merely for particular sectors would not do: " ... the addition of sector strategies doesn't produce a global strategy, though it helps to devise one and to implement it".[3]

As the cabinet and the bureaucracy attempted to come to grips with industrial strategy, however, the analytical difficulties and political risks came to appear more and more formidable, creating an increasingly defensive tone in federal spokesmen and a full scale retreat from the "global strategy" on which Pépin had insisted so uncompromisingly. The politics of industrial strategy became the reduction of

106

public expectations in order to minimize the deficit between such expectations and performance. In official pronouncements, industrial strategy peaked early; after 1972, it was downhill all the way.

Less than a year after Pépin's speech, he was out of the cabinet and the House of Commons, a victim of the Liberal reversal in the election of the fall of 1972. His successor as Minister of Industry, Trade and Commerce was Alastair Gillespie. As early as April 1973, Gillespie was "trying to dispel the expectation that, in today's complex and changing world, any government would be realistically expected to produce *one* grandiose . . . industrial strategy". He had little time for the idea "that government could examine Canada's overall industrial situation—nationally and internationally, now and in the future—and implement *one* all-purpose master plan that would become *the* bible for business". In short, Gillespie rejected the global strategy sought by Pépin in favour of "a coherent set of industrial policies", in particular, precisely those "strategies for sectors on an industry-by-industry basis" which Pépin had regarded as no substitute for an industrial strategy.[4] A year to the day after Pépin's speech, Gillespie was insisting to the Canadian Manufacturers' Association that " . . . the term 'An Industrial Strategy' is not as helpful or as accurate a statement as 'Objectives and Strategies for Canadian Industrial Development'", and emphasizing sector strategies.[5] Gillespie was mauled in parliamentary committee by opposition critics for failing utterly to substantiate his contention that "we have not abandoned an overall approach", when in fact he had little to offer beyond the litany that "a series of strategies" were necessary because of the unique circumstances of each industry.[6]

By 1974, Gillespie was making speeches on subjects like the General Agreement on Trade and Tariffs or "Canada's Industrial Future" without once mentioning industrial strategy or strategies.[7] In 1975, toward the end of his tenure as Minister of Industry, Trade and Commerce, Gillespie fully articulated the new official orthodoxy:

> I have steadfastly resisted the temptation to announce one master plan for industrial strategy development in Canada. You know, it sounds great, but when you look behind it, it is not much more than cosmetics. I would say that we do not need an industrial strategy for Canada because I think we need more than one industrial strategy—and I have mentioned 18 [or] . . . 19 industrial strategies that we are working on at the present time—because each industry has a unique set of problems, opportunities and constraints, which I have already dealt with on an industry-by-industry basis.[8]

Gillespie's successors in the portfolio, Don Jamieson and Jean Chrétien, avoided using the word "strategy" at all and held it delicately at

107

arm's length when others raised it. In the House of Commons, Chrétien stigmatized the idea of an "across the board strategy" as simultaneously protectionist, socialist and doctrinaire.[9]

After his appointment in April 1977, Jack Horner had a brief flirtation with the idea of an industrial strategy,[10] but the affair did not last. His deputy minister continued to try to defuse the proposition,[11] and his Department's *Report by the Second Tier Committee on Policies to Improve Canadian Competitiveness* of October 1978, was at pains to point out that the effort it represented was "not an industrial strategy for Canada".[12] In the following month, a departmental spokesman called the idea of industrial strategy "naive",[13] and Horner described industrial strategy as "a word which I used to shudder about".[14]

Finally, in one of his first announcements as President of the Board of Economic Development Ministers, Robert Andras echoed his colleague Horner: "I do not promise any 'Industrial Strategy' with all the T's crossed and I's dotted, because in a country like ours that isn't going to happen."[15]

This, then, is the somewhat murky history of the government's interpretation of industrial strategy—early enthusiasm followed by prolonged anticlimax. From an idea which the government was pleased to embrace and promote in its most ambitious form, industrial strategy was reinterpreted to fit existing industrial policy initiatives or, where this would not wash, rejected entirely. During this latter and longer phase, ambitious constructions of the idea of industrial strategy, entirely consonant with those in Pépin's first speeches, were attributed by official spokesmen to "certain circles",[16] or "several politicians and some academics",[17] whose "doctrinaire"[18] illusions were not shared by the government. Since the idea, no matter how assiduously ignored, seemed unwilling to go away, the Trudeau administration's involvement with it had to be repressed, and its advocacy projected onto others.

Behind this turnabout lies the not atypical history of a classic planning problem. The idea of industrial strategy raises a series of conceptual, administrative and political difficulties, each of which feeds upon the others. As the internally divided planning systems of the Trudeau era discovered, exploited or ignored these difficulties, ministers of Industry, Trade and Commerce found themselves, after Pépin's initial foray, backpedalling furiously from a public debate which the government had helped to create. Lacking either analytical clarity or philosophical consensus within the cabinet and the bureaucracy, the ministers did their best to reduce the policy question to no more than a political nuisance.

Industrial Strategy in the Bureaucracy and Cabinet

In order to understand the ambivalent federal posture toward the notion of industrial strategy, one must trace its emergence after 1971 as a political and bureaucratic issue to two factors already explored at some length. First, to diverse developments which appeared to threaten the viability of Canada's traditional economic strategy of doing what comes naturally behind the tariff wall. Second, to the reflexive affinity of the Cabinet Planning System for an idea which promised to bring objectives, coherence and a longer term perspective into what was regarded in the PCO as the chaos of industrial and regional development programs.

The Cabinet Planning System had focussed upon the issues implied by industrial strategy from the System's inception, before the explicit emergence of the idea itself. The first list of priority problems in November 1969 included three relevant items: tax reform, technology policy and foreign investment policy. Indeed, Pierre Trudeau had made the question of industrial development an important issue in his campaign for the leadership of the Liberal Party. It was natural that the Cabinet Planning System kept it before ministers. By 1971–72, industrial development was a priority problem as such, and the expression "industrial strategy" was being used in this connection by the Priorities and Planning Secretariat of the Privy Council Office. Given the souring of the economic picture and the Nixon administration's dissolution of the "special relationship", the PCO intensified its use of the Cabinet Planning System to try to create some movement toward a more systematic industrial development policy. The primary target of these efforts was the Department of Industry, Trade and Commerce (IT&C), and its then minister, Jean-Luc Pépin.

The Department of Industry had been established in 1963 to be "for the manufacturing industry what the Department of Agriculture is for farmers", as Prime Minister Pearson put it at the time.[19] Prominent in the promotion of the idea of the department were three of Pearson's closest economic counsellours: Walter Gordon, author of the *Report of the Royal Commission on Canada's Economic Prospects*[20] and Minister of Finance under Pearson; Maurice Lamontagne, also a minister under Pearson; and Tom Kent, his closest adviser on social and economic policy. All three were regarded as left-of-centre Liberals, ready to countenance an active role for the public sector in ensuring the health of Canadian industry.[21] Thus, the Department of Industry embodied from its origins the aspirations of an important minority theme in Canadian economic thought, a theme of nationalism and strong initiative by the state in industrial development.

This is not to say, however, that those aspirations were ever realized.

By 1968, the new Prime Minister had decided to combine the department with its older sister department, Trade and Commerce,[22] to form the Department of Industry, Trade and Commerce. Trade and Commerce represented the traditional interpretation of commercial policy as an element of foreign policy, or alternatively, of trade promotion as the nearest thing to industrial policy a trading nation would wish to undertake. The formation of IT&C thus brought together in a single entity instruments for structural intervention informed by an intellectual position which ultimately led to technological sovereignty, and instruments for trade promotion premised on assumptions largely consistent with those of free trade. There was an inevitable tension between the trade and industrial sides of the Department, and nationalist parliamentarians were quick to voice their fear that the prestige of the Trade and Commerce tradition would break the commitment to industrial development.[23]

Whatever the theoretical merits of the decision to merge Industry with Trade and Commerce, the resulting Department was to become one of the most unwieldy and unstable bureaucracies in Ottawa. The 1968 reorganization was followed by others at regular intervals over the decade. Ministers and deputy ministers came and went, while general directors and assistant deputy ministers multiplied and reshuffled apace. The split between the trade promotion and industrial development sides of the sprawling Department was, then, only the most fundamental of the organizational problems plaguing the evolution of industrial policy within IT&C.

By the early Seventies, IT&C operated a diverse range of promotional and incentive programs targeted on industry. On the one hand, these were intended to aid exports by Canadian firms, and on the other, to aid those firms directly in areas such as adjustment to changes in commercial policy, industrial design and research and development.[24] On the industrial development side, the Department was structured into vertical units known as the line branches, each responsible for assistance to a particular industry sector: chemicals, textiles, electrical and electronics, machinery, resource industries, etc. While this sectoral structure was the logical means for program delivery, since it simplified contact with the industry immensely, it also dominated the industrial side of the Department to the extent that the rapidly growing promotion and incentive programs of the early Seventies entirely escaped any horizontal policy co-ordination. The flow of benefits through the line branches created a community of interest between program managers in government and their industry clients, a powerful axis which proved extremely resistant to "program-bending" by agents external to the line branches. This kind of relationship was not confined to IT&C, and if co-ordination within the Department was difficult, co-ordination with other departments which operated programs affecting industrial development, such as Regional Economic Expansion (DREE), Manpower and Immigration, Environment and Transport was even more elusive. For reasons which have already been explored, Finance chose not to interpret its mandate to involve active leadership in the economic development area in general. Interdepartmental mechanisms were weak or non-existent, leaving the burdens of horizontal co-ordination almost entirely to the rarified level of the Cabinet Committees on Economic Policy and Priorities and Planning.

The lack of cohesion and co-ordination in the burgeoning programs run by IT&C, DREE and related departments naturally offended the Cabinet Planning System's policy aesthetic, its sense of a rational government, self-consciously pursuing explicit goals in a systematic fashion. From 1969 onward, the Cabinet Planning System, inspired by what it understood of the examples of countries like Sweden, France and Japan, pressed IT&C to move beyond the pell-mell development of new programs and expansion of existing ones to an overview of its industrial development policies. This exercise was undertaken through the Cabinet Planning System's instruments—notably the concept of the priority problem and, later, that of the policy thrust—approved by the Committee on Priorities and Planning and by full cabinet. It was seen as the logical parallel to the somewhat more successful efforts taking place to broach the problem of foreign investment in the Canadian economy, and it soon became identified with the idea of industrial strategy.

The pressure from the Cabinet Planning System on the Department of Industry, Trade and Commerce fell on a series of resistent deputy ministers and ambivalent ministers. While some of the more aggressive policy personnel in IT&C welcomed the PCO/cabinet intervention as an opportunity to break the autonomy of the line branches and the branches' intimate symbiosis with their industrial clients, the deputies, notably Jake Warren (1968–1971) and James Grandy (1971–1975), were, on the whole, sceptical about the PCO initiatives. Both deputies, and a large number of other officials, shared the essential reservations of the Finance Planning System about the Cabinet Planning System's ambitious construction of industrial development policy or industrial strategy. They felt they were being asked to do the impossible and the undesirable. They felt that the objectives and instruments which the Cabinet Planning System insisted be rationalized within a single industrial development framework were unrealistically broad, and that neither the analytical task involved, nor the historical background of

111

Canadian industrial development against which that task would have to be carried out, had been adequately considered. They feared the degree of government intervention, and particularly the degree of firm-level targeting of industrial development programs, implied by the PCO approach.

Given the Prime Minister's support for the Cabinet Planning System, neither ministers nor deputies of IT&C could afford a too explicit articulation of such concerns. Jean-Luc Pépin seems not to have felt them at all during his tenure as Minister, which ended with the election of 1972. It had been Pépin who expressed the government's early enthusiasm for industrial strategy in 1971–72. At this very point, however, the confrontation between the Finance and Cabinet Planning Systems over industrial strategy was clearly emerging, as were some of the fundamental intellectual and practical difficulties of the idea. The result was that the first half of the Seventies saw the lengthy, ardent, but unconsummated courtship by the Cabinet Planning System, of the reluctant bride, IT&C. The principal issue at stake was the nature of the dowry, industrial development policy. And of course the bride's rich uncle, the Department of Finance, played a central role, not altogether behind the scenes.

It is the continuing burden of the Department of Industry, Trade and Commerce that it is responsible for industrial development, while the principal instruments affecting corporate decision-making lie elsewhere, in the Department of Finance. Business perceptions of government policy are most influenced by commercial policy and especially by tax policy, which reside ultimately in the hands of Finance, and only secondarily by the promotional, incentive and regulatory instruments managed by IT&C. IT&C has had to accommodate its ambitions and tactics to this reality. At times, political and economic circumstances have favoured IT&C, at other times not. In the end, however, IT&C has been dependent on Finance for its influence upon framework policies critical to the IT&C mandate. In the matter of industrial strategy, therefore, IT&C found itself wedged uncomfortably between two planning systems sponsored by two power centres. Although on balance, IT&C shared the Finance Planning System's rejection of the Cabinet Planning System's approach to industrial development policy, it could not afford to alienate the PCO. It therefore presented, between 1970 and 1975, a series of policy compromises which attempted simultaneously to meet the Cabinet Planning System's terms of reference for a broad guage policy, to remain within the tolerance of the Finance Planning System's economic orthodoxy, and to put some order in the jumble of programs administered through the

112

line branches. IT&C also began a process of more formal consultation with the business community, a process which was ultimately to become the primary vehicle of a compromise strategy.

By 1971, it had become clear in the PCO that the then deputy minister of Industry, Trade and Commerce, Jake Warren, was not intellectually in tune with the Cabinet Planning System's notion of industrial policy. A number of Memoranda to Cabinet had been drafted to meet cabinet's demand for such a policy during 1970–71, but each had been rejected as failing to establish overall objectives for the industrial sector, and emphasizing instead a subsidy approach in which government reacts to private sector initiatives. By the fall of 1971, shortly after the shock of the Nixon trade policies, Warren had been given a senior diplomatic posting, amid rumours that his refusal to meet PCO expectations had been a major factor in his transfer.

Warren's successor was James Grandy, an economist who, like Warren, had had a distinguished career in the federal public service. After intensive public discussion of industrial strategy had begun over the winter of 1971–72, Jean-Luc Pépin spoke openly about the federal government's commitment to industrial strategy, and started a nationwide round of consultations with business on the subject. These consultations demonstrated that while there was agreement on a series of economic objectives—growth, employment, distributional equity, sovereignty, preservation of the environment—there was no agreement on their relative priority, nor on the nature of trade-offs between them. The consensus of the Fifties, centered on growth, had vanished. The resulting ambiguity about the framework of business perceptions within which policy had to be developed was to plague industrial policy-makers throughout the Seventies. The greater the ambitions for industrial strategy, the more serious this ambiguity became.

In early 1972, Grandy and Pépin attempted once again to meet the Priorities and Planning demand for an industrial development policy, and Pépin's own explicit public commitment to an industrial strategy. Where Warren had produced a very lengthy document which focussed on the department's subsidy/incentive programs and sought their expansion, the 1972 Memorandum emphasized a framework philosophy, rather than the operation-by-operation approach. It was very brief, and highlighted the arguments of orthodox theory in economic development regarding dangers of government selection of particular corporations as instruments for the realization of national objectives.

The discussion of this document in the Cabinet Committee on Priorities and Planning occasioned a classic confrontation between the Finance and Cabinet Planning Systems. Simon Reisman, then deputy minister of Finance (he had been deputy minister of Industry, 1964–68), took the opportunity to demolish in the presence of ministers, the notion of industrial development then being promoted by Pépin and by the Cabinet Planning System. In doing so, he extended the philosophy of the IT&C document further than Grandy had wished or been able to go, and he did so forcefully and categorically. Canada, said Reisman, already had an industrial strategy. It was unarticulated, and it was the only one really open to a nation in Canada's circumstances. Because of the location of primary markets, the strategy was centrist in its emphasis and focussed almost completely on the United States. There was very little Canadian policy could or should do, said Reisman, to alter these basic realities of economic geography. Instead, Canada should promote the basic momentum of industrial strength in the Montreal-Windsor corridor, raising the peripheral regions up behind the centre. The notion of "regional development" was essentially a kind of social policy, a redistributive mechanism for spreading the benefits of growth, a large step removed from a primarily market-oriented, non-interventionist strategy for maximizing economic development. Thus, to promote a strategy implying that government "pick winners" (and thus, necessarily, pick losers as well) was to misunderstand profoundly the forces underlying industrial growth. To introduce issues of regional distribution into industrial development policy was to confuse social and economic policy.

This was an entirely typical expression of the philosophy of the Finance Planning System. (The point about the separation of social and economic policy returned in the bitter debate over the Social Security Review of the mid-Seventies). Combined with the IT&C document, this perspective led in directions—incrementalism, centralism, continentalism—in which the Cabinet Planning System did not want to go. The result of the Priorities and Planning discussion was the kind of stalemate which would characterize the internal debate over industrial strategy for several years: no progress had been made toward an industrial strategy, but the Cabinet Planning System would keep the idea alive as a priority problem or, later, a policy thrust, hoping that some combination of changes in bureaucratic attitude, minister, or political circumstance would render the times more propitious for what it saw as an essential planning issue.

Ministerial attitudes toward the idea of industrial strategy, amorphous as it was, varied substantially. Few ministers had the time to become well versed in the subject matter, and many no doubt read the aspirations of their own regions into the concept. Central Ontario ministers identified with business, such as John Turner, Donald

MacDonald and Mitchell Sharp, tended to be unsympathetic, supporting, at least by their silence, the fight by Reisman, Grandy and others against the Cabinet Planning System's construction of the idea. Support for the idea seems to have come from ministers intellectually or ideologically disposed toward more systematic planning effort from the centre—such as Pépin, Bryce Mackasey, Gérard Pelletier, Otto Lang, and the Prime Minister—or from ministers who saw the debate as an opportunity to press regional claims to industrial development support. Although the personalities and issues changed somewhat, the same kind of divisions or ambivalence in cabinet about economic planning remained throughout the decade.

The election of 1972 returned a Liberal minority and removed the minister most identified with the idea of industrial strategy, Jean-Luc Pépin. In the aftermath of the election, however, "Optimum Economic Performance" was one of the government's three major themes. By early 1973, industrial development was one of five policy thrusts (along with social security, regional development, transportation and the urban environment), pursuant to the government's objectives to extend the benefits of economic growth to all regions, to secure national economic independence, and to contain inflation and increase employment opportunities while promoting stable economic growth. Industrial development remained a formal priority until 1975. In the spring of 1973, the responsible minister, Pépin's successor Alastair Gillespie, was asked by Cabinet to come forward with a Memorandum proposing the scope and objectives for the thrust toward industrial development, and outlining areas where the government ought to concentrate its efforts.

Although, by the standards of the Trudeau cabinet, Gillespie was moderately nationalist in orientation, he was far more sceptical than Pépin had been about the Cabinet Planning System's notion of industrial development, which by now embraced technology policy, domestic control of the economy, regional development, encouragement of entrepreneurship and export strategy. A former Minister of State for Science and Technology, Gillespie had few illusions about the PCO's ambitious standards and designs for comprehensive policy development.[25] In that portfolio, Gillespie had emphasized that Canada should not seek a science policy, but rather a series of science policies. His strategy for dealing with the Cabinet Planning System's demands in the industrial development area was much the same. The System's insistence on a "top-down" approach would be met by an analysis of the relationships of various industrial policies *inter se* and with contiguous policy areas. The heart and soul of the enterprise—from Gillespie

115

and IT&C's point of view—would be an approach to individual industries, specifically the sectoral strategy which he immediately began to advocate in his public speeches. Gillespie later spoke of "eighteen or nineteen industrial strategies"[26] and in April 1973, he stated "...it is my view, based on the consultations and work to date, that we must develop strategies for sectors on an industry-by-industry basis" and that industry itself must play a major role in the development of these strategies.[27] Gillespie saw the sectoral approach as the only way out of the pressure created by Cabinet Planning expectations, a way which promised at the same time the development of specific policies and programs of aid to industry within the not-too-distant future. He continued the process of consultation which Pépin had initiated.

Late in the winter of 1974, nearly a year after industrial development had been designated as a policy thrust, Gillespie and his department came forward with a Memorandum to respond to that designation. Once again, the document was a tremendous disappointment to the PCO planners. Less than ten pages in length, it was no more than a *tour d'horizon* of the status quo in industrial development programs. The document made no recommendations, thus endorsing completely the current policies and programs. It was scarcely long enough to touch a number of issues dear to the hearts of the PCO planners, such as the balance between primary and secondary industry, the role of the service sector as a creator of employment and growth in the so-called "post-industrial society", the trade-offs between such goals as international competitiveness and regional development, and the international bargaining potential of Canadian strength in certain commodity sectors. Once again, however, industrial development was retained as a policy thrust and Gillespie was specifically asked—since he was emphasizing the sectoral approach—to prepare for ministers an analysis of existing and possible sector strategies, as well as an overview of Canadian strengths and weaknesses in industrial development. The Cabinet Planning System was not going to surrender its focus on the subject.

Meanwhile, the continuing consultations with business, and the process of IT&C policy development goaded along by the Cabinet Planning System, were slowly beginning to generate some basic conclusions. By the summer of 1974, certain broad themes had become quite clear. First, the private sector's main concern was not with the lack of target-setting or indicative planning for industry by government. It was rather the multitude of conflicting and unco-ordinated policies being implemented in a variety of areas—regional development, environment, consumer affairs and others—which were having detrimental effects on the efficiency, costs and management capacity of industry.

Even if complete consistency in such policies would have to remain a distant ideal, business-government relations would remain problematic without greater co-ordination and increased sensitivity on the part of agencies whose programs and regulations affected industrial development. Second, industrial and trade policy must be seen within the context of macroeconomic policy. Detailed assessments of the prospects of approximately twenty industry sectors, developed in collaboration with representatives of each sector, showed that the major determinants of sector performance were often non-specific factors arising from the macroeconomic framework. Thus, the linkage between changes in the framework and their sectoral impacts would have to be scrutinized more systematically. This would require a sophisticated analytical capacity beyond the possibilities of the line branches. The development of an appropriate econometric model was begun in the Economic and Policy Analysis Branch of IT&C. The importance of macroeconomic policy to the health of industry was magnified by the international trends toward major regional trading blocs and toward cartelization.

The primary implication of both of these themes was the dependence of IT&C upon the co-operation of other actors—federal departments, other governments, corporations—for the achievement of its mission, plus the continuing lack of interdepartmental, intergovernmental and intersectoral machinery appropriate to that purpose. During 1974–75, the beginnings of such machinery were established on a formal and more permanent basis: interdepartmental committees, structures for federal-provincial co-ordination, consultative committees for each industry. The creation of this machinery and the proposal of a general framework for policy and co-ordination, were the major recommendations of Gillespie's last recourse to Cabinet on the subject of industrial development policy, in the winter of 1974–75.

The Cabinet Planning System was much more receptive to this initiative than it had been to the IT&C efforts of the previous five years. The Gillespie proposals included a set of objectives for industrial development policy, a definition of the federal government's role, the identification of seven major areas of government policy relevant to industrial development, an appendix describing sectoral strategies for twenty-three different industries, and specific recommendations as to structure and process for attempting to implement the analytical framework. Although the PCO planners were disappointed that IT&C had ignored certain issues (including the Cabinet Planning System's old favourite, the service industries), it supported the IT&C documents, and cabinet approved Gillespie's recommendations.

It should be noted that this consideration of industrial policy occurred six months after the election of July 1974, which returned the Liberals to the status of a majority government. It occurred, therefore, in the midst of, but independent of, the Priorities Exercise of 1974–75. Given the Cabinet Planning System's dominant role in that Exercise, it was to be expected that industrial development would be included. One of the sixteen priority policy areas was "National Industrial and Regional Development" (NIRD), which attempted to marry industrial strategy with regional development policy. It was developed under the rather isolated "core group" of central agency officials who managed the Priorities Exercise. The officials who wrote the NIRD Memorandum were from PCO and TBS. The resulting document, entirely separate from the ongoing efforts of IT&C, confirmed the worst fears of Finance and IT&C about the economic heresy and the impracticality of the planners. The NIRD document, in the eyes of those in the Finance Planning System or sympathizing with it, demanded far too much prescience on the part of public planners as to what ought to be produced and where, far too *dirigiste* policies of implementation, and far too little appreciation of the historical realities of industrial development in Canada. There was little explicit opposition, however, because the NIRD document fell along with the other priority policy area Memoranda, when the Priorities Exercise expired in the fall of 1975.

By that time, James Grandy had retired from the public service, Alastair Gillespie had become Minister of Energy, Mines and Resources and rather new issues were preoccupying their successors. The most important, if unanticipated, outcome of the introspection of 1974–75 was the program of wage and price controls. During 1975–76, government-business relations, and the internal policy development to support consultation, were dominated by the need to operate controls. Little overt attention was paid to industrial development policy. Beneath the surface, however, the foundations of the government's compromise approach to industrial strategy were being laid.

Although the controls period did not see a great deal of high profile activity on industrial development, the economic and political pressures created broke down the interdepartmental barriers in the economic and social policy areas. A deputy ministerial committee, the so-called DM-10 committee, advised cabinet collectively on the exit from controls and the economic challenges to follow. Systematic working relationships developed at senior levels, and these relationships were to be crucial to the reinvigorated effort in industrial development policy as the end of controls came into view. It had become evident that cabinet and its committees could not do the entire job of co-ordination and that machinery for such co-ordination would have to exist on a permanent basis, just below cabinet level.

One of the most important developments of this period was the decision to integrate commercial and industrial policy. The "Tokyo Round" of multinational trade negotiations (MTN) had begun in 1972, and the most critical phase of the MTN was, in 1976–77, about to begin. Commercial policy in Canada had traditionally been the property of a small group of senior officials in External Affairs, Finance and the trade side of IT&C. It had been developed as an adjunct of Canadian foreign policy rather than as an extension of industrial development policy. Until 1976–77, the Canadian role in the MTN had had little attention from ministers. At that point, Jake Warren was recalled from Washington to a newly-created post as "MTN Co-ordinator". The Secretary of State for External Affairs, Alan Mac-Eachen, was asked by the Prime Minister to chair a special ministerial committee on the MTN. The Interdepartmental Committee on Trade and Industrial Policy (ICTIP) was revitalized with the mandate (in part) to link Canada's commercial policy position as reflected in its role in MTN, with an industrial policy thrust rendered urgent by the increasingly evident weakness of the country's manufacturing sector. Warren and ICTIP would oversee and approve the development of policies to be submitted to the MacEachen committee. New machinery and momentum in commercial policy was only part of a series of changes, which will be described in the section which follows.

The frustrations of 1970–75 demonstrated a lack of internal consensus, notably between the Cabinet and Finance Planning Systems, as to what industrial policy could or should be, and a lack of demand for the Cabinet Planning System version from the primary actors for delivering the policy's benefits, that is, the corporate sector. IT&C reacted like other departments caught by the demands of the Cabinet Planning System. It attempted to respond to the form of the demands, while ignoring their content as specified by the problem definitions developed by the Cabinet Planning System. Neither of the industrial strategies was ever put before ministers as such. What developed instead was a slowly emerging consensus around a compromise approach, a middle ground which met IT&C's needs for renewal of its industrial development programs and the requirement for broader co-ordination of related policies. The Cabinet Planning System, in the throes of its last great effort, the Priorities Exercise of 1974–75, was forced to accept half a loaf; the sectoral/consultation approach was better than nothing at all.

Sectoral Strategy and the Board of Economic Development Ministers

According to Phidd and Doern, the mid-Seventies were a watershed for federal economic policy. Whereas the government "did not fully comprehend the complexities of the changes which occurred during the late 1960s and early 1970s",

> In retrospect it appears that by 1975 there was a clearer idea of the economic forces at work and four major shifts were made, as a result, in government policies. First, budgetary restraint programs were initiated in 1976 and subsequent years so that the annual growth rate of federal expenditures was reduced from over 28% in 1974–75 to under 9% in 1979 –80. Second, monetary policy became much more restrictive ... Third, the anti-inflation program helped to cool off the inflationary psychology prior to the impact of the new monetary and fiscal measures. Fourth, in co-operation with the private sector, the federal government launched a systematic review of government policies which affect economic and industrial performance.[28]

Chapter 3 dealt with some of the implications of the first three of these shifts of policy.

This section will deal with the fourth initiative, which can be seen within the context of this broader redirection and new emphasis upon economic policy within the Trudeau ministry. It was not until 1975–76 that the government began to act as if the traditional preoccupations of fiscal conservatism—the viability of private enterprise, the level of taxation, government spending, deficit financing—might become issues which could swing significant numbers of votes away from the Liberal Party. The realization dawned slowly. It was not fully manifested until the major budget cuts of the summer of 1978 and the structural changes which followed. The establishment of the Board of Economic Development Ministers may be interpreted as the creation of an instrument to marry aggressive industrial development policies with the "fiscal responsibility" of the budget cuts.

Before all this could occur, however, industrial development policy had to be resurrected from the broader economic debates and feverish activity of the controls period. In 1976, Prime Minister Trudeau named Jean Chrétien, then President of the Treasury Board, as Minister of Industry, Trade and Commerce. As part of the bargain, it was rumoured, Chrétien insisted that his deputy minister at the Treasury Board, Gordon Osbaldeston, be named deputy minister of IT&C. At any rate, Osbaldeston, a former trade commissioner and head of the Trade Commissioner Service, was duly transferred to IT&C in December 1976. In Chrétien and Osbaldeston, IT&C gained a team with the mutual confidence hitherto lacking in the portfolio. Both were tough, ambitious pragmatists skilled in the politics of their respective domains. One would have to go back to the combination of C. M. Drury and Simon Reisman in the old Department of Industry to find comparable philosophical consistency between a minister and deputy in this policy area. Furthermore, Chrétien and Osbaldeston could operate in government councils turning toward values congenial to industrial interests, and without a strong Cabinet Planning System to second-guess their efforts. Finally, they could work in concert with Mac-Eachen and Warren to take advantage of the government's engagement to a tighter integration of commercial and industrial policy.

By 1977, the elements of the Chrétien/Osbaldeston strategy were essentially in place: the sectoral approach, emphasis on consultation with business, and the interdepartmental machinery (notably ICTIP) were all legacies of the end of the Gillespie/Grandy efforts in 1974–75. ICTIP was a senior committee chaired by Osbaldeston, which included the deputies of all of the economic departments. Its re-emergence, as the DM-10 committee wound down toward the end of the controls period, took advantage of the working relationships which had developed in DM-10. ICTIP was the forum for planning and coordination of the centrepiece of the government's approach to industrial development policy, the process of consultation which began with Enterprise 77. Enterprise 77 was the consultation to end all consultations. Interviews about business' needs from public policy were held in 5,000 industrial firms across the country and the results were fed into ICTIP.

Here is how Osbaldeston described the process leading to the sectoral consultation approach:

> I went over to the department . . . The question of industrial strategy or strategies was flying around. Government had somehow or other [to] come down on that issue so they turned to their advisors and asked that they come up with some alternative, either in terms of process or of policy, to meet the requirement . . . I think industrial strategy requires some kind of consensus if it is going to survive the afternoon's newspapers . . . I wasn't really anxious to go into the marsh into which a number of my predecessors dashed to disappear forever. We decided we would go about it another way . . . what are the facts relative to our industrial structure by sector? Why did it happen? If you don't like it, how do you change it?[29]

The results of this very extensive series of consultations had two general implications. The first was that business' prime complaint about the federal government lay, as ever, in the inconsistency of direction and the inequity of costs of the diversity of federal policies and regulations which affect industrial development. The second was that a somewhat more focussed and sustained series of consultations would be required to develop sector strategies for the various industries. Profiles of the problems and opportunities in each industry sector had been developed in the IT&C line branches under the co-ordination of the Department's central policy staff. In some important cases, sector profiles were rewritten outside the line branches. The sector profiles were finalized within IT&C and were approved by ICTIP.

In November 1977, a Memorandum to Cabinet from IT&C summarized the results of Enterprise 77 and the policy development that went with it. The document examined the prospects for Canadian manufacturing in the 1980s within the framework of the multilateral trade negotiations then in progress, the results of the Enterprise 77 interviews, and a review of the various policies affecting industrial development. IT&C proposed for federal-provincial approval a new industrial policy thrust: twenty-three sectoral task forces (twenty-one manufacturing industries, plus construction and tourism). After discussion by provincial deputy ministers of industry in December 1977, by their ministers in January 1978, and by the First Ministers' Conference of February 1978, the so-called Tier 1 committees were convened.

These committees, or sectoral task forces, each composed of management, labour, academic, federal and provincial representatives, met during the first half of 1978. Their task was to distill the sector profiles developed in IT&C, the results of the Enterprise 77 interviews, and their own experience in the industry, and to elaborate a sectoral strategy for each industry. The product of this Tier 1 exercise was some twenty-three sectoral reports.[30] Senior officials of Industry, Trade and Commerce had briefed each sectoral task force intensively during the exercise.

The next step was Tier 2. A Tier 2 committee, composed once again of business, labour and academic representatives, who had generally not been involved in Tier 1, was designated

> ... to identify and make recommendations about factors and policies that cut across sector lines ... to pull together the common threads runn ng through the reports, to make recommendations on broad economic policy and on issues important generally to manufacturing and tourism.[31]

The Tier 2 committee's report identified nine areas where public sector initiatives could help industrial development: trade and multilateral trade negotiations, manpower, labour relations, taxation, research and development, energy, transportation costs, regional development and government purchasing policies. In each area, specific recommendations as to the direction of government policies were made.

By the time the Tier 2 report emerged in the fall of 1978, the government's industrial policy machinery was changing dramatically. Prime Minister Trudeau had returned from the economic summit meeting in Bonn in the summer of 1978 to face serious economic and political problems. The failure of his invitation to ministers and departments in the spring of 1978 to help the government meet its restraint commitment, plus the renewal of that commitment, indicated the need for drastic action. Hence the draconian and unilateral declaration of the budget cuts of August 1978. Further, progress at the MTN indicated that trade liberalization would indeed make significant progress, despite the desultory beginnings at the Tokyo Round. This was consistent with Canadian policy but it raised the issue of the delivery of adjustment assistance to business and labour in industries which would be exposed by tariff reductions, notably those in Québec. None of the existing departments and agencies in the economic area appeared to have the appropriate breadth and mandate to undertake such a function. Finally, the earmarking of some of the funds for economic development purposes had set off a wild scramble among the economic ministers to claim shares of those funds. However, given the way the cuts themselves had been made, there was no longer a credible expenditure decision-making process within which that competition could be managed.[32]

A new mechanism for allocating resources and delivering services was clearly needed in the economic development sector. Other unfilled functions were also emerging in that sector. The series of consultations undertaken within Enterprise 77, Tier 1 and Tier 2 had shown that business was unhappy both at the fragmentation of federal policy and at the multiple points of access to government which this fragmentation required of the private sector. IT&C had begun to move in the direction of co-ordinating and focussing the industrially-relevant policies of as many as thirteen or fourteen other federal departments, but as long as the Department had major programs and policies of its own, its undertaking these newer "central agency" functions was viewed with suspicion by other departments.[33]

The product of these pressures was a new cabinet committee, the Board of Economic Development Ministers, to be chaired by the incumbent of a new portfolio. This minister, the President of the Board of Economic Development Ministers, was to be supported by a Ministry of State for Economic Development, established by Order in Council under the *Ministries and Ministers of State Act* of 1971. The new committee and portfolio were announced in late November 1978, as part of a cabinet shuffle which was intended to revitalize the government as it went into the pre-election period. The BEDM, as it was known, was to be the primary instrument for the advancement of industrial development policy, which had slowly emerged over the last two years as a major priority for a government anxious to solidify a wavering constituency in the pro-private enterprise, fiscally conservative middle class.

According to the Order in Council establishing the portfolio, the President was to "formulate and develop policies with respect to:"

a) The most appropriate means by which the Government of Canada may, through measures within its field of jurisdiction, have a beneficial influence on the development of industries and regional economies in Canada,

b) The integration of programs and activities providing direct support to industry including their co-ordination with other policies and programs of the Government of Canada, and

c) The fostering of co-operative relationships with respect to industrial development with the provinces, with business and labour, and with other public and private organizations.

In short, what ought the federal government to do in the area of industrial and regional development, how ought this to be done, and how ought it to be related to the activities of the provinces, business, labour and other actors?

The Order in Council went on to bestow upon the President the following powers, duties and functions:

a) He shall, in concert with and as the President of a board of Ministers to be called the Board of Economic Development Ministers,

   (i) define an integrated federal approach to the provision of direct support to industry and economic development in Canada both by industrial sector and by region,

  (ii) review and concert proposals by departments prior to their consideration by Treasury Board or by the Governor in Council, and

 (iii) develop mechanisms to improve and to integrate program delivery at the local or regional level;

b) He shall advise the Treasury Board on the allocation of financial, personnel and other resources to federal programs that provide direct support to the development of economic enterprise in Canada;

c) He shall lead and co-ordinate the efforts of the Government of Canada to establish cooperative relationships with the provinces, business, labour and other public and private organizations, for the industrial development of the economy; and

d) In respect of research and policy development, he may
   (i) initiate and co-ordinate research and policy studies,
   (ii) initiate proposals for new policies, programs and activities, and
   (iii) evaluate existing and proposed policies, programs and activities to ensure their consistency with federal industrial development policies and recommend changes therein.[34]

In his announcement of the creation of the BEDM, the Prime Minister saw its function as "to focus and co-ordinate our economic policies" and he referred explicitly to the need to allocate the resources freed by the summer budgetary cuts and earmarked for economic development. He saw the Board's role having to do "essentially with the microeconomic problems, assigning priorities to expenditures by the various departments of government in the area of economic development" while the Minister of Finance "remains the lead economic minister, particularly as regards the macroeconomy".[35]

According to its first and only President, Robert Andras, speaking at the First Ministers' Conference at the end of November 1978:

> The Board will integrate federal economic development policies supporting growth. It will review and co-ordinate economic proposals made by departments before those proposals go ahead to Cabinet or Treasury Board. It will develop more effective ways to deliver government programs in the country. Ministers who are members of the Board will channel their major proposals through my Ministry and the Board. Here, I must say that the Ministers will continue to run their own affairs and to propose major economic policy. But they achieve a new focus for their economic policy proposals [:] A Board of Ministers which when agreed on a proposal, will present it as coming from one agreed unit. The focus of economic development within the government will be, if you like, greater than the sum of the individual parts.
>
> It will be my role, and my Ministry's, working with the Board, to review and advise upon the spending of resources, from the departments involved, in the areas of enterprise development, employment, regional expansion, resource industries, and research and development.[36]

Jack Horner, then Minister of Industry, Trade and Commerce, saw Andras' role as flowing from the ongoing industry sector studies and "from the cuts the federal government made in August, cuts which freed up certain amounts of money in which the government wanted to get, I suppose, the biggest bang for its buck, and believing that they could get the biggest bang for their buck if they brought about better co-ordination between various departments".[37]

By early 1979, Andras had added the encouragement of small business (in co-operation with the Minister of State for that purpose), and the issue of deregulation, to the resource allocation, co-ordination and consultation functions of the BEDM.[38]

125

In addition to Andras and Horner, the Board was composed of the Ministers of Regional Economic Expansion, Employment and Immigration, Labour, Small Business, Energy, Mines and Resources, Science and Technology and Revenue, as well as the Deputy Prime Minister. On the Board as ex-officio members were the Minister of Finance and the President of the Treasury Board, though what precisely was to be understood by "ex-officio status" in this case has never been explained.

The Ministry of State for Economic Development was established with a few dozen of the best and brightest of the federal government's economic policy personnel, on secondment from their respective departments. At their head as Secretary of the Ministry was Gordon Osbaldeston, transferred from Industry, Trade and Commerce. His two principal lieutenants were also veterans of IT&C's sectoral consultation exercises. The quality of the Ministry of State's personnel was a clear signal to the bureaucracy that the government meant business with its new economic policy machinery, because of and notwithstanding the looming election.

The BEDM represented a departure from the principles underlying existing machinery of government in a number of ways. First, its mandate to combine policy and resource allocation decision-making— for that was what its role of "advising" the Treasury Board meant— was entirely new as a formal responsibility of a cabinet committee. It signified a new approach to expenditure management, an approach which has continued to develop, and the full implications of which have not yet become clear. At a minimum, it represented a recognition that the responsibility of the Treasury Board for the essence of resource decision-making on a proposal-by-proposal basis had been no more than nominal for sometime, and that the cabinet committee system had proven incapable of providing the elements of information and control necessary for effective expenditure management. Thus, responsibility for both policy and resource decision-making was to be vested explicitly in a single committee of ministers, who could be held accountable by the Prime Minister and cabinet colleagues for management of and performance in the sector in question.

A second feature, another departure, was the creation of a new central agency in the form of the Ministry of State, to serve as an enlarged secretariat to the new cabinet committee, the Board of Economic Development Ministers. This Ministry of State, because it had a clear mandate to co-ordinate, and because it had no programs of its own, could more effectively play the role of broad interdepartmental leadership which IT&C had sought to play, *faute de mieux*, in 1977 and 1978. At the same time, the exclusive devotion of the entire Ministry to the economic development sector provided more thorough support to the cabinet committee than a much smaller PCO secretariat would have been in a position to provide. In contrast to previous practice in the PCO, and somewhat more in line with what went on in support of the Treasury Board, the Ministry of State provided a three page "Assessment Note" on each departmental proposal. These Assessment Notes, in part analogous to, although shorter than, the briefing notes which cabinet committee chairmen received from PCO secretariats, went to *all* ministers on the Board of Economic Development. They reflected discussion of the proposal by a shadow committee of deputy ministers, chaired by Osbaldeston, and including the deputies of the departments represented on the Board.

These innovations—combining policy and resource decision-making, supporting a cabinet committee with a separate secretariat answering to the chairman and with a shadow committee of deputy ministers—were not new ideas. They had been discussed within the PCO sporadically at various points during the Trudeau administration. During Planning Phase II in 1971–72, and again during the Priorities Exercise in 1975, various organizational mechanisms for improving policy support, coordination and follow-up for cabinet committees, along the lines of the BEDM initiatives, had been considered but not implemented. Likewise, the idea of sectoral budgets to be assigned to particular cabinet committees had been floated during Planning Phase II and again in the mid-Seventies. BEDM represented the application of these general ideas to the economic sector in lieu of their application across the whole range of cabinet committees and policy sectors, as well as in lieu of a more sweeping reorganization of the economic departments themselves.[39] It also represented a first definitive step toward one of the major features of the Clark reforms in the central decision-making process in 1979, ten months later.

BEDM and the Ministry of State for Economic Development also implied a concertation of industrial policy and a co-ordination of industrial development programs which might open the door to a more focussed federal intervention in structural factors. These structural factors had, since the energy crisis, been perceived increasingly as most significant constraints upon the Canadian economy. The intellectual tradition in the PCO and elsewhere, which was suspicious of the macroeconomic orthodoxy, perceived the new structures as equipped to undertake somewhat stronger initiatives in this regard.

In the event, however, BEDM and the Ministry were not able to go beyond the logic of the sectoral approach. The particular climate of a pre-electoral period and the subsequent change of government resulted in a pause in the momentum of activities (and a change in name from the BEDM to the Cabinet Committee on Economic Development). Perhaps the lingering influence of the Department of Finance on the Ministry staff, as well as in interdepartmental discussion, made itself felt. In any case, its primary role was as a lead card for a Liberal administration, newly convinced of the importance of growth and industrial development, in an election in which economic issues would play a major part. The principal means of doing this was to accelerate the pay-off to the Enterprise 77 – Tier 1 – Tier 2 sequence.

In February 1979, the BEDM published its response to the Tier 2 report of the previous fall, which had summarized the sectoral task force recommendations in nine major areas.[40] The report identified the BEDM's functions (priorities in economic development, effective and co-ordinated delivery of programs, evaluation of policies and programs, aid to small business)[41] and responded specifically to the forty-six recommendations which the Tier 2 committee had put forward. In forty-three of these, the government "was able to agree with the recommendation or with the underlying principles involved", while in three cases (mortgage tax deductibility, value-added taxes, removal of sales taxes on construction materials and equipment) the government disagreed.[42] The further work by government required by its responses and the timing within which this work was to be undertaken were summarized in an annex to the report.

The Tier 2 recommendations were relatively general. Although the government's positive reactions were welcome, the very conception of the Tier 2 overview precluded the inclusion of sector-specific measures. Given its short pre-electoral existence, the BEDM scarcely had the time to tackle all twenty-three sectors. In April 1979, Robert Andras claimed substantial progress in the forest products, shipbuilding, automotive and book publishing sectors, as well as a number of other worthy activities:

> [The BEDM] set out policies for the planning and supply of the electrical needs of the Maritime Provinces; assisted in the development of a policy for the Labrador liner mill; examined the problems of the Canadian footwear industry; responded to the recommendations by business and labour on furthering economic growth; adopted measures for reducing the time and irritation imposed by government paperwork on Canadian businessmen; and sought through new publications to make it easier for business people to find out the range of direct and indirect programs of assistance for the private sector.[43]

Much of this amounted to a potentially more effective kind of "fire-fighting" in the economic development area. So-called "fire-fighting", the rescue of plants or industries in trouble, constitutes, in practice, a very significant part of the public sector's role in industrial development in Canada.

By far the most important of the BEDM's accomplishments was its realization of federal-provincial agreements on a major program in pulp and paper modernization. This program represented the culmination of two and a half years of analysis and negotiation by the Department of Regional Economic Expansion, intended to protect an industry deeply threatened by superior technology and lower labour and material costs in the United States. The forestry policy involves a federal commitment over several years of $250 million for modernization and of half a billion dollars in general forestry assistance programs, which were already in place. More important, the policy represents the beginnings of a national strategy for a particular industry sector, a strategy which comprehends a disparate range of interests and forces: the beggar-thy-neighbour mentality of provincial industrial policies, the competitive pressure from foreign producers and the implications of certain foreign owners controlling foreign markets.

The relatively brief life of the Clark government provided little indication of any fundamental departure from the Liberal approach to industrial development policy. Despite a change in nomenclature, the cabinet committee/ministry of state structure remained essentially intact. Gordon Osbaldeston, the principal architect of federal industrial policy during the last half of the Seventies, remained as Secretary of the Ministry of State. The Conservative minister, Robert de Cotret, who was also Minister of Industry, Trade and Commerce, refused to commit himself in public to any specific approach to an industrial strategy. He was suspicious of government propping up weak industries but gave little indication as to what this might imply.[44] After considerable talk about industrial strategy while in opposition, especially by Sinclair Stevens, who became President of the Treasury Board, the Conservative approach while in office might be characterized as "business as usual", meaning an extension of the sectoral consultative approach. The showpiece of this approach was to have been a National Economic Development Conference to be held in 1980.

Conclusion

What are we to make of the government's approach? Sectoral consultation represents a compromise, an incrementalist expedient to maintain a degree of movement in industrial policy without the political pressures from threatened interests which the adoption of either of the "bold alternatives" for an industrial strategy would inevitably create. It

129

is regarded within the bureaucracy as the only realistic and practicable approach given Canadian circumstances.[45] According to Osbaldeston, after the consultation process, it is quite possible

> ... that one will perceive what some may want to call an industrial strategy. However, I don't think that is a requirement. The problems at the moment in the industrial area can be handled by the technique being used to explore them. I don't want to suggest for a moment that the process we now [1978] have in play is suitable for seeking consensus on broad national goals. It is not. It is not intended to. It may shed a little background information for people attacking these problems, and indeed, it may not give rise to an industrial strategy. It may point a direction. It may raise some interesting background material for those who want to tackle those marshy problems.[46]

It remains to be seen, however, whether it can move Canadian industrial policy from an essentially reactive enterprise, preoccupied with weakness and with repulsing threats to Canadian jobs and industries, to an enterprise which creates strength and exploits opportunities for growth. Proponents of a more aggressive approach are apt to see Canada's manufacturing sector as rapidly declining and, short of greater governmental vision and resolve, likely to produce more and more enfeebled sectors to sponge up attention and resources which might better be spent on building new industries for the future.

Of course, the critics are themselves divided. The free traders, and the economically orthodox generally, see the consultation process as an endless series of corporate pleadings for government handouts; the total demands on the federal government emerging from the twenty-three sectoral task forces of Tier 1 were estimated to be on the order of $4 billion. They feel that in the sectoral approach, the government has created a monster with an insatiable appetite. Proponents of technological sovereignty, on the other hand, see the problem not as growing out of consultation as such but out of the rigidity underlying the sectoral approach. According to the Science Council, for example,

> There can be little doubt that many senior officials within the government are reluctant either to embark on an exercise involving a comprehensive review of industrial structure or to develop a co-ordinated industrial strategy to tackle Canada's economic problems ... It would seem that the government regards the problem as too complex and has decided to rely on a number of *ad hoc* policies ... There would seem to be an ideological aversion on the part of federal officials to become involved in any policy which requires government co-operation with industry. As a result of official commitments to *laissez-faire*, government has failed to solve the serious problems now facing Canadian industry ... The reality is that many countries are now moving progressively toward "political" economies in which market forces are manipulated for strate-

gic national purposes. Partial recognition of this fact is evident in the federal government's recent establishment with industry of 23 sector working parties to advise the government on industrial policy. However, this initiative has not been sufficient to fill the policy vacuum created by the reluctance of the federal government to formulate or to implement an industrial strategy.[47]

Again, official circles would tend to see this kind of criticism as unrealistically ambitious. As Osbaldeston puts it, "I guess I have ended up...wondering whether we should perhaps learn to walk before we run or to put it another way...whether we should not be concentrating on the exercises that deal with well-defined areas as opposed to dealing with the broader national objectives right off the mark."[48]

It may be idle to expect a Canadian cabinet to embrace a more ambitious and aggressive industrial policy in the absence of enthusiasm for the idea in the business and financial community (as evidenced by the "popular" debate over industrial strategy) and in the absence of intellectual consensus in business, academic and bureaucratic circles (as evidenced by the "sophisticated" debate over industrial strategy). Democratic governments are nothing if not risk averse. It is most unlikely that any government will remain in office long enough to benefit from the fruits of its industrial strategy initiatives, since there is general agreement that these would not emerge before ten to twenty years from the implementation of a strategy. On the other hand, the costs of such an initiative are, politically speaking, identifiable and relatively imminent. The crucial elements in the political calculus then become the relative costs of incrementalism versus those of an ambitious strategy, over the life of an administration. Hitherto, the costs of incrementalism in the area of industrial development have not been so clear and so generally accepted as to outweigh in the minds of ministers and senior officials the potential costs of an industrial strategy, but there is nothing inevitable about this situation.

Perhaps, indeed, this is too simplistic a perspective. Canada is more likely to back into an industrial strategy than to embrace one explicitly. The industrial implications of supply/infrastructure problems, such as capital investment, transportation and, especially, energy, which in themselves raise planning challenges of extreme urgency, but somewhat less ideological controversy, may well prove to be the critical path to a more coherent development strategy.[49] That development strategy will inevitably seek employment, sovereignty, growth and distribution of national income as ultimate goals, and hence will comprehend industrial development. In other words, technological sovereignty, with its emphasis on research and technology, and free trade, with its emphasis on commercial policy, may represent policy approaches to industrial strategy which are too frontal, too explicit, to be practicable in the current political and intellectual climate. This is not to say that the instruments comprehended by these alternatives will not be central elements in an eventual development strategy, but simply to point out that neither as such has yet generated a sufficient consensus of support within the relevant communities. It may be that they are not as appropriate entry points to industrial strategy as more indirect, "back doors" to a development strategy, such as energy. It may also be that the two major alternatives which have emerged hitherto are not as mutually exclusive as their respective proponents portray them, and that a medium term development strategy might well profit from elements of each.

The implication of this perspective would be a need to redefine industrial strategy horizontally in the light of serial consideration of the central supply/infrastructure factors, beginning with and emphasizing those most pressing on the public agenda. Research and development would be only one among such factors. Such a redefinition would not see energy or transportation policies as "contextual factors" to be subordinated to an explicit, technologically oriented industrial strategy, but as the most urgently needed foundations to a development strategy, because they are those around which a degree of public support for a concerted planning approach may more easily be rallied. This logic is the logic of the transition of lead agency from the Department of Industry, Trade and Commerce, with a vertical conception of industrial policy, to the Ministry of State for Economic Development, with a horizontal conception of development.

The great danger in such an approach is that what it may gain in short term political feasibility, it may lose in long term economic effectiveness. This at least would be the position of some proponents of technological sovereignty and of some proponents of free trade: that the approach of building on planning for supply factors, where a sense of crisis may be more perceptible and general, and where ideological confrontation is less pronounced, may well be inviting the tail to wag the dog. To return to an earlier metaphor, such an approach might merely prolong the essentially defensive posture of Canadian industrial policy. However, since such proponents have hitherto failed to bring business, government, and labour along with them on the road to either bold alternative, at least no further than what they regard as so much timid talk in the sectoral consultation exercises, the risks of political realism may appear to many of their sympathizers preferable to the as yet strictly prospective benefits of analytical purity.

132

The Clark Reforms 7

The election of a Progressive Conservative government in May 1979 signalled the advent of major changes in the central decision-making process. The new Prime Minister, Joe Clark, had taken a special interest in the operations of the Privy Council Office when he was a backbencher in opposition, and he was on record as seeing the Trudeau approach as too rationalistic or technocratic in nature. Well before the election, he had asked certain close political associates to prepare plans regarding changes in senior personnel, and in machinery, which a Conservative government would wish to consider. This so-called "Transition Team" consulted dozens of people in business, politics and academic life, but the bulk of the work was done by five or six people, all of them confidants of Clark.

The Clark reforms represented a significant rethinking of the basic assumptions underlying the design of the central decision-making process. The reforms can, however, be seen as the logical extension of the principles first manifested in the Board of Economic Development Ministers and of ideas about the resource allocation process being mooted in the PCO and TBS some months before the May election. That is, it was Clark who decided to adopt and to take political responsibility for the reforms, but it was not he or his people who conceived most of them. They were less the implementation of a blueprint prepared by the Transition Team than the result of an attempt by the Privy Council Office and the Treasury Board Secretariat to meet needs perceived before the arrival of the new Prime Minister, in ways which turned out to be compatible with his general ideas.

Given the brief life of the Clark government, it is not possible to provide a satisfactory assessment of the effectiveness of its reforms in the central decision-making process. A description of these innovations makes it clear that they constitute a set of responses to an analysis of decision-making in the Seventies which is largely consistent with the one emerging from earlier chapters of this study.

The Clark reforms involved two basic interrelated elements: (i) the restructuring of cabinet and the cabinet committee system, and (ii) the integration of policy and resource decision-making within an expenditure budget process based on a five year fiscal plan. The critique of the Trudeau system implicit in the Clark initiatives reflected a number of themes which had been raised and debated repeatedly in Ottawa over the previous decade. The full Canadian cabinet of some thirty-plus ministers is too large and cumbersome for effective collective decision-making. The emphasis on collegiality and collective responsibility in the Trudeau committee system caused intolerable delay and regularly frustrated the initiatives of ministers and senior officials. The Prime Minister and the Privy Council Office played too strong a role in the decision-making process relative to individual ministers and departments yet, at the same time, co-ordination at the level of the major policy sectors—economic, social, foreign and defence—was inadequate. Individual departmental ministers were overburdened with a myriad of responsibilities and obligations. Finally, the nominal separation of policy and resource decision-making, and the lack of data on the medium term impact of such decisions, led to the breakdown of the expenditure budget process and the failure to plan effectively within resource limits.

The Clark reforms were composed of four sets of changes:

(i) the Clark cabinet committee system;
(ii) increased numbers of Ministers of State;
(iii) the new expenditure management system;
(iv) the development of sectoral policy secretariats.

The Cabinet Committee System

The Clark cabinet committee system involved the retention, transformation or demise of the Trudeau cabinet committees, the creation of an Inner Cabinet and the substantial diminution of the role of full cabinet. The following committees emerged from the Clark reorganization. The *Economic Development Committee* inherited the responsibilities of the Economic Policy Committee, the Board of Economic Development Ministers and part of those of the Government Operations Committee. The *Social and Native Affairs Committee* took over the responsibilities of the Social Policy Committee, the Culture and Native Affairs Committee and the environmental and northern policy responsibilities of the Government Operations Committee. The *Economy in Government Committee* assumed parts of the responsibilities of Government Operations, Priorities and Planning and the Treasury Board.

The External Policy and Defence Committee was rechristened the *Foreign Policy and Defence Committee*. The *Legislation and House Planning* and *Federal-Provincial Relations Committees* were retained. The *Treasury Board* was retained with modified responsibilities. Thus, the Priorities and Planning, Culture and Native Affairs and Government Operations Committees disappeared as separate entities.

The most innovative aspect of the Clark reorganization was the establishment of an Inner Cabinet consisting of the chairpersons of cabinet committees, the ministers of central agencies and regional ministers where a region was not already adequately represented under the first two criteria. Thus the Inner Cabinet of 1979–80 consisted of:

Joe Clark	Prime Minister
Robert de Cotret	Chairman, Economic Development
Flora MacDonald	Chairwoman, Foreign Policy and Defence
Walter Baker	President of the Privy Council. Chairman, Legislation and House Planning
William Jarvis	Chairman, Federal-Provincial Relations
David MacDonald	Chairman, Social and Native Affairs
Sinclair Stevens	President of the Treasury Board. Chairman, Economy in Government
John Crosbie	Minister of Finance
Jacques Flynn	Minister of Justice
Roch LaSalle	Minister of Supply and Services (Québec)
Ray Hnatyshyn	Minister of Energy, Mines and Resources (Saskatchewan)
John Fraser	Postmaster General and Minister of the Environment (British Columbia)

The Inner Cabinet took over most of the responsibilities of the Priorities and Planning Committee and became the analogue to the full cabinet in the Trudeau system, as the senior forum for collective decision-making by ministers. Thus, the Inner Cabinet was to set the major priorities for the government, approve the work program of the cabinet committees, make decisions of major political importance, determine overall fiscal policy and allocate resources to major policy sectors. At least as important to the conception of the Inner Cabinet as what it was supposed to do, was what it was *not* supposed to do. It was not supposed, as was the full cabinet in the Trudeau regime, to provide final approval of every decision taken by the other committees of the Clark system, nor was it to be the court of last resort for ministers who wished to appeal against such decisions. Within their work programs and spheres of responsibility, cabinet committee decisions were to be regarded as final government policy. Appeals to Inner Cabinet by ministers dissatisfied with committee decisions were supposed to be allowed only on a basis of exception and with the specific permission of the Prime Minister.

Thus, the theory of the Clark cabinet committee system was that major decisions were to be made by a subgroup of the cabinet composed of the most senior ministers, while sectoral decisions were to be within the full responsibility of other subgroups of ministers most concerned with that policy sector. In practice, it is unclear to what extent this power of sectoral decision-making, substantially independent of Inner Cabinet, was ever devolved upon cabinet committees during 1979-80. The Cabinet Agenda retained a bipartite structure analogous to the Main Agenda and the Annex of the Trudeau era, indicating that a significant number of cabinet committee decisions were at least brought to the attention of Inner Cabinet. It was unlikely that a new and inexperienced government could have resisted the temptation to reopen in Inner Cabinet the more politically sensitive decisions of committees. That kind of self-denying ordinance, however, represents precisely the kind of discipline required to gain full advantage of the efficiencies which are supposed to reside in a two-tiered cabinet system.

Under the Clark system, full cabinet still met regularly, but it was not to have decision-making functions. Its purpose was to be the exchange of information and the co-ordination of political strategy. When should a certain announcement be made? How should it be explained? Full cabinet was not supposed to reopen policy decisions, but to subserve essentially political discussion.

Thus, in theory at least, there was under Clark no single forum consisting of all ministers and providing for final approval of all government policies. There was no structural entity which itself embodied the principle of collective responsibility that lies at the root of parliamentary cabinet systems, as full cabinet had been under Trudeau. Rather, it was the system as a whole, organized in hierarchical fashion, which had to support or render operational the principle of collective responsibility.

Again unlike the Trudeau system, the membership of Inner Cabinet and cabinet committees was public information. The Appendix shows the membership and responsibilities of the Conservative cabinet committees of 1979-80.

Ministers of State

The Progressive Conservative government made far more extensive use of the status of Minister of State than its predecessor. The expansion took place in the category of Ministers of State whose role was to lighten the load on the ministers of major departments. Apparently the Prime Minister and his Transition Team would have named even more such ministers, had the Privy Council Office not strongly advised otherwise. These Ministers of State "to assist" were, according to the Prime Minister, to help the departmental minister to "strengthen operational and policy control" over the department, with "The precise division of responsibilities within these ministries [to] be determined in consultation with Mr. Clark."[1] In addition to the Ministers of State for Economic Development, Science and Technology and Federal-Provincial Relations, the Clark cabinet included the following Ministers of State "to assist":

Martial Asselin	Minister of State for CIDA, assisting the Secretary of State for External Affairs
Perrin Beatty	Minister of State (Treasury Board)
Robert Howie	Minister of State (Transport)
Steven Paproski	Minister of State for Fitness and Amateur Sport, and Multiculturalism, assisting the Minister of National Health and Welfare, and the Secretary of State, respectively.
Ronald Huntington	Minister of State for Small Business and Industry, assisting the Minister of Industry, Trade and Commerce
Michael Wilson	Minister of State for International Trade, assisting the Minister of Industry, Trade and Commerce.

In the original plan for the Clark cabinet, these Ministers of State "to assist" were not to sit regularly on cabinet committees. They would attend only for the discussion of items where the policy had been developed under their supervision. Under this approach, their access to the collective decision-making process would have been sporadic and indirect at best. Thus, although the Clark cabinet was called "two-tiered", its original conception implied three classes of minister: (i) ministers who were on Inner Cabinet and on certain committees; (ii) ministers who were on committees but not on Inner Cabinet; and (iii) those Ministers of State who were on neither Inner Cabinet nor committees.

By October 1979 however, this unrealistically hierarchical approach was dropped, and the Ministers of State "to assist" were added to the appropriate cabinet committees. The Appendix lists committee members in the same order as the official listing issued in that month; it will be noted that the Ministers of State in question were generally included at the end of the lists for their respective committees.

The Expenditure Management System

A third element in the Clark reforms in central decision-making was the new expenditure management system. Under Trudeau, the theory of the resource allocation process separated policy decisions, which were taken in the operational and planning committees of cabinet, from resource decisions, which were supposed to be taken by the Treasury Board. Clark changed this approach by substantially elaborating some of the principles implicit in the resource allocation role of the Board of Economic Development Ministers and by introducing a five-year planning horizon as advocated by the Lambert Commission. Based on recommendations developed principally in the Treasury Board Secretariat and the Privy Council Office, he restructured the expenditure budget process.

According to the official account of the new system, it involved two fundamental reforms:

(i) The preparation and publication of a longer term fiscal plan encompassing government revenues and expenditures over a five-year period—i.e. setting out the overall financial constraint within which choices must be considered.

(ii) The establishment of specific expenditure limits for policy sectors, related to the government's priorities, and assignment of the responsibility for managing a particular policy sector's resources within the established limits to the appropriate policy committee of cabinet.[2]

The fiscal plan was to encompass "the total spectrum of revenues and expenditures to provide a clear picture of the planned role of the government in the economy". Overall expenditure limits, as well as specific limits to apply to each of nine budgetary envelopes designated for nine policy sectors, were to be established. These limits, which were to be made public after they were established, were not simply for the current and coming fiscal years, but were also "planning projections" to apply to the three subsequent fiscal years. This five-year fiscal plan was to permit ministers to appreciate the medium term expenditure implications of current decisions to spend or save. It was to permit departments to plan over the five-year period with a more

138

realistic grasp of resource limitations. It was to provide a public base line against which the impact of changes in political engagements and economic circumstances could be assessed by parliamentarians, provincial governments, the media and private sector planners.[3] The five-year fiscal plan would provide the information necessary to make intelligent adjustments to expenditures. The fact that it was public would create a need to explain such adjustments to Parliament. As with any other mechanism to make administrative information public, it was in one sense a self-denying ordinance intended to constitute a continuing discipline, in the public interest.

Thus, the fiscal plan was to implement the first of the four principles which the government saw an underlying the new system: "Establish Known Limits":

> The setting of limits, for the government as a whole and for policy sectors over a five-year period, is the essential device to shift the decision-making process from a focus on new initiatives to the necessity to make real choices and trade-offs in full view of fiscal consequences.[4]

The government's second principle was to "Put First Things First", to establish "priorities and fiscal limits *before* developing expenditure plans, so that the development of detailed spending plans and program forecasts does not create *de facto* priorities that cannot be changed except in a marginal and/or arbitrary way". Third, the government wished to "Make Decisions Where They Can Best be Made", to avoid "the clear and constant danger of a handful of decision-makers who could not possibly know all there is to know being overloaded with responsibility". Thus, "more people [must] be given greater responsibility in more specialized areas" and there must be "a decentralization of decision-making in order to reduce issues to a human size". Finally, since "Spending in a political system carries its own reward", the government must "Place Responsibility for Saving with Those Who Spend", not simply with a lonely and beleaguered President of the Treasury Board. Accordingly, the Clark Cabinet committee system ensured "that groups of ministers who want to spend must also save".[5]

If the fiscal plan was one major element in the realization of these principles, then management by committees of resource allocation within policy sectors was the other. The new expenditure management system was to work thus. After departments provide program forecasts to the Treasury Board Secretariat, it would not be the responsibility of the President and the Board to conduct a series of one-on-one negotiations with each minister and his department in order to reduce the department's "B" budget forecasts to the minimum or to force an "X" budget down the minister's throat. Rather, the President of the Treasury Board and the Minister of Finance would, after reviewing departmental forecasts, the Fiscal Framework for the year in question, and the projections for that year in the current fiscal plan, recommend to the Inner Cabinet an overall expenditure target, composed of specific expenditure limits for each of nine budgetary envelopes. Each item of expenditure, each program, was assigned to one of the envelopes, and each envelope was in turn assigned to Inner Cabinet or a committee: Fiscal Transfers to the Provinces, Public Debt (both assigned to Inner Cabinet), Economic Development (Economic Development), Services to Government, Parliament (both assigned to Economy in Government), Justice and Legal Affairs, Social and Native Affairs (both assigned to Social and Native Affairs) and External Affairs and Aid, Defence (both assigned to Foreign Policy and Defence). Details are included in the Appendix.

Once Inner Cabinet had "established overall expenditure limits and allocated resources *among* policy sectors in accordance with the overall priorities and objectives of the government" and on the basis of the recommendations of the President of the Treasury Board and the Minister of Finance, it became the responsibility of the cabinet committees to "allocate the resources *within* each policy area or "envelope" subject to the limit established, and to Inner Cabinet's ensuring that any reallocation is in keeping with overall objectives and priorities."6 Thus, it was the responsibility of the committees to decide which program must be curtailed in order to meet the aggregate spending limitations within the envelope. To the extent that ministers on a particular committee wished to undertake new initiatives involving expenditures, existing activities within the envelope would in all likelihood have to be cut in order to create the resources for such initiatives. This was how the new system attempted to "Make Decisions Where They Can Best be Made" and to "Place Responsibility for Saving with Those Who Spend". As noted, Inner Cabinet was to have had final responsibility for approving the overall spending plans resulting from committee decisions, on the basis of which Estimates would have been prepared. The underlying goal of the reorganization, then, was to render each policy or program decision simultaneously a resource allocation decision, that is, a decision to reduce the margin of manoeuvre left at any one time within the budgetary envelope, or a decision to reallocate resources if the ceiling had already been reached. Substantial decision-making was decentralized to the level of the cabinet committees, by giving them the mandate and the means to fulfil it. Where the Cabinet Planning System of the early Seventies had sought optimal solutions on a government-wide scale, the new expenditure management system suboptimized on a sectoral scale.

According to the Clark government, the committee system was reorganized "with the intention of giving significantly greater decision-making authority to the policy committees of Cabinet and thereby to individual Ministers in the area of their responsibility, while still ensuring that the work in one policy sector is consistent with the overall work and priorities of the government."[7]

It should be noted that the new system of expenditure management left the Treasury Board, as a committee of ministers, with a reduced but rather clearer role in management policy: responsibility for the approval of submissions from departments in the areas of program management, administrative policy, personnel policy, financial management and the like, as well as the promulgation of regulations and guidelines in these areas. The President of the Treasury Board who was, along with the Minister of Finance, an ex-officio member of all the policy committees of cabinet, had the responsibility of monitoring the technicalities of the management of envelopes by advising on "the current state of commitments in each envelope and anticipated demands on each envelope". In particular, he was to ensure "that the Chairman is aware whenever there is a danger that an envelope may be breached in a current or future year". That is, he was to play the role of a kind of expert scorekeeper to ensure that the ignorance or self-interest of certain actors did not cause inadvertant overcommitment of resources. The President could also play a somewhat stronger role in advising "on specific policy or program proposals before Committees in light of the analytic work of the Treasury Board Secretariat and the Controller General, with particular emphasis on efficiency and effectiveness criteria."[8] Clearly, however, the President, the Board and the Program Branch of the Secretariat no longer held their one-time singular, formal and leading role in determining what programs would be expanded or cut in the expenditure budget process.

The new expenditure management system focussed the intense interdepartmental competition for funds within a particular envelope, on the committee responsible for the envelope. The minister who was chairperson of the committee had the important responsibility to "lead policy and program development in the policy sector" and to ensure:

> ... that the Committee has the information necessary to give full consideration to trade-offs that must be made among departments in that sector, and to agree on broad allocations for departments and programs within the envelope assigned. This would include recommendations and decisions on cutting back expenditures and reallocating the savings to other programs.[9]

The fourth aspect of the Clark reforms—the establishment of sectoral policy secretariats—was intended to support committee chairpersons in the performance of these roles.

Sectoral Policy Secretariats

Under the Trudeau government, the primary responsibility for briefing and supporting the chairpersons of cabinet committees lay with the secretariats to each committee, located in the Privy Council Office. The four to eight officials in each of these secretariats were ultimately responsible, through the Secretary to the Cabinet, to the Prime Minister. Clark took two measures to alter what he saw as the overcentralization of power and the narrowness of the support given chair-persons under the Trudeau system. First, he altered the role of the PCO and its secretariats by instructing Assistant Secretaries that their primary responsibility was to the chairperson of their committees and not to himself as Prime Minister. Furthermore, major personnel changes in the PCO, which more or less coincided with the election, left the Office with persons of different experience and expertise from their predecessors at the Assistant Secretary, Deputy Secretary and Secretary levels. These PCO personnel would have the opportunity to establish new working relationships and new ground rules for PCO-departmental interaction.

Second, Clark provided alternative sources of advice to committee chairpersons by establishing sectoral policy mandates outside PCO. The primary example, of course, was the Ministry of State for Economic Development which Clark had inherited from the dying hours of the Trudeau administration. Its mandate—to brief ministers collectively, to co-ordinate the policy sector through interdepartmental machinery and to support the resource allocation role of the Board of Economic Development Ministers—was transposed and further formalized with respect to the Board's successor in the Clark system, the Economic Development Committee. It was to be the model for a second innovation in sectoral policy machinery, the Ministry of State for Social Affairs, which was to play a similar role with respect to the Social and Native Affairs Committee. The new Ministry of State was in the process of formation when the Clark government fell. It was to have answered to the chairman of the Social and Native Affairs Committee, David MacDonald, who was also Secretary of State and Minister of Communications. Of the other three policy committees, Federal-Provincial Relations had an extensive secretariat of its own, the Federal-Provincial Relations Office, although this Office ultimately answers to the Prime Minister. The Economy in Government Committee, chaired by the President of the Treasury Board, had the resources

142

of the Treasury Board Secretariat and the Office of the Controller General to call on. Finally, there was discussion of establishing a sectoral policy secretariat within the Department of External Affairs, to serve the Foreign Policy and Defence Committee, although this initiative did not develop very far before the government fell. In sum, then, Clark was in the process of establishing potentially powerful policy bureaucracies on a decentralized basis, and he was establishing them largely outside the range of direct prime ministerial influence. These secretariats were to answer to the chairpersons of cabinet committees, but they were to be composed of at least a few dozen professional officers, as opposed to less than ten in the PCO secretariats. They were to play a critical role in briefing committees collectively, and chairpersons in particular, with respect to what were to be, at least in theory, significant powers of independent policy and resource decision-making. In a sense, they were to combine many of the functions of the PCO secretariats and the directorates of the Program Branch of the Treasury Board Secretariat, but neither of the latter were dismantled or reduced in size.

Requiem

A number of open questions remain about the Clark reforms. First, in light of the norms underlying behaviour and expectations in previous Canadian cabinets, could a cabinet on the Clark model maintain the necessary solidarity? This is no marginal issue, when the Inner Cabinet, the ultimate decision-making body, contained only twelve of the nearly thirty ministers, leaving many major portfolios, such as Transport and Health and Welfare, outside. Would it be possible to maintain unity when a subset of cabinet ministers makes a politically controversial decision, the consequences of which have to be borne by ministers who have had no opportunity to participate in the decision?

Second, could co-ordination and cohesion be maintained when the Inner Cabinet did not routinely approve cabinet committee decisions, as the full cabinet did under the Trudeau system? Would there not be a danger that the committees might take their independent responsibilities in different or contradictory directions? Would Inner Cabinet approval of major priorities, committee work programs and overall expenditure plans be sufficient to prevent internal contradiction or competition in government policies? Put another way, could Inner Cabinet respect the independence of committees required by the decentralized Clark model? Would full cabinet be able to restrain itself from reopening policy decisions?

Third, how would Ministers of State "to assist" relate to their departmental ministers? Clark's idea was to reduce the burden on departmental ministers by giving them a ministerial colleague to undertake certain specific policy functions within the portfolio. Historically, however, the ambiguity of the relationship has caused considerable difficulties, sometimes greater than the benefits accruing. Under Trudeau, there were major battles between departmental ministers—who must bear ultimate responsibility for the entire portfolio, including its Estimates and submissions to the Treasury Board—and Ministers of State. Would not the extensive use of Ministers of State "to assist" in the Clark government have led to the same frustrations? Ministers of State without very distinct program or policy responsibilities are liable to exercise very marginal influence indeed. Sooner or later they find themselves speaking to the press about possible government plans or policies which are primarily the responsibility of other ministers, with predictable effects on the unity and cohesion of cabinet.

Fourth, how would the sectoral policy secretariats and the PCO committee secretariats relate to one another? What role would the directorates of the Program Branch of the Treasury Board Secretariat play in briefing cabinet committees? Would the interaction among these various sources of policy advice to chairpersons and committees be co-operative, competitive or even hostile? The relative novelty of the innovations and their different stages of development preclude final assessment. Nevertheless, it seems clear that the Ministry of State for Economic Development had succeeded in developing stable and effective working routines in support of the cabinet committee, as well as in the interdepartmental machinery beneath the committee. There was no evidence of major contention between the Ministry of State and PCO or TBS. These changes in form should not be taken to indicate that the desired improvements in the substance of policy had necessarily been achieved, however. The Ministry of State for Social Affairs remained in embryonic form; even its title had not yet been formally announced when the government fell. In support of the Economy in Government Committee, the Treasury Board Secretariat, with its far greater reach and resources, apparently dominated the attention of the chairperson of the Committee and President of the Board, Sinclair Stevens.

A fifth question of considerable interest focusses on the degree to which the Clark reforms clarified the process of policy-making in the economic sector, in particular the role of the Minister of Finance. The most that can be concluded on this subject is that while the Clark government witnessed the continuing incremental progress of collective decision-making into the historical prerogatives of the Minister of Finance, it did not resolve the ongoing tension around the issue.

Indeed, in some ways the situation became more complex, with three powerful competitors surrounding the Minister of Finance, John Crosbie: Robert de Cotret, Minister of Economic Development and Trade, Sinclair Stevens, President of the Treasury Board, and James Gillies of the Prime Minister's Office. There was considerable rivalry, even animosity, among these, the leading economic policy decision-makers on the Clark team. The structural reforms did little to reduce this. For the first time since the committee system emerged, the Minister of Finance did not chair his own committee. Crosbie demanded of the Prime Minister that he be permitted to bring major economic policy questions for collective decision to Inner Cabinet, thereby avoiding having to bring them to the Economic Development Committee chaired by de Cotret. He also succeeded in keeping the central macroeconomic issues off the work programs which were assigned to the cabinet committees, giving himself the flexibility to manage these issues as he would. For the same reasons, the two budgetary envelopes principally within the purview of the Minister of Finance, Fiscal Transfers and Public Debt, remained the responsibility of the Inner Cabinet. Likewise, Crosbie's new deputy minister, Grant Reuber, was rumoured to have made the independence of economic policy-making in the Department of Finance a condition of his appointment. On the other hand, the linkage between the budget, campaign promises and the future of the government meant that the major issues of the budget of December 1979 were extensively discussed in Inner Cabinet, more so than for previous budgets. The relationship between the collective responsibility of cabinet and the individual responsibility of the Minister of Finance in the area of economic policy rested, as always, on an ambiguous series of compromises tending slowly toward the former. It could not have been otherwise in a government with a slender minority and under severe political pressure.

The Clark reforms represented a coherent attempt to resolve certain persistent flaws in the central decision-making process. The arrival of the new government, headed by a Prime Minister with the courage to innovate despite a precarious political situation, created a window through which a breath of fresh air ventilated the corridors of power. Significant features of the Clark reforms appear likely to be retained by the new Trudeau administration which arrived in February 1980. The budgetary envelope system, or something very much like it, will remain. The resurrected Priorities and Planning Committee will play a role more reminiscent of the role of the Inner Cabinet under Clark than of its namesake under the Trudeau cabinet committee system of the Seventies. Like Clark, Trudeau in 1980 will attempt to focus decision-making responsibilities in appropriate committees and to minimize the process of appeal by ministers dissenting from committee decisions. As the individual minister loses his theoretical right to involvement in each and every government policy decision, he gains the power and responsibility, along with specific colleagues, to manage his particular policy sector.

The question as to whether the Progressive Conservative government of 1979–80 was critical to the ultimate emergence of these initiatives is perhaps moot. The fact is that it greatly facilitated both their implementation before the 1980 election *and* the prospect of further reform of the machinery of government by the new Liberal administration. The reappointment of Michael Pitfield as Secretary to the Cabinet signals among other things a continued commitment to the search for structural and procedural solutions to the problems of governing.

Conclusion 8

The first seven years of the Trudeau ministries were those in which formal planning systems had the greatest currency in Ottawa, and the greatest impact on the governing process. The overriding feature of planning during this period was the coexistence of three planning systems whose interactions frustrated rather than fostered cohesion in federal policy-making. While there was no absolute theoretical inconsistency among the three systems, their embodiment in separate departments, their differing time frameworks, their distinct intellectual/disciplinary bases, their characteristic postures within the central decision-making process, and their advocacy by the strongest personalities at the senior management level, meant that they in fact operated at cross-purposes more often than in harmony.

The agency philosophy of the Department of Finance created a planning system almost by default, since it emerged as such when it found no echo, no niche, in the more elaborate central decision-making process which Pierre Trudeau brought with him to office in 1968. Embattled bureaucratically by the creation of new portfolios representing what had hitherto been regarded as secondary economic objectives, as well as by a cabinet committee system demanding a greater collective role in economic policy-making, the Department fought tenaciously to preserve inviolate its core functions of demand management. In doing so, it had recourse to the values of a mature and well-articulated intellectual discipline. Macroeconomics provided explicit criteria by which major government initiatives could be evaluated and Finance's willingness to do so made of its agency philosophy a *de facto* planning system. The Finance Planning System represented a unique and intellectually consistent approach to planning as defined in this study. It sought in matters of process to protect the prerogatives of the Minister and the Department at the expense of collective ones and, in matters of substance, to "fine tune" the economy and to protect the market as the dominant mechanism for the allocation of

147

resources. Unlike the other planning systems, the Finance Planning System never claimed to be such. Also unlike the other planning systems, the Finance Planning System would probably have emerged even without its primary protagonist, Simon Reisman. When he was deputy minister of finance during 1970–74, however, Reisman epitomized the Finance Planning System, and gave its articulation within the central decision-making process a particular force and flavour.

The Finance Planning System may be said to have disappeared with the retirement of Reisman and the implementation of wage and price controls in the fall of 1975. The concerns which underlay it remained stronger than ever, but the economic situation had developed in such a way as to destroy its primary competitor, the Cabinet Planning System, and to demand actions which left the Department's traditional aloofness a luxury Finance could no longer afford.

The Treasury Planning System was unthinkable without its creator, Douglas Hartle, Deputy Secretary–Planning to the Treasury Board, 1969–73. He was its manager, its theoritician, its spokesman, and his departure presaged its ultimate demise. He was also at times its burden, when his vigorous advocacy overstepped the unwritten norms of bureaucratic culture. The Treasury Planning System was based on planning theory and microeconomics and, in principle, it was to confine itself to the evaluation phase of the strategic planning process. The Treasury Planning System could not find a home in the central decision-making process. Indeed the Planning Branch's philosophy never became the agency philosophy of the Secretariat as a whole, since the Planning Branch never succeeded in establishing a consistently co-operative relationship with the Program Branch of the Treasury Board. Hartle's frustration with the incoherence of the theory of the Cabinet Planning System led him to articulate a full-blown alternative, and his inability to use for evaluation purposes the objectives produced by the Cabinet Planning System led him to try to begin to implement that alternative.

In the end, the Treasury Planning System was an artistic success but a commercial failure. It was the most intense and technically productive episode in the continuing enterprise of implementing evaluation in the federal bureaucracy. It was an important portal of entry and training ground for some extremely talented public servants. On the other hand, an evaluation up to its own rigorous standards of the Planning Branch of the Treasury Board Secretariat could not, given its ambitious objectives, but conclude in the negative. One thing is certain. No such systematic evaluation was done when the shell that remained of the Planning Branch was finally dismantled in 1978. Instead, the economy and the Prime Minister's political instincts dictated a major budget cut. The call went out to round up all the usual suspects, and among that melancholy company were at least two products of the planning enthusiasm of happier days: the Planning Branch of the Treasury Board Secretariat and the Ministry of State for Urban Affairs.

The third planning system, the Cabinet Planning System, was the one in contrast to which the agency philosophies associated with the other two may be said to have defined themselves. It rested on intellectual bases a good deal more eclectic and less mature than the Finance and Treasury Planning Systems. It held a virtual monopoly on the key element in the central decision-making process: the cabinet committee system. The Cabinet Planning System, unlike the other systems, styled itself explicitly as such. It was supported ultimately by the personal interest of the Prime Minister, through the person of Michael Pitfield, Assistant Secretary to the Cabinet, 1967–69, Deputy Secretary to the Cabinet–Plans, 1969–73, and Secretary to the Cabinet, 1975–79. The Cabinet Planning System emphasized the establishment of objectives and the choice of priorities in a longer term framework. It sought to provide ministers with an overview of government activities and an opportunity to redirect those activities in some more general way than by a sequence of policy and program decisions taken solely on the basis of departmental Memoranda. It attempted to stimulate ministers and departments to ask fundamental questions and to face issues which they might have preferred to avoid. It asked "what kind of Canada do we want in the year 2000?" It sought, according to some of its proponents, "to help ministers to understand what it was they were doing". Like the Privy Council Office as a whole, it emphasized its reliance on "the views of ministers", and jealously protected its claim on the interpretation thereof.

The Cabinet Planning System had an extremely important impact upon the atmosphere of cabinet decision-making, the nature of "planning" issues coming forward, the considerations which were regarded as fundamental in the discussion of such issues, the timing with which decisions were taken, and the image of policy-making which was projected from the cabinet secretariat to the bureaucracy at large. It represented an instinct for *innovation*, as opposed to the conservatism of the Finance Planning System, and for *initiation*, as opposed to the at least equal emphasis on *termination* and *reallocation* of the Treasury Planning System. While many of those of its projects which depended upon other departments and agencies for their fruition (i.e. projects involving substantive policy) ultimately came to nothing, its own failure to support the Finance or Treasury Planning Systems ensured their final frustration.

149

The Cabinet Planning System died in the fall of 1975, when the Priorities Exercise of 1974–75 dissolved into the imposition of wage and price controls. While the importance of the position of Assistant Secretary to the Cabinet—Priorities and Planning remained, the Secretariat to the Committee shrunk markedly, and no further major planning exercises emerged.

The period between October 1975 and May 1979 saw the emergence of a series of economic and political crises whose urgency diverted attention and resources to purposes that precluded planning on a governmental scale. Wage and price controls consumed much of the political and bureaucratic energy of 1975–76. The last four years of the decade witnessed a struggle to come to terms with the economic policy implications of stagflation. Economic issues took centre stage, but shared it with constitutional ones. The election of a Parti Québecois government precipitated the intergovernmental crisis which characterized the period from late 1976 onward. National unity provided an attractive set of opportunities for the most aggressive and capable policy analysts, and a specific direction for political attention. Finally, the Prime Minister's conversion to fiscal conservatism, on the road from the Bonn economic summit in the summer of 1978, led to dramatic budget cuts and structural innovation. In much of this, the government was reacting rather than acting, and any resemblance to the ideals of the Cabinet Planning System was strictly coincidental. Furthermore, the problems of 1975–79 were in part the product of the planning failures of 1968–75. It should not be overlooked, however, that the economic and intergovernmental crises provided frameworks which reduced the key issues to a more manageable set than, for example, the Priorities Exercise had elicited. Such frameworks could have stimulated more efficient planning efforts, had a more realistic groundwork been laid in 1974–75.

The experience of planning in Ottawa during the Trudeau era permits a few general conclusions about planning. The first of these is *the irrelevance, in a political and bureaucratic context, of the means/ ends distinction on which planning theory is predicated.* This is as true given the incentives of the executive branch, as it is in the national political arena. The Treasury and Cabinet Planning Systems made much of the search for objectives and priorities. Nevertheless, what divided the three systems internally was their inability either to share the means to formulate and implement policy, or to entrust them to one another. Their differences, if any, on ultimate objectives were rarely engaged. Likewise, at the level of national politics, what made many ministers so uncomfortable about the Cabinet Planning System

150

was precisely its preoccupation with objectives abstracted from tangible programs. As Phidd and Doern have observed,

> Economists tend to speak of instruments and goals as if they were always in a "means-end" relationship. However, it is very difficult in political terms to draw clearcut lines between means and ends because policy is not necessarily made in that way . . . Processes and instruments become ends in themselves especially in a democratic state.[1]

Why should this be so? In strictly pragmatic terms, public sector decision-makers sense what academics and practitioners of the so-called "policy sciences" have until recently rarely admitted: that the analytical tools of the social sciences are inadequate to link courses of action sufficiently tightly to objectives, such as to permit the development of courses of action, or means, as a more or less mechanical extension from the identification of objectives. To the contrary, decision-makers recognize that courses of action will be regarded by voters as professions of goals, or incarnations of policies, in ways that decision-makers must at all costs anticipate. Thus, custody over and control of courses of action, means, instruments or programs are what is ultimately at stake in the micropolitics of the executive branch. Planning theory begins with objectives, and in doing so, vastly overrates the strength and conviction of policy analysis. It is frustrated, not by the sheer perversity of "politics", but by the politicians' entirely rational instinct for a dialectic between means and ends in order to control the margin between public accomplishment and popular expectation. If there are to be "objectives" or "goals" for general consumption, grandiose and persuasive they must indeed be. They must not, however, be confused with the particular ends of particular programs, through the aggregation of which most governments govern most of the time.

The primacy of means in the political dynamics of the executive, or at least their inseparability from ends, highlights a second theme which emerges from the Canadian experience. This is that *executive power is finite, and planning may either diffuse or focus it.* Here again, the Cabinet Planning System seems to embody the most suspect premises: its endorsement of "countervailing ideas in the policy process" and its suspicion of what it seems to have regarded as the anti-spending inflexibility of the Finance Planning System and the Treasury Board Secretariat. There are at least three important ways in which executive power is limited. The first, and least important for present purposes, is *constitutional* and refers to the role of the legislative and judicial branches. The second, fully recognized by the Finance and Treasury Planning Systems and the Treasury Board Secretariat as a whole, is *economic*, and refers to resource scarcity. The third and most elusive is *sociological* and refers to the finite aggregate supply of ministerial commitment and attention. Partisan arguments have been made that the Trudeau cabinet committee system overstepped or distorted *constitutional* limits on executive power relative to the legislature and the judiciary, but these need not be pursued here. Likewise, the examination of the failure to integrate planning and policy with resource allocation during most of the Trudeau era suggests that *economic* limitations were given short shrift and echoes the Lambert Commission's conclusions:

> Planning is effective only if it is undertaken in an environment in which there are real and finite limits to resources. Planning will never be successful if it is conducted on the assumption that resources are inexhaustible.[2]

Perhaps the most interesting and certainly the least examined limit on executive power is the *sociological* one. Implicit in the multifarious initiatives of the Cabinet Planning System was the notion that a Record of Decision or a letter from the Prime Minister could set in motion a policy-making exercise which would, given this one impetus, produce useful proposals for ministerial decision-making at some subsequent point. Planning was to take the policy-making enterprise into more issues in a more interconnected way and within a longer term framework. Planning was not only to improve the quality of policy, it was to increase the total capacity of the policy-making institution. In the event, these assumptions were largely negated. The majority of the Cabinet Planning System's projects came to naught because cabinet approval at a particular time (often owing principally to the Prime Minister's presumed support) proved inadequate, in the absence of continuing ministerial interest and support, to bring them to fruition. No matter how analytically strong were the evaluations of the Treasury Planning System, they expired when they emerged without strong ministerial advocacy. The Cabinet Planning System, and the fragmentation of the three planning systems, diffused rather than focussed power. As Phidd and Doern point out,

> In political terms, who or what organization will command sufficient instruments to *mobilize* power, rather than constrain power? The timely mobilization of power is often as necessary a characteristic of effective government and economic management as is the capacity to constrain and diffuse power.[3]

Ends cannot be distinguished from means. Means consume power. Power is finite. Therefore, planning must focus power. It follows that *planning cannot be pluralistic.* It is ironic that the Cabinet Planning System was criticized for overcentralization even as its agency philosophy embraced "countervailing ideas in the policy process" and it coexisted with two other distinct, if *de facto*, planning systems. With an elaborate formal central decision-making process, and a multiplicity of planning and evaluation groups, the Trudeau government rarely faced explicitly the fact "that the political meaning of co-ordination can only be contemplated when one acknowledges that such co-ordination involves in part the temporary victory of one or two . . . objectives over other values and objectives, the use of one or more instruments over other instruments, and the relative triumph of one department over another and of one or more ministers over others".[4]

According to Shonfield, if the commitment to national planning means anything, it implies at least a clear pattern of relationships between the disparate organs of authority on which a coherent social and economic policy depends.[5] Such "a clear pattern of relationships" existed in Canada almost exclusively in the theory of the central decision-making process as it was articulated by senior officials. In a 1965 passage whose relevance to the Canadian experience of 1968–75 is startling, Shonfield wrote:

> To a large extent planning in a capitalist context, as we have come to know it since the war, is a matter of tightening the hierarchical structure of government, compelling all the departments which have significant long-term consequences into a *single intellectual framework*, determined at the highest level of administration. New lines of authority are established, and at each level of power there is a more precise definition of the area in which choice and local initiative are allowed. Planning thus requires a high degree of explicitness in the relations between the different departments of government and a clear division of responsibilities.[6]

The need for a single intellectual framework, a framework patently lacking in Canada, leads to a final point. *Planning cannot create political conviction.* If a single agency philosophy failed to dominate, it was because Canadian political culture and a relatively hospitable socioeconomic environment failed to provide the impetus. If planning systems ran at cross-purposes, it was because no sufficient ministerial consensus in support of any particular one existed. Without political conviction based on popular perceptions, the planning enterprise is like a hothouse plant, with bright flowers and no roots.

Consider one of the most serious economic developments during the period we have examined, the energy crisis of 1973. It is generally believed that the great lesson is that Western planning was faulty. Most of the relevant data were at hand, yet few foresaw the crisis. We were indeed caught with our collective pants down, but this is not the "energy lesson". The real energy lesson has only emerged over the years since the crisis. It is rather more important than the inevitable call for more and better planning. It is simply that even when a crisis as profoundly threatening as the energy supply situation arises, the fragmentation of power, the clash of interests and the short run political disincentives to coercion of the electorate enormously reduce the prospects of mobilizing sufficient collective will to act decisively.

Envoi: Planning in the Eighties

What does all this portend for planning in the Eighties? Will we see a more focussed and concerted effort to establish and pursue a limited number of national goals? The Eighties will see difficult times. Many of the preoccupations of planning in the late Sixties and first half of the Seventies will become altogether dispensable luxuries. A few others will assume an importance which may generate the required consensus behind a particular intellectual framework or planning philosophy. In the end, then, the prospects for planning depend more on public attitudes than on the institutional factors that have been the principal preoccupation of this study. We have learned, during the Seventies, something about how, or rather how not, to organize and think about planning.

Implicit in many of the planning efforts between 1968 and the mid-Seventies was an optimism which rested ultimately—despite a lot of shallow rhetoric about participation—on the esoteric soft technology of management systems and planning techniques. Such systems and techniques depended directly upon technocratic expertise, and those who had or could feign such expertise were forever seeing their systems' failures to "take" as the product of self-interest and obscurantism. These failures can now be traced to the anti-political assumptions of the systems themselves, notably the idea that such instruments could be so compelling in use as to dispel that *melange* of ambition and idealism, ignorance and wisdom, selflessness and self-interest, which characterizes any kind of collective decision-making. By assuming that some of these untidy overheads of democracy could be substantially reduced, and by attempting to focus political decision-making on priorities and objectives rather than the surveillance of the management of specific programs and policies, the planning systems lost their legitimacy in the eyes of political men, even those who wanted to believe.

Planning is a search for overriding criteria against which decision-making about the relationships and relative priority of policies and programs may be undertaken. It is not thereby a way to eliminate the

154

regular inconsistency, frequent perversity and occasional chaos of policy-making in a democracy. It is not a way to expand the intrinsic limits to the power of a parliamentary cabinet, though it may yet prove to be a way to focus and mobilize that power. It is not a way to avoid painful choices among competing interests, though it may yet prove to be a way to force them to the political forefront.

These points have been made before, but a disillusioned view of planning arrived relatively late in the Government of Canada. Planning may define issues, politicians may articulate them, and attempt to lead public opinion. Inevitably, however, planning without public consensus and support becomes sterile and diffused. Such support, and the bureaucratic and ministerial co-operation required to build on it, can form around only a very limited number of issues at any one time. Such political resources must be husbanded with great care, and this is where the institutional lessons may come into play. Planning systems which are unduly pluralistic, which fail to force choice, will squander political resources, just as management control systems which have the same features will squander financial resources. Planning systems which are unduly elaborate and insular will identify false problems and fail to confront real ones.

There is a certain clarity about the priority issues of the Eighties, a clarity which had no parallel in 1970. The economy and the constitutional ground rules for the political community are the critical issues facing Canadians.

The economic problems of the Seventies and in particular the plight of Canadian manufacturing—"desperate" or merely "extremely serious" depending upon whom is consulted—seem to have generated a degree of public consensus around economic development as a priority. The social and cultural experiments of the late Sixties and early Seventies appear as expensive self-indulgence, now largely irrelevant in the face of grimmer realities. The skilful political marshalling of the sentiment, and the articulation of a concerted strategy in response to it, represent a substantial political opportunity. It should be recognized, however, that the adoption of such a concerted approach would still be seen by the two principal parties as at best a high risk/high return alternative, quite out of character with recent Canadian political history and party traditions. Thus far, only the New Democratic Party, whose third party status lowers the risk/return ratio substantially, has shown any serious interest in this option. As there is little reason in the short term to expect significant improvements in Canada's economic performance (indeed, the reverse), the major parties may well revise their approaches, particularly if their traditional "rolling compromise" political strategies[7] begin to roll in the wrong direction.

155

The first indicators of such an eventuality may have been detectable in the Clark administration of 1979–80, and its demise. For ideological as well as practical reasons, economic issues constituted a primary motif of the government's approach to the people. Furthermore, there emerged the beginnings of the kind of hierarchical decision-making structure which would appear to be a necessary, if not sufficient, condition for the identification and pursuit within government of a manageably small number of major priorities. However, the Clark government showed little inclination to follow the implications of the structural and procedural changes to the point of substantial innovations in the substance of policy, with the possible exception of the energy sector. It had little opportunity to do so. It may be that the precipitate return to opposition will push the party toward more distinctive alternative policies. However, to the extent that the electoral defeat is interpreted as the consequence of the substance of a tough-minded budget which asked citizens to "bite the bullet", there will be resistance to highly defined alternative policies. It remains for a party —perhaps one whose leadership personnel is quite different from that of either major party at the moment— to realize the potential benefits in terms of policy-making and planning which might arise from a determined effort to articulate a very few major priorities and to marshall the political, financial, and bureaucratic resources to achieve them.

As for constitutional reform and national unity, the Conservative legacy is even more ambiguous. The Clark government simply did not have the time to unveil its vision of a "community of communities". It made a virtue of necessity by avoiding open confrontation with the Government of Québec. It seems probable, however, that the Eighties will demand a more articulated view of the constitutional future.

There are two points of particular interest which arise from the current critical stage of constitutional development. The first is that the process of debate within Québec represents a paradigm example for planning: the articulation of distinctive objectives and planning criteria by each of two parties, the development of a program by the government in accordance with its objectives, and a high level of popular interest and involvement in a choice between parties which is also a genuine choice between policies. Only this degree of public involvement could legitimize a type of planning with extensive and systematic consequences for a range of policies, a type which would satisfy the most ambitious of the normative definitions of planning in the academic literature.

The second point is that the two issues of economic and constitutional development may well become systematically intertwined, to the point where Canada as a whole may face the kind of existential crisis now faced by Québec. If economic stagnation leads to the development of support for more ambitious industrial strategies, with all that implies for international trade and foreign investment policy, Canada will have to face elemental questions of its social, cultural and political identity. If the constitutional reform process falters in its ultimate test, Canadians in Québec and elsewhere will have to face precisely the same issues. Economic and constitutional uncertainty would tend to fuse in a crisis which, ironically, would genuinely ask "What kind of Canada do we want in the year 2000?"

In such a crisis, there would be pressure on the major parties to polarize into a vaguely nationalist and centralist Liberal Party and a continentalist and decentralist Progressive Conservative Party. The acid test would be each party's ability to articulate a coherent and attractive view of Canada's economic and constitutional future, in particular vis-à-vis the United States. The "rolling compromises" underlying each party position would be truly distinct, and this is very much a prerequisite for comprehensive national planning based on a popular mandate awarded to one of these two positions.

This speculative scenario, then, illustrates the general thesis that planning must be rooted in politics in a way it generally was not during the Seventies. No amount of sophistication can compensate for a political system which is predicated on personality rather than policy. The technocratic planning theories of the Sixties and Seventies have been irreparably devastated by the critiques of both right and left, by the conservative spokesmen for economic freedom and by the neo-marxists, and no satisfactory post-positivist theory of planning has been developed in their place. There are no obvious technical solutions. We are, then, older and sadder. Perhaps we are a little wiser as well.

Appendix
The Clark Cabinet
Committee System, 1979– 80[1]

I. *Inner Cabinet*
        Clark   (Chairman)
        Flynn
        Baker
        F. MacDonald
        Crosbie
        D. MacDonald
        LaSalle
        Fraser
        Jarvis
        Stevens
        Hnatyshyn
        de Cotret

- Fiscal Arrangements Envelope, FY 1980–81: $3.6 Billion

  Municipal Grants
  Subsidies under BNA Act
  Federal-Provincial Fiscal Arrangements
  Utilities Income Tax Transfers
  Reciprocal Taxation

- Public Debt Envelope, FY 1980–81: $9.8 Billion

  Interest and Amortization

II. *Economic Development Committee*
        de Cotret   (Chairman)
        MacKay   (Vice-Chairman)
        F. MacDonald
        McGrath
        Lawrence

Crosbie
Alexander
Mazankowski
Epp
Fraser
Jarvis
Stevens
Wise
Atkey
Hnatyshyn
Grafftey
Huntington
Wilson

- Economic Development Envelope, FY 1980–81: $8.4 Billion

Agriculture
   Canadian Dairy Commission
   Canadian Livestock Feed Board
   Farm Credit Corporation

Communications

Consumer and Corporate Affairs

Economic Development — Ministry of State

Employment and Immigration
   Department and activities of Canada
   Employment and Immigration Commission
   relating to job creation and employment services

Energy, Mines and Resources
   Energy
   Oil Import Compensation Payments
   Sarnia-Montreal Pipeline
   Minerals
   Earth Sciences
   Atomic Energy Control Board
   Atomic Energy of Canada Ltd.
   National Energy Board

Environment
   Forestry

Fisheries and Oceans

Industry, Trade and Commerce, including industrial
support and grain programs
Canadian Commercial Corporation
Federal Business Development Bank
Foreign Investment Review Agency

Labour

Northern Pipeline Agency
Public Works Lands Co. Ltd.

Regional Economic Expansion, including Cape Breton
Development Corporation

Science and Technology
National Research Council
Natural Sciences and Engineering Research Council
Science Council of Canada

Supply and Services, industrial programs
Unsolicited Proposals for R & D
Source Development Fund

Transport
Air Canada
Canadian Transport Commission

Treasury Board—employment funds

This envelope "consists of those government programs that are
directly related to the key economic sectors, including resources, manufacturing and tourism as well as horizontal policy activities such as competition policy, regional development
and transportation."[2]

III. *Social and Native Affairs Committee*
        D. MacDonald   (Chairman)
        Crombie   (Vice-Chairman)
        Flynn
        Nielsen
        Lawrence
        Crosbie
        Alexander
        Mackay
        Epp

Jarvis
McKinnon
Stevens
Atkey
Grafftey
Howie

- Social and Native Affairs Envelope, FY 1980–81: $23.5 Billion

    Central Mortgage and Housing Corporation, community services and home insulation

    Canadian Radio-Television and Telecommunications Commission

    Employment and Immigration
    Contribution to UI Account
    Immigration

    Environment – Environment Programs and Parks

    Indian Affairs and Northern Development

    Labour
    Canada Centre for Occupational Health and Safety

    National Health and Welfare
    Health and Social Service Programs
    Established Programs Financing
        Hospital Insurance
        Extended Health Care
        Medicare
    Canada Assistance Plan
    Old Age Security
    Family Allowance
    Medical Research Council

    Secretary of State
    Canada Council and other cultural agencies
    Canadian Broadcasting Corporation
    National Library and Public Archives
    Social Sciences and Humanities Research Council
    Status of Women

    Veterans Affairs

This envelope "consists of all social programs including major statutory programs that involve direct payments to individuals from the federal government (income maintenance), or to support essential social services through arrangements with the provinces (Established Program Financing)."[3]

- Justice and Legal Envelope, FY 1980–81: $1.2 Billion

  Justice
  Canadian Human Rights Commission
  Law Reform Commission of Canada
  Supreme Court of Canada
  Tax Review Board

  Solicitor General
  Correctional Services
  National Parole Board

  Royal Canadian Mounted Police

This envelope "consists of those government programs aimed at achieving justice and protection of the individual. Ninety per cent of the expenditures are allocated to the two major programs—RCMP and Correctional Services."[4]

IV.   *Foreign Policy and Defence Committee*
                F. MacDonald   (Chairman)
                McKinnon   (Vice-Chairman)
                Asselin
                McGrath
                Crosbie
                Mazankowski
                Stevens
                Wise
                Atkey
                de Cotret
                Paproski
                Wilson

- External Affairs Envelope, FY 1980–81: $1.6 Billion

  External Affairs
  Canadian International Development Agency
  International Development Research Centre
  International Joint Commission

- Defence Envelope, FY 1980–81: $4.9 Billion

  National Defence
  Defence Services
  Defence Services-Pensions
  Military Pensions

V. *Economy in Government Committee*
  Stevens   (Chairman)
  Baker   (Vice-Chairman)
  Nielsen
  Crosbie
  D. MacDonald
  Alexander
  LaSalle
  Fraser
  Crombie
  Grafftey
  Beatty
  Paproski
  Huntington

- Parliament Envelope, FY 1980–81: $0.1 Billion

  Parliament
  The Senate
  House of Commons
  Library of Parliament

This envelope "has been defined for those elements outside the direct control of the government."[5]

- General Government Envelope, FY 1980–81: $3.9 Billion

  Finance
  Administration
  Anti-Dumping Tribunal
  Inspector General of Banks
  Anti-Inflation Board
  Auditor General
  Insurance
  Tariff Board

  Governor General and Lieutenant
  Governors

National Revenue

Post Office

Privy Council
    Chief Electoral Officer
    Commissioner of Official Languages
    Economic Council of Canada
    Public Service Staff Relations Board

Public Works
    National Capital Commission

Secretary of State
    Public Service Commission
    Representation Commissioner

Supply and Services—Administration and Services
    Canadian Arsenals Ltd.

Treasury Board
    Comptroller General
    Statistics Canada

This envelope "includes those programs and activities of government whose primary purpose is to provide support and services to program departments or are primarily service oriented (Post Office). It also includes Executive Functions (mainly central agencies) and agencies which report to Parliament but for which the government retains a financial and management responsibility."[6]

VI.   *Federal-Provincial Relations Committee*
        Jarvis   (Chairman)
        Flynn   (Vice-Chairman)
        Asselin
        Nielsen
        Lawrence
        Crosbie
        D. MacDonald
        Mazankowski
        Crombie
        Howie

VII.   *Legislation and House Planning Committee*
    Baker (Chairman)
    Flynn (Vice-Chairman)
    McGrath
    Lawrence
    MacKay
    Epp
    McKinnon
    Crombie
    Beatty
    Howie

VIII.   *Treasury Board*
    Stevens (Chairman)
    Crosbie (Vice-Chairman)
    Nielsen
    LaSalle
    Wise
    Hnatyshyn

Notes

Introduction

[1] The terms "policy" and "program" are frequently used in this study, in much the same sense as the following definitions, developed by the Treasury Board Secretariat:

Policy—A government policy is a statement by the government of a principle or set of principles it wishes to see followed, in pursuit of particular objectives, which may be stated in such a way as to suggest possible courses of action (programs) and as to indicate how success of the policy may be measured (criteria).

Program—A course of action or instrument to implement a policy (or policies), sometimes involving legislative mandates and usually, public expenditures. (A program also has objectives, which will in general be more operational than those of a policy, and be suggestive of possible criteria against which accomplishment of the objectives may be measured).

These definitions are quoted in George Szablowski, "The Optimal Policy-Making System: Implications for the Canadian Political Process", in Thomas A. Hockin, (ed.), *Apex of Power: The Prime Minister and Political Leadership in Canada* (2nd ed., Scarborough, Prentice-Hall, 1977), p. 208. A policy, then, is a posture, a set of guidelines to direct action with respect to a public issue. A program is a specific activity, conceived within the context of a policy, for example, a subsidy program, a fiscal transfer program, a regulation program, or a program to provide services in a particular sector, such as industrial development, defence, welfare, cultural affairs, or communications.

[2] Cf. Peter Aucoin, "Theory and Research in the Study of Policy-Making", in G. Bruce Doern and Peter Aucoin (eds.), *The Structures of Policy-Making in Canada* (Toronto, Macmillan, 1971), pp. 30-33.

Chapter 1

[1] Canada, Royal Commission on Financial Management and Accountability, *Final Report* (Ottawa, Supply and Services, 1979), pp. 63-64.

[2] The one indispensable reference is Aaron Wildavsky, "If Planning is Everything, Maybe it's Nothing", *Policy Sciences* 4 (1973), pp. 127-153. For

167

thoughtful Canadian discussion, see Peter Aucoin, "Theory and Research in the Study of Policy-Making" in G. Bruce Doern and Peter Aucoin (eds.), *The Structures of Policy-Making in Canada* (Toronto, Macmillan, 1971), pp. 10-38 and "Public Policy Theory and Analysis" in G. Bruce Doern and Peter Aucoin (eds.), *Public Policy in Canada. Organization, Process, and Management* (Toronto, Macmillan, 1979), pp. 1-26.

[3] For two recent attempts to describe the Trudeau approach in detail, see Richard French, "The Privy Council Office: Support for Cabinet Decision-Making", in Richard Schultz, Orest M. Kruhlak and John C. Terry (eds.), *The Canadian Political Process* (Toronto, Holt, Rinehart and Winston, 3rd ed., 1979), pp. 363-394, and M. J. Kirby, H. V. Kroeker, and W. R. Teschke, "The Impact of Public Policy-Making Structures and Processes in Canada", *Canadian Public Administration* 21 (1978), pp. 407-417.

[4] On ministerial time, see Gordon Robertson, "The Changing Role of the Privy Council Office", *Canadian Public Administration* 14 (1971), pp. 499-500 and Michael Pitfield, "The Shape of Government in the 1980s: Techniques and Instruments for Policy Formulation at the Federal Level", *Canadian Public Administration* 19 (1976), pp. 16-17.

[5] Quoted in Stephen Duncan, "Emasculated Mandarins", *Financial Post*, (January 25, 1975).

[6] M. J. Kirby, H. V. Kroeker and W. R. Teschke, *op. cit.*, p. 410.

[7] Quoted in J. R. Mallory, "The Two Clerks: Parliamentary Discussion of the Privy Council Office", *Canadian Journal of Political Science* 10 (1977), p. 14.

[8] For purposes of this discussion, the following cabinet committees are omitted: the Board of Economic Development Ministers, the Security, Intelligence and Emergency Planning Committee, the Special Committee of Council, and various *ad hoc* committees which met relatively rarely.

[9] See Richard Schultz, "Prime Ministerial Government, Central Agencies, and Operating Departments: Towards a More Realistic Analysis", in Thomas A. Hockin, (ed.), *Apex of Power: The Prime Minister and Political Leadership in Canada* (Scarborough, Prentice-Hall, 2nd. ed., 1977) pp. 229-236 and Richard French, "The Privy Council Office: Support for Cabinet Decision-Making", in Richard Schultz, Orest M. Kruhlak and John C. Terry (eds.), *The Canadian Political Process* (Toronto, Holt, Rinehart and Winston, 3rd. ed., 1979), pp. 375-383.

[10] Douglas Hartle, *The Draft Memorandum to Cabinet* (Toronto, Institute of Public Administration of Canada, 1977); Hubert L. Laframboise, "Moving a Proposal to a Positive Decision: A Case History of the Invisible Process", *Optimum* 4:3 (1973), pp. 31-42.

[11] Cf. M. J. Kirby, H. V. Kroeker and W. R. Teschke, "The Impact of Public Policy-Making Structures and Processes in Canada", *Canadian Public Administration* 21 (1978), p. 413: Stephen Duncan, *Financial Post*, (September 20, 1975).

[12] George Radwanski, *Trudeau* (Toronto, Macmillan, 1978), pp. 163-165. The parting shots of sometime Trudeau ministers like Eric Kierans and Paul Hellyer were consistent with this line of argument. See, e.g., "Trudeau a Monarch of all he Surveys?", *Ottawa Journal* (November 13, 1969). See also Frank Jones, *Toronto Star* (May 30, 1969); Peter Riegenstrief, *Toronto Star*

(February 28, March 2, 1970); Ben Tierney, *Montreal Gazette* (May 1, 1970); Pierre O'Neil, *La Presse* (September 13, 1971); "Mandarins...", *Montreal Gazette* (September 16, 1972).

[13] See, e.g., Douglas Fisher, *Toronto Telegram* (October 26, 1971); Claude Lemelin, *Le Devoir* (October 7, 1974); Christina Newman, *Globe and Mail* (January 4, 1975); Stephen Duncan, *Financial Post* (January 25, 1975).

[14] On the Treasury Board see, *inter alia*, Douglas Hartle, *The Expenditure Budget Process in the Government of Canada* (Toronto, Canadian Tax Foundation, 1978); Michael Hicks, "The Treasury Board of Canada and its Clients: Five Years of Change and Administrative Reform 1966-71", *Canadian Public Administration* 16 (1973), pp. 182-205; A. W. Johnson, "Management Theory and Cabinet Government", *Canadian Public Administration* 14 (1971), pp. 73-81, and "The Treasury Board of Canada and the Machinery of Government of the 1970's", *Canadian Journal of Political Science* 4 (1971), pp. 346-366; Canada, Royal Commission on Financial Management and Accountability, *Final Report* (Ottawa, Supply and Services, 1979).

[15] *Financial Administration Act*, R.S., c. 116, s. 3 (Hereafter cited as *FAA*).

[16] The Federal-Provincial Relations Office has been organizationally separate from the Privy Council Office since 1975, but it still answers to the Prime Minister, notwithstanding Ministers of State for Federal-Provincial Relations, whose responsibilities are technically no more than to assist the Prime Minister.

[17] *FAA*, s. 5 (1).

[18] *FAA*, s. 5 (2).

[19] *FAA*, s. 5 (4).

[20] *FAA*, s. 5 (1) and (5), respectively.

[21] Sweeping changes in its mandate have been proposed by the Lambert Commission. See Canada, Royal Commission on Financial Management and Accountability, *Final Report* (Ottawa, Supply and Service, 1979), pp. 36-47.

[22] Douglas Hartle, *The Expenditure Budget Process in the Government of Canada* (Toronto, Canadian Tax Foundation, 1978), p. 14.

[23] A. W. Johnson, "Management Theory and Cabinet Government", *Canadian Public Administration* 14 (1971), pp. 73-81; Michael Hicks, "The Treasury Board of Canada and its Clients: Five Years of Change and Administrative Reform 1966-71", *Canadian Public Administration* 16 (1973), pp. 195-205.

[24] Which included, during much of the Trudeau administration, the following divisions: Industry and Natural Resources; General Government Services; Transport, Communications and Science; Social and Manpower; Defence, External, and Cultural Affairs; Management Information Systems; Estimates.

[25] Which included the following directorates: Contract Review, Real Property and Contract Policy; Employee Administrative Services; Planning and Evaluation; and the Information Systems Division.

[26] Which included the following divisions: Staff Relations, Personnel, Planning and Coordination.

[27] Royal Commission on Financial Management and Accountability, *Final Report* (Ottawa, Supply and Services, 1979), p. 44.

[28] Hubert L. Laframboise, "Counter-Managers: The Abandonment of Unity of

Command", *Optimum* 8:4 (1977), pp. 21-22. Cf. his "Administrative Reform in the Federal Public Service: Signs of a Saturation Psychosis", *Canadian Public Administration* 14 (1971), pp. 303-325.

[29] Cf. Michael Hicks, "The Treasury Board of Canada and its Clients: Five Years of Change and Administrative Reform 1966-71", *Canadian Public Administration* 16 (1973), pp. 190-91.

[30] Richard W. Phidd and Bruce Doern, *The Politics and Management of Canadian Economic Policy* (Toronto, Macmillan, 1978), p. 468. Cf. A. W. Johnson, "The Treasury Board of Canada and the Machinery of Government of the 1970's", *Canadian Journal of Political Science* 4 (1971), p. 350.

[31] See for example the publications of Hartle, Johnson, Kroeker, Phidd and Doern, and the Royal Commission on Financial Management and Accountability, cited elsewhere in this chapter.

[32] This account draws heavily on A. W. Johnson, *op. cit.*, pp. 354-355.

[33] *Ibid.*, p. 354.

[34] See Thomas Hockin, "The Cabinet and the Public Service: Remarks of Mitchell Sharp, J. Chrétien, *et al*", in his *Apex of Power: The Prime Minister and Political Leadership in Canada* (Scarborough, Prentice-Hall, 2nd. ed., 1977), pp. 186-187.

[35] Hubert L. Laframboise, "Administrative Reform in the Federal Public Service: Signs of a Saturation Psychosis", *Canadian Public Administration* 14 (1971), p. 321.

[36] A. W. Johnson, *op. cit.*, p. 350.

[37] Douglas Hartle, *The Expenditure Budget Process in the Government of Canada* (Toronto, Canadian Tax Foundation, 1978), p. 27.

Chapter 2

[1] See Richard Bernstein, *The Restructuring of Social and Political Theory* (Philadelphia, University of Pennsylvania Press, 1978), pp. xi-xxiv, 3-54.

[2] Cf. Peter Aucoin and Richard French, *Knowledge, Power and Public Policy*, (Ottawa, Information Canada, 1974), esp. p. 77.

[3] "Notes for Remarks by the Prime Minister at the Harrison Liberal Conference", (Typescript, Harrison Hot Springs, B.C., November 21, 1969), first brought to our attention by Bruce Doern, "The Development of Policy Organizations in the Executive Arena", in Bruce Doern and Peter Aucoin, (eds.), *The Structures of Policy-Making in Canada* (Toronto, Macmillan, 1971), pp. 64-65.

[4] "Notes . . . ", p. 4.

[5] "Notes . . . ", p. 7. Italics added.

[6] "Notes . . . ", p. 10.

[7] George Radwanski, *Trudeau*, (Toronto, Macmillan, 1978), pp. 147-150.

[8] *Ibid.*, pp. 145-147; Michael J. Kirby and Hal V. Kroeker, "The Politics of Crisis Management in Government: Does Planning Make Any Difference?", in C. F. Smart and W. T. Stanbury (eds.), *Studies on Crisis Management*, (Montreal, Institute for Research on Public Policy/Butterworth, 1978), p. 183.

[9] M. J. Kirby and H. V. Kroeker, *op. cit.*, p. 182; M. J. Kirby, H. V. Kroeker, and W. R. Teschke, "The Impact of Public Policy-Making Structures and

Processes in Canada", *Canadian Public Administration* 21 (1978), pp. 407-410; Douglas Hartle, *The Expenditure Budget Process in the Government of Canada*, (Toronto, Canadian Tax Foundation, 1978), pp. 3-5.

[10] "Federalism, Nationalism and Reason" in *Federalism and the French Canadians* (Toronto, Macmillan, [1964] 1968), p. 203, quoted in Bruce Doern, "The Development of Policy Organizations in the Executive Arena", in Bruce Doern and Peter Aucoin, (eds.), *The Structures of Policy-Making in Canada* (Toronto, Macmillan, 1971), p. 61. Cf. Herman Bakvis, "French Canada and the 'Bureaucratic Phenomenon", *Canadian Public Administration* 21 (1978), pp. 121-124.

[11] Douglas Hartle, *Public Policy Decision-Making and Regulation* (Montreal, Institute for Research on Public Policy/Butterworth, 1979), pp. 72-73.

[12] Cf. Hubert L. Laframboise, "Administrative Reform in the Federal Public Service", *Canadian Public Administration* 14 (1971), p. 315.

[13] Richard W. Phidd and Bruce Doern, *The Politics and Management of Canadian Economic Policy* (Toronto, Macmillan, 1978), p. 5.

[14] *Ibid.*, p. 467; cf. Peter Aucoin, "Theory and Research in the Study of Policy-Making" in Bruce Doern and Peter Aucoin (eds.), *The Structures of Policy-Making in Canada* (Toronto, Macmillan, 1971), p. 25.

[15] George Szablowski, "The Optimal Policy-Making System: Implications for the Canadian Political Process", in Thomas A. Hockin, (ed.), *Apex of Power: The Prime Minister and Political Leadership in Canada* (Scarborough, Prentice-Hall, 2nd. ed., 1977), p. 198.

[16] Cf. Douglas Hartle, *The Expenditure Budget Process in the Government of Canada* (Toronto, Canadian Tax Foundation, 1978) and "Techniques and Processes of Administration", *Canadian Public Administration* 19 (1976), pp. 21-33; M. J. Kirby and H. V. Kroeker, "The Politics of Crisis Management in Government: Does Planning Make Any Difference?", in C. F. Smart and W. T. Stanbury (eds.), *Studies on Crisis Management* (Montreal, Institute for Research on Public Policy/Butterworth, 1978), pp. 179-195; Michael Pitfield, "The Shape of Government in the 1980s. Techniques and Instruments for Policy Formulation at the Federal Level", *Canadian Public Administration* 19 (1976), pp. 8-20.

[17] Cf. George Szablowski, "The Optimal Policy-Making System: Implications for the Canadian Political Process", in Thomas A. Hockin, (ed.), *Apex of Power: The Prime Minister and Political Leadership in Canada* (Scarborough, Prentice-Hall, 2nd. ed., 1977), pp. 197-210 and "Decisional Technology and Political Process in Canada" (Unpublished Ph.D. thesis, McGill University, 1979); Laurent Dobuzinskis, "Rational Policy-Making: Policy, Politics and Political Science", in T. A. Hockin, *op. cit.*, pp. 211-228.

[18] See A. W. Johnson, "The Treasury Board of Canada and the Machinery of Government of the 1970's", *Canadian Journal of Political Science* 4 (1971), pp. 346-366.

[19] M. J. Kirby, H. V. Kroeker, W. R. Teschke, "The Impact of Public Policy-Making Structures and Policies in Canada", *Canadian Public Administration* 21 (1978), pp. 407-417; Michael Prince, "Policy-Advisory Groups in Government Departments", in Bruce Doern and Peter Aucoin (eds.), *Public Policy in Canada. Organization, Process, and Management* (Toronto, Macmillan, 1979), pp. 275-300.

[20] Douglas Hartle, *A Theory of the Expenditure Budget Process* (Toronto, Ontario Economic Council/University of Toronto Press, 1976), pp. 74, 84-85.

[21] For example, A. W. Johnson, *op. cit.*

[22] Richard W. Phidd and Bruce Doern, *The Politics and Management of Canadian Economic Policy* (Toronto, Macmillan, 1978), p. 229.

[23] *Ibid.*, p. 7.

[24] *Ibid.*, p. 534. The developments outlined here are a major theme in Phidd and Doern's analysis.

[25] See, *ibid.*, pp. 38, 58, 88-89; Ronald Anderson, *Globe and Mail* (February 28, 1975).

[26] Douglas Hartle, *The Expenditure Budget Process in the Government of Canada* (Toronto, Canadian Tax Foundation, 1978), pp. 11-12. In a different context, Bruce Doern described Finance as "almost a 'government within a government'." See "Economic Policy Processes and Organization" in Bruce Doern and Peter Aucoin (eds.), *Public Policy in Canada. Organization, Process, and Management* (Toronto, Macmillan, 1979), p. 100.

[27] Colin Campbell and George Szablowski, *The Super-Bureaucrats. Structure and Behaviour in Central Agencies* (Toronto, Macmillan, 1979), p. 14.

[28] Douglas Hartle, *Public Policy Decision-Making and Regulation* (Montreal, Institute for Research on Public Policy/Butterworth, 1979), pp. 77, 85.

[29] Douglas Hartle, *The Expenditure Budget Process in the Government of Canada* (Toronto, Canadian Tax Foundation, 1978), p. 11.

[30] C. Campbell and G. Szablowski, *op. cit.*, p. 86, quoting an official from the Department of Finance.

[31] R. Phidd and B. Doern, *op. cit.*, p. 558.

[32] Canada, Royal Commission on Financial Management and Accountability, *Final Report* (Ottawa, Supply and Services, 1979), esp. pp. 21-36.

[33] A. W. Johnson, "The Treasury Board of Canada and the Machinery of Government of the 1970's", *Canadian Journal of Political Science* 4 (1971), p. 347.

[34] Douglas Hartle, "A Proposed System of Policy and Program Evaluation", *Canadian Public Administration* 16 (1973), p. 245.

[35] George Szablowski, "The Optimal Policy-Making System: Implications for the Canadian Political Process", in Thomas A. Hockin (ed.), *Apex of Power: The Prime Minister and Political Leadership in Canada* (Scarborough, Prentice-Hall, 2nd. ed., 1977), pp. 197-210, and "Decisional Technology and Political Process in Canada", (Unpublished Ph.D. thesis, McGill University, 1979).

[36] Hubert Laframboise, "Administrative Reform in the Federal Public Service: Signs of a Saturation Psychosis", *Canadian Public Administration* 14 (1971), p. 317. See also his "Counter-Managers: The Abandonment of the Unity of Command", *Optimum* 8:4 (1977), pp. 18-28.

[37] See Douglas Hartle, "Techniques and Processes of Administration", *Canadian Public Administration* 19 (1976), pp. 21-33, and other post-1976 publications.

[38] Canada, Royal Commission on Financial Management and Accountability, *Final Report* (Ottawa, Supply and Services, 1979), p. 86.

[39] Henning Frederikson, "Operational Performance Measurement Systems" in

172

K. Kernaghan (ed.), *Public Administration in Canada* (Toronto, Methuen, 3rd. ed., 1977), p. 178.

[40] Treasury Board, "Planning-Programming-Budgeting System in Canada", in K. Kernaghan (ed.), *op. cit.*, p. 174.

[41] "The Public Servant as Advisor: The Choice of Policy Evaluation Criteria", *Canadian Public Policy* 2 (1976), pp. 424-438.

[42] "A Proposed System of Policy and Program Evaluation", *Canadian Public Administration* 16 (1973), p. 243.

[43] *Ibid.*, pp. 249-250.

[44] Hartle in 1973 took the term "priority problem" to mean "priority", but this was his misunderstanding of the lexicon of the Cabinet Planning System. See the discussion in the next section of this chapter.

[45] *Ibid.*, p. 245.

[46] *Ibid.*, p. 265. Italics added.

[47] "The Public Servant as Advisor: The Choice of Policy Evaluation Criteria", *Canadian Public Policy* 2 (1976), p. 438.

[48] Bruce Doern, "The Development of Policy Organizations in the Executive Arena", in Bruce Doern and Peter Aucoin, (eds.), *The Structures of Policy-Making in Canada* (Toronto, Macmillan, 1971), pp. 39-78 and Donald Gow, *The Process of Budgetary Reform in the Government of Canada*, (Ottawa, Economic Council of Canada, 1973), p. 29.

[49] Laurent Dobuzinskis, "Rational Policy-Making: Policy, Politics, and Political Science" in Thomas A. Hockin (ed.), *Apex of Power: The Prime Minister and Political Leadership in Canada* (Scarborough, Prentice-Hall, 2nd. ed., 1977), p. 211.

[50] Bruce Doern, " . . . Policy Organizations . . . ", *op. cit.*, p. 67.

[51] Laurent Dobuzinskis, *op. cit.*, p. 220; George Szablowski, in Thomas A. Hockin, *op. cit.*, pp. 198-200.

[52] Michael J. Kirby and Hal V. Kroeker, "The Politics of Crisis Management in Government: Does Planning Make Any Difference?", in C. G. Smart and W. T. Stanbury (eds.), *Studies on Crisis Management* (Montreal, Institute for Research on Public Policy/Butterworth, 1978), p. 185. Note the key words, "comprehensive", "systems", and "*best* policies".

[53] *Ibid.*, pp. 179-195.

[54] Michael Pitfield, "The Shape of Government in the 1980s: Techniques and Instruments for Policy Formulation at the Federal Level", *Canadian Public Administration* 19 (1976), p. 11.

[55] Michael J. Kirby and Hal V. Kroeker, *op. cit.*, p. 187.

[56] Donald Gow, *The Process of Budgetary Reform in the Government of Canada* (Ottawa, Economic Council of Canada, 1973), p. 41.

[57] Richard W. Phidd and Bruce Doern, *The Politics and Management of Canadian Economic Policy* (Toronto, Macmillan, 1978), pp. 100-101.

[58] *Ibid.*, p. 101.

[59] See, for example, Geoffrey Stevens, *Globe and Mail* (August 21, 1973).

[60] Michael J. Kirby and Hal V. Kroeker, *op. cit.*, p. 188.

[61] Privy Council Office, "Policy Planning and Support for Ministerial Decision-Making in Canada" in Thomas A. Hockin (ed.), *Apex of Power: The Prime Minister and Political Leadership in Canada* (Scarborough, Prentice-Hall, 2nd. ed., 1977), p. 49.

[62] *Ibid.*, p. 50.

[63] Though in his 1973 article Hartle did so confuse them. Cf. Douglas Hartle, "A Proposed System of Policy and Program Evaluation", *Canadian Public Administration* 16 (1973), pp. 243, 254 and his *The Expenditure Budget Process in the Government of Canada* (Toronto, Canadian Tax Foundation, 1978), p. 3. See also Donald Gow, *op. cit.*, p. 44; Robert J. Jackson and Michael M. Atkinson, *The Canadian Legislative System* (Toronto, Macmillan, 1974), p. 59; Peter Aucoin and Richard French, *Knowledge, Power and Public Policy* (Ottawa, Information Canada, 1974), p. 16.

[64] Donald Gow, *op. cit.*, p. 45.

[65] Peter Regenstrief, *Toronto Star* (February 28, 1970).   0).

[66] Robert J. Jackson and Michael M. Atkinson, *op. cit.*, p. 59.

[67] Bruce Thordarson, *Trudeau and Foreign Policy. A Study in Decision-Making* (Toronto, Oxford University Press, 1972).

[68] L. A. Rossetto, "A Final Look at the 1971 White Paper on Defence", *Queen's Quarterly* 84 (1977), pp. 61-74.

[69] Donald Gow, *op. cit.*, p. 44; Bruce Doern, "The Development of Policy Organizations in the Executive Arena" in Bruce Doern and Peter Aucoin, *The Structures of Policy-Making in Canada* (Toronto, Macmillan, 1971), p. 62.

[70] Cf. Privy Council Office, "Policy Planning and Support for Ministerial Decision-Making in Canada", in Thomas A. Hockin (ed.), *Apex of Power: The Prime Minister and Political Leadership in Canada* (Scarborough, Prentice-Hall, 2nd. ed., 1977), p. 50.

[71] See Peter Aucoin and Richard French, *Knowledge, Power, and Public Policy* (Ottawa, Information Canada, 1974), and David M. Cameron, "Urban Policy", in Bruce Doern and V. Seymour Wilson, (eds.), *Issues in Canadian Public Policy*, (Toronto, Macmillan, 1974), pp. 228-252.

[72] Michael Pitfield, "The Shape of Government in the 1980s: Techniques and Instruments for Policy Formulation at the Federal Level", *Canadian Public Administration* 19 (1976), p. 13.

[73] Michael J. Kirby and Hal. V. Kroeker, *op. cit.*, p. 192.

[74] Richard W. Phidd and Bruce Doern, *op. cit.*, p. 102.

[75] Robert J. Jackson and Michael M. Atkinson, *op. cit.*, p. 61.

[76] *Ibid.*, p. 61.

[77] *Ibid.*, pp. 60-61.

[78] Douglas Hartle, "A Proposed System of Policy and Program Evaluation", *Canadian Public Administration* 16 (1973), p. 250.

[79] Douglas Hartle, *The Expenditure Budget Process in the Government of Canada* (Toronto, Canadian Tax Foundation, 1978), pp. 19-21.

Chapter 3

[1] Douglas Hartle, *Public Policy Decision-Making and Regulation* (Montreal, Institute for Research on Public Policy/Butterworth, 1979), p. 13.

[2] Hal V. Kroeker, *Accountability and Control. The Government Expenditure Process* (Montreal, C.D. Howe Research Institute, 1978), pp. 49-50.

[3] Richard Phidd and Bruce Doern, *The Politics and Management of Canadian Economic Policy* (Toronto, Macmillan, 1978), p. 19.

[4] Hal V. Kroeker, *op. cit.*, p. 50.

⁵ Colin Campbell and George Szablowski, *The Superbureaucrats. Structure and Behaviour in Central Agencies* (Toronto, Macmillan, 1979), pp. 93-94.

⁶ On the Social Security Review, see Rick Van Loon, "Reforming Welfare in Canada", *Public Policy* 27 (Fall 1979), pp. 469-504, esp. pp. 495-496.

⁷ Canada, Royal Commission on Financial Management and Accountability, *Final Report*, (Ottawa, Supply and Services, 1979), p. 44.

⁸ See Douglas Hartle, "Techniques and Processes of Administration", *Canadian Public Administration* 19 (1976), pp. 25, 30-31; Hubert L. Laframboise, "Moving a Proposal to a Positive Decision: A Case History of the Invisible Process", *Optimum* 4:3 (1973), p. 38; and cf. A. W. Johnson, "The Treasury Board of Canada and the Machinery of Government of the 1970's", *Canadian Journal of Political Science* 4 (1971), pp. 358-359.

⁹ Paul McCracken *et al, Towards Full Employment and Price Stability. Summary* (Paris, OECD, June 1977), pp. 16-17.

¹⁰ *Ibid.*, p. 25.

¹¹ *Ibid.*, pp. 26-36.

¹² *Ibid.*, pp. 39-41.

¹³ Canada, *The Way Ahead: A Framework for Discussion* (Ottawa, October 1976), p. 5.

¹⁴ *Ibid.*, p. 7.

¹⁵ Federal-Provincial Conference of First Ministers, *Notes for Remarks by the Prime Minister of Canada Introducing the Discussion of General Economic Policies* (Ottawa, Document 800-7/046, February 13, 1978), p. 5.

¹⁶ *Ibid.*, p. 3.

¹⁷ See First Ministers' Conference on the Economy, *Industrial Development Issues*, (Ottawa, Industry, Trade and Commerce, Document 800-9/013, November 27-29, 1978), p. 4.

¹⁸ First Ministers' Conference, "Remarks by the Honourable Jack H. Horner", (Typescript, Ottawa, Industry, Trade and Commerce, November 28, 1978), p. 3.

¹⁹ *Industrial Development Issues*, (Note 17), pp. 4-5.

²⁰ See Douglas Hartle, *The Expenditure Budget Process in the Government of Canada* (Toronto, Canadian Tax Foundation, 1978), pp. 43-45 and Richard D. French, "The Privy Council Office: Support for Cabinet Decision-Making", in Richard Schultz, Orest M. Kruhlak, and John C. Terry (eds.), *The Canadian Political Process* (Toronto, Holt Rinehart and Winston, 3rd ed., 1979), pp. 380-381.

²¹ Bruce Doern and Richard Phidd, "Economic Management in the Government of Canada: Some Implications of the Board of Economic Development Ministers and the Lambert Report", (Typescript of paper presented to the Canadian Political Science Association, May 1979), p. 21.

²² Canada, Royal Commission on Financial Management and Accountability, *Final Report*, (Ottawa, Supply and Services, 1979), single quote edited from separate passages on pp. 68, 69, 71, 74.

Chapter 4

¹ Michael J. Kirby and Hal V. Kroeker, "The Politics of Crisis Management in Government: Does Planning Make Any Difference?", in C. F. Smart and W. T. Stanbury (eds.), *Studies on Crisis Management* (Montreal, Institute for

Research on Public Policy/Butterworth, 1978), pp. 189-190, from *Toronto Star* (November 7, 1975). The general themes were later publicized officially in *The Way Ahead*. See Canada, *The Way Ahead: A Framework for Discussion* (Ottawa, October 1976).

[2] Douglas Hartle, *A Theory of the Expenditure Budgetary Process* (Toronto, Ontario Economic Council/University of Toronto Press, 1976), p. 84.

[3] George Radwanski, *Trudeau* (Toronto, Macmillan, 1978), pp. 294-299.

[4] Hugh Winsor, *Globe and Mail* (May 14, 1976).

[5] George Radwanski, *Financial Times* (March 29, 1976); see also *Financial Times* (July 28, 1975).

[6] George Radwanski, *Trudeau* (Toronto, Macmillan, 1978), p. 304; see pp. 288-304.

Chapter 5

[1] Science Council of Canada, *Forging the Links. A Technology Policy for Canada* (Ottawa, Supply and Services, February 1979), p. 19. Italics added.

[2] Cf. H. L. Laframboise, "Here Come the Program-Benders!" *Optimum* 7:1 (1976), pp. 40-48.

[3] Cf. Richard W. Phidd and Bruce Doern, *The Politics and Management of Canadian Economic Policy* (Toronto, Macmillan, 1978), p. 112.

[4] *Ibid.*, p. 23.

[5] Science Council of Canada, *Forging the Links. A Technology Policy for Canada* (Ottawa, Supply and Services, February 1979), p. 56.

[6] Richard W. Phidd and Bruce Doern, *The Politics and Management of Canadian Economic Policy* (Toronto, Macmillan, 1978), p. 536.

[7] Richard Simeon, "Federalism and the Politics of an Industrial Strategy" in Science Council of Canada, *The Politics of an Industrial Strategy: A Seminar* (Ottawa, Science Council of Canada, 1979), pp. 6, 23, 22-23, respectively.

[8] *Ibid.*, p. 42.

[9] Cf. K. H. Norrie, "Regional Economic Conflicts in Canada: Their Significance for an Industrial Strategy" in Science Council of Canada, *The Politics of an Industrial Strategy: A Seminar* (Ottawa, Science Council of Canada, 1979), pp. 55-83.

[10] Science Council of Canada, *Forging the Links. A Technology Policy for Canada* (Ottawa, Supply and Services, February 1979), pp. 40, 21, respectively.

[11] See, in general, Roy MacLaren, "Structuring Industry-Government Relations: The Problems of the Canadian Context" in Science Council of Canada, *The Politics of Industrial Strategy: A Seminar* (Ottawa, Science Council of Canada, 1979), pp. 89-104.

[12] Gordon Sharwood, *Financial Post* (July 8, 1978).

[13] *Minutes of Proceedings and Evidence of the Standing Committee on Finance, Trade and Economic Affairs*, 26 (June 5, 1973), p. 31. See also, Canadian Chamber of Commerce, *A Compendium of Business Viewpoints on National Industrial Strategy* (Montreal, Canadian Chamber of Commerce, 1973).

[14] See Science Council of Canada, *Forging the Links. A Technology Policy for Canada* (Ottawa, Supply and Services, February 1979), p. 39; Richard W.

Phidd and Bruce Doern, *The Politics and Management of Canadian Economic Policy* (Toronto, Macmillan, 1978), pp. 472, 479.

[15] Canada, *Foreign Direct Investment in Canada* (Ottawa, Information Canada, 1972), pp. 442-443.

[16] J. Douglas May, "Investment Incentives as Part of an Industrial Strategy", *Canadian Public Policy* 6 (1979), p. 71.

[17] Cf. Science Council of Canada, *Forging the Links. A Technology Policy for Canada* (Ottawa, Supply and Services, February 1979), p. 19.

[18] In treating the alternatives as industrial strategies we follow K. H. Norrie, "Regional Economic Conflicts in Canada: Their Significance for an Industrial Strategy" in Science Council of Canada, *The Politics of an Industrial Strategy: A Seminar* (Ottawa, Science Council of Canada, 1979) pp. 55-83.

[19] R. J. Wonnacott, "Industrial Strategy: A Canadian Substitute for Trade Liberalization?" *Canadian Journal of Economics* 8 (1975), p. 539, n. 3, referring to *Canadian Forum* (January/February 1972), reprinted in A. Rotstein, (ed.), *An Industrial Strategy for Canada* (Toronto, New Press, 1972).

[20] See K. H. Norrie, *op. cit.*, pp. 66-73 and A. E. Safarian, "Foreign Ownership and Industrial Behaviour: A Comment on 'The Weakest Link'" *Canadian Public Policy* 5 (1979), p. 328.

[21] See J. N. H. Britton, "Locational Perspectives on Free Trade for Canada", *Canadian Public Policy* 4 (1978), pp. 4-19; M. J. Gordon, "A World Scale National Corporation Industrial Strategy" *Canadian Public Policy* 4 (1978) pp. 54-55; J. N. H. Britton and J. M. Gilmour, *The Weakest Link. A Technology Perspective on Canadian Industrial Underdevelopment* (Ottawa, Science Council of Canada, Supply and Services, 1978), pp. 22, 153-155; and cf. R. Dauphin, *The Impact of Free Trade in Canada* (Ottawa, Economic Council of Canada, Supply and Services, 1978) and L. A. Skeoch with B. C. McDonald, *Dynamic Change and Accountability in a Canadian Market Economy* (Ottawa, Supply and Services, 1976), pp. 34-37.

[22] R. J. Wonnacott, "Industrial Strategy: A Canadian Substitute for Trade Liberalization?" *Canadian Journal of Economics* 8 (1975), pp. 536-547; S. Globerman, "Canadian Science Policy and Technological Sovereignty", *Canadian Public Policy* 4 (1978), pp. 34-45; A. E. Safarian, "Foreign Ownership and Industrial Behaviour: A Comment on 'The Weakest Link'" *Canadian Public Policy* 5 (1979), pp. 318-335; D. J. Daly, "Weak Links in the 'Weakest Link'", *Canadian Public Policy* 5 (1979), pp. 307-317.

[23] J. N. H. Britton and J. M. Gilmour, *op. cit.*, p. 162.

[24] *Ibid.*, pp. 162-166. For the view of the Science Council as a corporate entity, cf. Science Council of Canada, *Forging the Links. A Technology Policy for Canada*, (Ottawa, Supply and Services, 1979).

[25] J. N. H. Britton and J. M. Gilmour, *ibid.*, p. 45.

[26] *Ibid.*, pp. 130-131.

[27] *Ibid.*, p. 166.

[28] *Ibid.*, pp. 166-170.

[29] *Ibid.*, p. 171. See pp. 170-180.

[30] *Ibid.*, p. 174.

[31] *Ibid.*, pp. 178-180; M. J. Gordon, "A World Scale National Corporation Industrial Strategy", *Canadian Public Policy* 4 (1978), pp. 46-56, esp. p. 52.

[32] *Ibid.,* p. 180-182.
[33] *Ibid.,* pp. 182-186.
[34] *Ibid.,* p. 182.
[35] *Ibid.,* p. 187. Note, however, that the Science Council of Canada was unwilling to go as far as Britton and Gilmour on the matter of regulation of technology imports. Science Council of Canada, *Forging the Links. A Technology Policy for Canada* (Ottawa, Supply and Services, 1979), pp. 54-56.
[36] Britton and Gilmour, *ibid.,* p. 187.
[37] Economic Council of Canada, *Looking Outward* (Ottawa, Information Canada, 1975), p. 185; see also R. J. Wonnacott, *Canada's Trade Options* (Ottawa, Economic Council of Canada/Information Canada, 1975) and D. J. Daly and S. Globerman, *Tariff and Science Policies: Applications of a Model of Nationalism* (Toronto, Ontario Economic Council/University of Toronto Press, 1976).
[38] A. Breton, *A Conceptual Basis for an Industrial Strategy* (Ottawa, Economic Council of Canada/Information Canada, 1974), p. 23.
[39] Economic Council of Canada, *op. cit.,* pp. 172-177.
[40] A. Breton, *op. cit.,* p. 23.
[41] Economic Council of Canada, *op. cit.,* pp. 112-118, 174-178.
[42] Britton and Gilmour, *op. cit.,* pp. 159-160, 152, respectively.

Chapter 6

[1] *Minutes of Proceeding and Evidence of the Standing Committee on Finance, Trade and Economic Affairs,* 13 (November 30, 1978), p. 14.
[2] David Crane, *Vancouver Sun* (January 24, 1972); Ronald Anderson, *Globe and Mail* (March 15, 1972); *Minutes of Proceedings and Evidence of the Standing Committee on Finance, Trade and Economic Affairs* 4 (March 12, 1972), pp. 12, 40-41.
[3] J. L. Pépin, "Industrial Strategy—Notes for a Speech to the Annual General Meeting of the Canadian Manufacturers' Association" (Typescript, Industry, Trade and Commerce, presented in Edmonton, June 5, 1972). Pépin had given a similar speech to the Chamber of Commerce in Hamilton in April, 1972.
[4] Alastair Gillespie, "Towards a Coherent Set of Industrial Policies—Notes for a Speech to the Canadian Club" (Typescript, Industry, Trade and Commerce, presented in Toronto, April 16, 1973).
[5] Alastair Gillespie, "How Do We Continue to Grow from Here?—Notes for a Speech to the Annual Meeting of the Canadian Manufacturers' Association" (Typescript, Industry, Trade and Commerce, presented in Toronto, June 5, 1973).
[6] *Minutes of Proceedings and Evidence of the Standing Committee on Finance, Trade and Economic Affairs* 14 (May 8, 1973), p. 14; see pp. 13-20.
[7] Alastair Gillespie, "GATT Means Opportunity—Notes for a Speech to the Canadian Electrical Manufacturers' Association" (Typescript, Industry, Trade and Commerce, presented in Toronto, September 24, 1973); "Canada's Industrial Future—Notes for a Speech to the Conference Board" (Typescript, Industry, Trade and Commerce, presented in Winnipeg, April 3, 1974).

[8] *Minutes of Proceedings and Evidence of the Standing Committee on Finance, Trade and Economic Affairs*, 44 (May 5, 1975), pp. 15-16.

[9] *Hansard* (November 9, 1976), p. 903.

[10] Ronald Anderson, *Globe and Mail* (November 17, 1977).

[11] Gordon F. Osbaldeston, "The Policy Environment and Canadian Corporate Performance" (Typescript, Industry, Trade and Commerce, presented at McMaster University, March 20, 1978), p. 7.

[12] Canada, Industry, Trade and Commerce, *A Report by the Second Tier Committee on Policies to Improve Canadian Competitiveness* (Ottawa, Industry, Trade and Commerce, October 1978), p. 5.

[13] *The Gazette*, (Montreal, November 1, 1978).

[14] *Minutes of Proceedings and Evidence of the Standing Committee on Finance, Trade and Economic Affairs* 13 (November 30, 1978), p. 15.

[15] Robert Andras, "Remarks", (Typescript, Ottawa, Ministry of State for Economic Development, November 28, 1978), p. 2.

[16] Gordon F. Osbaldeston, *op. cit.*

[17] Alastair Gillespie, "Towards a Coherent Set of Industrial Policies—Notes for a Speech to the Canadian Club" (Typescript, Industry, Trade and Commerce, presented in Toronto, April 16, 1973).

[18] *Hansard* (November 9, 1976), p. 903.

[19] J. E. Hodgetts, *The Canadian Public Service. A Physiology of Government 1867-1970* (Toronto, University of Toronto Press, 1973), p. 103.

[20] Canada, Royal Commission on Canada's Economic Prospects, *Final Report* (Ottawa, Queen's Printer, 1958).

[21] John D. Harbron, "Industry Dept. . . . " *Toronto Telegram* (July 17, 1968).

[22] See O. M. Hill, *Canada's Salesman to the World. The Department of Trade and Commerce, 1892-1939* (Montreal, Institute of Public Administration of Canada/McGill Queen's University Press, 1977).

[23] See, for example, *Minutes of Proceedings and Evidence of the Standing Committee on Finance, Trade and Economic Affairs* 31 (April 1, 1969), p. 12; and *Minutes of Proceedings and Evidence of the Standing Committee on Miscellaneous Estimates* 20 (May 12, 1970), p. 13.

[24] The most thorough discussion of the department is to be found in Richard W. Phidd and Bruce Doern, *The Politics and Management of Canadian Economic Policy* (Toronto, Macmillan, 1978), pp. 263-314.

[25] See Peter Aucoin and Richard French, *Knowledge, Power and Public Policy* (Ottawa, Science Council of Canada/Information Canada, 1974).

[26] *Minutes of Proceedings and Evidence of the Standing Committee on Finance, Trade and Economic Affairs*, 44 (May 5, 1975), pp. 15-16.

[27] Alastair Gillespie, "Towards a Coherent Set of Industrial Policies—Notes for a Speech to the Canadian Club" (Typescript, Industry, Trade and Commerce, presented in Toronto, April 16, 1973), p. 12.

[28] Bruce Doern and Richard Phidd, "Economic Management in the Government of Canada: Some Implications of the Board of Economic Development Ministers and the Lambert Report", (Typescript of paper presented to the Canadian Political Science Association, May 1979), pp. 36-37.

[29] In W. Dodge (ed.), *Consultation and Consensus: A New Era in Policy Formulation?* (Ottawa, The Conference Board in Canada, December 1978), pp. 75-76.

[30] For example, *A Report by the Sector Task Force on the Canadian Automotive Industry* (Ottawa, Industry, Trade and Commerce, 1978). The other sectors included printing, cement and concrete, textile and clothing, construction, electrical, electronics, fertilizer, food and beverage, footwear, forest products, processed fruit and vegetable, furniture, machinery, iron and steel, non-ferrous metals, oceans, petrochemicals, plastics, shipbuilding, urban transportation, tourism.

[31] Canada, Industry, Trade and Commerce, *A Report by the Second Tier Committee on Policies to Improve Canadian Competitiveness* (Ottawa, Industry, Trade and Commerce, October 1978), p. 2.

[32] Bruce Doern and Richard Phidd, "Economic Management in the Government of Canada: Some Implications of the Board of Economic Development Ministers and the Lambert Report", (Typescript of paper presented to the Canadian Political Science Association, May 1979), p. 21.

[33] *Ibid.*, p. 19.

[34] "Proposed Order in Council, Section 18, Ministries and Ministers of State Act", (Typescript, Ottawa, Privy Council Office, 1978).

[35] "Text of Prime Minister's Remarks to Press', (Typescript, Ottawa, November 24, 1978), pp. 1-2, quoted in Doern and Phidd, *op. cit.*, p. 11.

[36] Robert Andras, "Remarks-Board of Economic Development Ministers" (Typescript, Ottawa, Ministry of State for Economic Development, November 28, 1978).

[37] *Minutes of Proceedings and Evidence of the Standing Committee on Finance, Trade and Economic Affairs* 13 (November 30, 1978), p. 15.

[38] See Doern and Phidd *op. cit.*, p. 12. This paper provides a more extensive account of the BEDM.

[39] On this last point, see Doern and Phidd, *ibid.*, p. 19.

[40] Canada, Board of Economic Development Ministers, *Action for Industrial Growth. Continuing the Dialogue* (Ottawa, Board of Economic Development Ministers, February 1979).

[41] *Ibid.*, pp. 4-5

[42] *Ibid.*, p. 9.

[43] Robert Andras, "Notes for Remarks to the Montreal Board of Trade", (Typescript, Ottawa, Board of Economic Development Ministers, April 3, 1979), pp. 8-13, as summarized in Doern and Phidd, *op. cit.*, p. 15.

[44] Robert de Cotret, "Notes for Remarks to the Canadian Chamber of Commerce" (Typescript, Ottawa, Ministry of State for Economic Development, September 23, 1979), p. 5.

[45] See for example, Gordon Ritchie, "Trade and Technology—Comments", *Canadian Public Policy* 4 (1978), pp. 373-378.

[46] In W. Dodge, (ed.), *Consultation and Consensus: A New Era in Policy Formulation?* (Ottawa, The Conference Board in Canada, December 1978), pp. 77-78.

[47] Science Council of Canada, *Forging the Links. A Technology Policy for Canada* (Ottawa, Supply and Services, February 1979), pp. 20-21.

[48] In W. Dodge, *op. cit.*, p. 77.

[49] After this had been written, Pierre Trudeau made a major campaign address to the Toronto Ad and Sales Club on February 12, 1980. The once

and future Prime Minister told his audience that "Canada's best industrial strategy is to maintain favorable energy prices". See *Toronto Star* (February 12, 1980), p. A 10.

Chapter 7

[1] Office of the Prime Minister, "Press Release", (Typescript, Ottawa June 4, 1979), p. 3.
[2] Canada, Department of Finance, *The New Expenditure Management System. A Paper Outlining the Envelope System for Allocating and Controlling Expenditures of the Government of Canada* (Ottawa, December 1979) pp. 7-8.
[3] *Ibid.*, p. 9.
[4] *Ibid.*, p. 6.
[5] *Ibid.*, p. 7.
[6] *Ibid.*, p. 8.
[7] *Ibid.*, p. 7.
[8] *Ibid.*, p. 14.
[9] *Ibid.*, p. 13.

Chapter 8

[1] Richard W. Phidd and Bruce Doern, *The Politics and Management of Canadian Economic Policy* (Toronto, Macmillan, 1968), p. 22.
[2] Canada, Royal Commission on Financial Management and Accountability, *Final Report* (Ottawa, Supply and Services, 1979), p. 83.
[3] Richard W. Phidd and Bruce Doern, *op. cit.*, p. 130. Italics in the original.
[4] *Ibid.*, p. 115.
[5] The words are Shonfield's, but they have been rearranged with a change of tense. Andrew Shonfield, *Modern Capitalism. The Changing Balance of Public and Private Power* (London, Oxford University Press, 1965), p. 317.
[6] *Ibid.*, p. 316. Italics added.
[7] Parties struggle to achieve a series of "rolling compromises among ... conflicting interests". See Douglas Hartle, *A Theory of the Expenditure Budget Process* (Toronto, University of Toronto Press, 1976), p. 31.

Appendix

[1] From Canada, Department of Finance, *The New Expenditure Management System. A Paper Outlining the Envelope System for Allocating and Controlling Expenditures of the Government of Canada* (Ottawa, December 1979), pp. 18-22; *Financial Post* (November 17, 1979); "Cabinet Committee Membership", (Typescript, Ottawa, Privy Council Office, October 19, 1979).
[2] Finance, *ibid.*, p. 11
[3] *Ibid.*
[4] *Ibid.*
[5] *Ibid.*
[6] *Ibid.*

Index

Techniques", as priority problem, 62
Reisman, Simon, 28, 45, 64, 67, 75, 113–114, 115, 121, 148
Research and development, 29, 40, 87, 95, 97, 98, 104, 110, 122, 125, 131, 132
Resource allocation, x, 59–74, 126, 134, 135, 138–142. *See also* Expenditure budget process
Resources, conservation of, 79
Resources, ownership and control of, as priority problem, 51; sharing of, as priority policy area, 80
Reuber, Grant, 145
Revenue, Minister of, 126
Robinson, Russell, 36
Royal Commission on Canada's Economic Prospects, Report of, 109
Royal Commission on Financial Management and Accountability, 1–2, 11, 31, 33, 36, 59, 63–64, 73–74, 138, 152
Royal Commission on Government Organization, 33, 35
Royal Commission on Taxation, 36

Science and Technology, Minister of State for, 137
Science and Technology, Ministry of State for, 51, 54, 76, 115, 126
Science Council of Canada, viii, 87, 89, 90, 92, 96, 98, 130–131
Science policy, as priority problem, 51, 52, 54
Second Tier Committee. *See* Tier 2
Secretary of State, 137, 142
Secretary to the Cabinet, 7, 76, 142, 146
Sectoral policy secretariats, 134, 14. 143, 144
Sectoral strategy, 106, 107, 116, 117, 119–130, 132
Sharp, Mitchell, 115
Shonfield, Andrew, 152–153
"Shop Canadian" program, 70
Simeon, Richard, 89–90
Small Business, Minister of State for, 125, 126, 137

Social Affairs, Ministry of State for, 142, 144
Social and Native Affairs, committee of cabinet, 134, 135, 140, 142
Social justice, as priority problem, 51, 52
Social Policy, committee of cabinet, 5, 134
Social security, 79
Social Security Review, 32, 48, 63, 114
Socialism, 18, 89, 91, 108
"Special relationship", in Canada-U.S. economic policy, 94–95, 109
Speech from the Throne, 48, 49, 79, 84
Stabilization policy, 13, 28, 30, 31, 32, 59–62, 67, 69, 93
Stagflation, 59, 69, 74, 150. *See also* Inflation
Stanfield, Robert, 75
Stevens, Sinclair, 129, 135, 144, 145
Stewart, Ian, 36, 68
Strategy, industrial. *See* Industrial strategy
Structural problems, in the economy, 28, 67, 73, 88, 92–93, 95, 97, 104, 110, 127
Submission, Treasury Board, 10–11, 12, 35, 141, 144
Summit conference, Bonn, West Germany, 71, 72, 123, 150
Supplementary Estimates. *See* Estimates
Supply, 14
Supply and Services, Minister of, 12, 135
Supply factors, in the economy, 92–93, 94, 104, 131, 132
Supply management, of the economy, 67, 72–73
Systems analysis, 19, 22, 42, 50
Szablowski, George, 42

Tariff policy, 87, 91, 94, 97, 98, 100–101, 104, 123
Tax, income. *See* Income tax
Tax expenditures, 74

190